PASCAL FOR OUR TIME

Pascal for Our Time

Romano Guardini

Translated by
Brian Thompson

HERDER AND HERDER

1966
HERDER AND HERDER NEW YORK
232 Madison Avenue, New York 10016

Original edition: *Christliches Bewusstsein. Versuche über Pascal*. Deutscher Taschenbuchverlag GmbH & Co. KG, München, 1962.

Nihil obstat: Patrick A. Barry
Censor Librorum

Imprimatur: ✠ Robert F. Joyce
Bishop of Burlington
May 9, 1966

Library of Congress Catalog Card Number: 66–22605
© 1966 by Herder and Herder, Inc.
Manufactured in the United States

Things have diverse qualities, and the soul diverse inclinations; for nothing is simple, of that which presents itself to the soul, and the soul never presents itself simply to any object. Thence it comes that one weeps and laughs about one and the same thing.

PENSÉES, fr. 112

Contents

Preface

The inquiries in this book were guided by the question: How does it come about, when a man believes? Not only when he is religious, or searching, but believes, in the distinct and full sense which the word has in the language of Scripture and the Church? What is the structure of the Christian consciousness based on such belief? How does a life determined by such belief realize itself?

The question was not to be answered abstractly, through an analysis of the phenomena of Christian existence, but from a starting point in concrete reality. It would thus lead to the attempt to consider a great and determined man and to find the answers in his existence.

But this man had to be himself of a special kind. It was not sufficient that he be a fervent Christian; he had also to have that brisk theoretical interest, which allowed his own existence to become a problem for him and impelled him to justify it intellectually. On the other hand, no mere theorist would do, but only a philosopher or theologian whose thought was the expression of existence; a man who not only thought existentially, but existed thoughtfully. Finally, there was still another condition to fulfill: that he be situated in real history; that his time live in him, and that he feel himself impelled to justify his believing existence in it, to make his existence comprehensible to it, and through it, to himself.

All this appears to be present in Pascal. In him are found the earnestness and passion of a faith attained through experience and decision, the audacity and energy of the Christian life; at the same time, there is in him the alertness and the craving for knowledge of the born researcher—who in addition exhibits the rare combination of scientific, psychological, and theological endowment. He is at once a scholar and a man of the world: a not easily repeated possibility of an historical moment, since the modern scientific consciousness had fully emerged, but was not yet supported by the rationalizing technologies of modern scientific activity, but was rather based on the personal initiative of the inquiring personality as well as on the freely forming group. Lastly, there is a final piece of luck: modern consciousness is there, but that which preceded it has not yet disappeared. In Pascal, both still coexist, and we can thus witness the stimulating process of emergence. We see the colliding realities experienced by an inner self, the thence-arising questions thought out by a mind which has not undergone those impoverishments of the image of the world, those atrophies of the experiencing organs, which make the modern period so much poorer than the Middle Ages. Pascal's experience of the world has several reactions more, his image of man is by several elements richer, the arch of his consciousness is by several measures more broadly drawn, than would have been the case as little as fifty years later.

To this man the question is to be addressed: What happens when a man believes? What is the structure of the Christian consciousness based on such belief? How does a life determined by such belief realize itself?

Pascal has been called a "great Christian." No less a man than Nietzsche honored him as such. The designation is supposed to express something lofty; in reality, however, it discloses a questionableness, which the simply religious sense feels. "A great Christian"—what is that? A great entrepreneur, statesman, scholar, philosopher: this is clear; but a "great Christian"? Can one be "great" in that which constitutes the essence of the Christian condition? Obviously, only if either "Christian" or "great" changes its immediate meaning. There is indeed someone who

10

lives under the highest standards of what is Christian, the saint, but he would passionately defend himself from being called great. Not only through humility and in order to protect himself from *hubris,* but because he feels that he is thereby—through a modern, unchristian confusion of categories—brought into a false order of values. He will think of Mt. 11, 25 and of its re-valuation of natural values, among which precisely that great-ness belongs. On the other hand, there is the greatness of the religious man, the genius of religious experience, of religious knowledge and mastery of life, also in Christianity. But this greatness does not stem from Christianity itself, it is introduced into it. If the task of becoming a Christian is satisfied, then this greatness is also baptized and transformed. But residues always remain, and often a great deal therein remains "residue." The danger is very great that the heart withdraw behind the duties of Christian thought, imagination, creation, and formation, and evade its real duty, becoming Christ-like—and what misery, what weakness, what profound sterility can hide beneath all this agitation and violence!

One points out such a possibility when one calls a believer gifted with genius a "great Christian." The suspicion arises that what is meant by the word consists precisely in the fact that he is not simply a Christian, not simply a believing and loving disciple. Moreover, the most profound decision of his life could be precisely whether he transforms his "greatness" into Christian terms; whether he overcomes its illusions and attachments and is capable of sacrificing, in the sense allotted to him, precisely this greatness, which has its potentialities, but also its dangers.

Pascal was certainly not a saint. Perhaps he was really only a "great Christian." We ourself tend to the opinion that here lies the genuine "Pascal problem," from a Christian point of view. But then one does not do him justice, as long as one sees in him either the saint or the secular religious genius. He was certainly neither, but rather a man in whom the decision for Christ and genuine worldly greatness lay in bitter struggle; and indeed, precisely when he thought and struggled as a Christian. Precisely

11

then did the darkest aspect in him break through. It is precisely in his religious creation and struggle that Pascal's demon emerged.

It is for just this reason that his personality gives such a profound answer to the question of how it comes about, when a man believes.

We do not make any claim exhaustively to present the world of this great mind and glowing heart. The six chapters of this book raise only several of the many questions which could be raised.

More essential is the following: Pascal belongs to that class of men who cannot be defined. One can in the last analysis only conjecture who he really was and how he thought about the problems of Christian existence. It was not given to him to express himself definitively. What he left behind are for the most part fragments.

The *Lettres écrites à un provincial* break off after the eighteenth, at the moment when the problem attains the proper plane.

Of the great work, which was to give the synthesis of his views, the apology of Christianity, we have only a mass of notes. It is already an illusion when one thinks of them as "*pensées.*" The title, which was only added later, gives the impression that it is a collection of "maxims and reflections," the first of those books full of subtle remarks about human existence, so subtle precisely in their apparent negligence, which go from the Duc de La Rochefoucauld to Chamfort to Joubert and Valéry. In reality, however, it is not at all a matter of "fragments" in the sense of a literary form, but of preliminary notes, out of which the work itself was yet to arise; of memory props for the great construction planned. As long as Pascal was sure of his faculties, he worked without such aids. He worked out problems in a never-failing memory and then wrote the work down in a single stroke. Only when his bodily state was so disturbed that his memory no longer obeyed him did he decide to make notes. They were not seldom written down in the most unfavorable state of health;

they were sometimes dictated, occasionally to a third party completely devoid of understanding, perhaps a servant. Completely irrespective of the fact that they are in part undecipherable with complete certainty—see the facsimile edition of Léon Brunschvicg—, their full meaning could often only be clear to their author. Sometimes they contain Pascal's own opinion, sometimes that of a conversational partner or an adversary under attack; they thus often present dialectical remarks, which were only to receive their proper meaning in context. The *Pensées* are a workshop abandoned in complete confusion. Even the arrangement into which the existing editions bring them is already an interpretation. Besides, it is not sure to what extent the original has been preserved. Family and friends had to take into account the critical disposition of the public and the mistrust of the authorities. Finally, they were intent on the elaboration of the legend. Pascal had to be the hero of the family and the classic champion of Port-Royal: genius, ascetic, Jansenist saint. It remains uncertain how many of the notes disappeared, and what was added to them from other contexts, letters, or fragments of treatises.

The most important source for the knowledge of a man, personal notes and letters, is almost completely lacking in Pascal's case. No personal recollections exist. The *Vie de Blaise Pascal* by his sister Gilberte is invaluable as the first coherent portrayal by someone closely associated with Pascal. But it is precisely the decisive establishment of the Pascal canon by family and party. Of letters, very little is preserved. The correspondence which would have given the most important information about his personal life and his inner religious life, namely, that with his close friend, the Duc de Roannez, and his sister, is almost completely destroyed; only a few extracts remain, just enough to show us what a deplorable loss we have suffered. And that Pascal's final attitude, which determines all that preceded it, and with which the final chapter of this book is to deal, is veiled in complete silence, has symbolic meaning for his entire life.

Our task consists in the interpretation of a subject which, in the final analysis, remains inscrutable.

Pascal's personality was continually in the most intensive movement. His society tried in vain to harness it in its own, much too simple forms. He repeatedly came into conflict with what surrounded him more or less closely. He was an eruption of forces under high pressure, which, working ceaselessly, laid hold of ever new objects, came into tension with one another in their manifestations, and never attained to a comprehensive self-articulation. The reality "Pascal" known to us is less a figure than an outline, an outline situated in the most powerful movement towards such a figure; less a being than a combat and becoming. To be sure, in a Latin sphere. Never chaos, then; not even in that positive sense, as I tried to show it in a Dostoevski.[1] Throughout, there is a will to clarity and precision. A powerful constructive energy is at work. Pascal was not only an engineer himself; his own existence strives towards the form of a great construction. But this form was not able to come forth. We must take care not to consider this fragmentary character according to the romantic concept of the "fragment." In Pascal there is nothing of the floating indetermination which ceaselessly seeks to define itself without ever succeeding. In the abstract, he could define himself; he repeatedly succeeds in doing so. But repeatedly a new impulsion coming from the inner self shatters the existing definition, in order to forge ahead to a new one. Pascal is thus event in process, perpetual destruction and reconstruction.

Thence stems the particular character of the influence he exercises: He is not a teacher, nor did he have any pupils. He is not a methodical guide, but a stimulating power, a moving shock. Thus Pascal—as he has come down to us—belongs in that group of minds, so different among themselves, whose first member was Socrates. A builder of the greatest energy, yet whose effect in history is rather that of a moving force. A mind animated by an absolute will to clarity, which nonetheless stands in disturbing indetermination—but an indetermination which

14

stems not from a lack of precision of the mind, but from the tensions of the forces at work in himself. They were so powerful and so violently opposed that the task of bringing them to completion could not be successfully accomplished in the meagerly allotted creative period. Actually, Pascal always left the game of his life drawn. He let problems be and put his heart into God's hand. He drew his life to a close not by proof and definition, but by silence. The silence of the last six months—this is what determines, from the end, this entire life plunged in unfathomable distress and unceasing combat.

Such are the hidden strata which make a rational penetration of this life impossible. For this reason, it cannot be reduced to any form. Not that it evaded the *ratio,* and indeed the most penetrating *ratio,* but because the forces erupting from within repeatedly called into question the form which had been proper but a moment before. Pascal should have lived to be eighty. What false sentimentality lies in the veneration of youth cut short in its development! As if the fragment were of fuller significance than the arch deployed to its full extent! Pascal should have lived to be very old, for this great master of dialectic would then have been able to create a construction of such precise calculation, of so great a span, with such exact foundations and vast reaches, that everything would have found room within it. But he was only thirty-nine years old when he died, after he had lived, in his own words, not a single day from the twentieth year on without pain, and had become incapable in the final years of all regular work.

One can therefore only try, we repeat, to give but an interpretation of something which remains ultimately unascertainable. The norms of this interpretation, however, are determined by the interpreter's own decisions in life. How can one otherwise explain such contradictory interpretations? There is first of all the image of Pascal of the official family tradition, devised by the biography of him by his sister, Gilberte Périer, which shows him as the towering mind, the strict ascetic, the exemplary champion of Port-Royal—and opposed to this picture is a very

15

recent essay which sees in him a nature of somber sensuality and the most powerful ambition, which forces his final adherence to the faith with tragic violation of his own nature, at the price of the most grievous sufferings of body and soul. There is the Pascal of traditional apologetics, whose knowledge of spiritual and Christian things is used in the wrangling with modern problems—and opposed to it, contemporary views which see him, in Kierkegaardian terms, as an isolated loner, fighting against the Church; or make him into the forerunner of Ivan Karamazov and of his legend in the Grand Inquisitor; or even group him together with Nietzsche and see at the very bottom of his religious struggle a Titanism which rejects faith.

Because all this is so, this book can only be an essay, a hypothesis which proves itself correct to the extent that it helps one to understand this life more completely and more profoundly.

I have already said that this investigation will be in no way exhaustive. The first chapter deals with the decisive crisis in Pascal's life and inquires about its significance for his existence. The second attempts to describe Pascal's image of man and his situation in the world, whereby the problems brought up in the first chapter are further discussed, and Pascal's place in the evolution of intellectual history is determined. The third speaks about his conceptions of society, culture, and education, and develops more fully the historical factor. The questions about the nature of man and his relationship to God are taken up anew in the fourth chapter, where Pascal's theories of knowledge and value, both in general and from a Christian point of view, are developed. The fifth chapter examines a special theorem, the "argument of the wager," and thence obtains a certain historical context. The sixth finally unrolls the whole of Pascal's life once more and attempts to show what constitutes, in our opinion, the essential of this life on the human and Christian planes.

Many questions remain to be asked. For example, Pascal's thought concerning the Christian reality in its objectivity, concerning the history of salvation, the Church, Scripture, the sacraments—in relationship with his concept of expression in general, of corporality in the broadest sense, symbol and word. Or concerning the Christian world of values in its relationship to heart, will, and freedom, thus the Christian ethos; or the nature and possibility of Christian culture, and so forth.

We could not go into these questions, nor have we dealt with such problems customarily associated with Pascal as the question of the essence of grace, of freedom, of predestination—in short, what is connected with the concept of Jansenism. It seemed to us that Pascal is misinterpreted from different sides: by his friends and followers as by his Molinist adversaries, both of whom see in him simply the "Jansenist," but in opposite lights. By psychologists, philosophers, and historians, not themselves believers, who treat him from general historial points of view, and who, according to their mood or the necessity of their thesis, overlook his Christianity, or limit it, or declare it false, or even discover it with an earnestness which seems comic to the believer, in order to proclaim him as *"the"* Christian— whereby there sometimes arises a snobbery of Christianity, which is one of the strangest phenomena which our twisted human nature is capable of producing. And finally, what is perhaps the worst misinterpreter, namely, the solidified philosophical-theological terminology, which seizes the living man and does him violence.

We had the perhaps presumptuous desire to get close to Pascal himself. And since one cannot know another man without certain stylizations, they were to be as far as possible only those which were given along with the eyes and the perceptive presuppositions of the observer himself. He has thus dared to leave aside the literature about Pascal, except in the case of the most essential information; to stick completely to the texts, and through these texts, to interrogate the man and the thinker about that which seemed important to him. This rendered the inquiry fragmentary, but it has in exchange, perhaps, the chance of a more open view. In that it dispensed itself from the question, by

17

now tiresome, of the extent to which Pascal shared the views of Jansenius and Arnauld, it has perhaps gained a somewhat fresher impression, and the chance of seeing who the living Pascal was.

CHAPTER I

The Mémorial

1.

THE RELIGIOUS DECISION IN PASCAL'S LIFE

We begin with the analysis of a small text which is certainly one of the most powerful expressions of religious experience which we possess. It is the *Mémorial,* a note which does not even require a full page of a book to print. It was found after Pascal's death, sewn into his coat, written twice by his own hand, first quickly on paper, then once more on parchment, in the most careful of scripts, with precise lines indicating the sense.[2]

The way in which Pascal treated this "memorial"—every time he had a new coat made, he took care to sew in the two pages himself—tells us that it was very important to him. We must thus ask ourselves what life gave them birth.

Pascal was one of the greats in the intellectual sphere. When he died in 1662, he was only thirty-nine years old. His writings treated subjects of the most varied kind—mathematics, logic, humanities, pedagogy, theology—and the critical edition fills an imposing row of books. His outer and inner fate, it is true, has brought it about that for the most part they remain fragmentary.

Pascal was an ardent mind. Great conceptions arose in him; he was profound, broad, and audacious. At the same time, he stood in an entirely spontaneous proximity to reality. His theoretical thinking was borne by direct contact with things. On the basis of experience he created neatly thought-out theories; the theories, in turn, in the form of masterly ordered observation and reliable experimentation, prepared scientific experience. The sure thrust of his thinking struck the nerve of the problem; he knew how to draw out its fullness and unfold it precisely and clearly. The "reduplication" of this thinking was a magnificently intensive and lucid language—"*ce style âpre, noble, sobre, ardent, concentré, impétueux, et magnifique,*" as Stowski says. But this great mind lived in a body sick from earliest childhood on. Whatever he created, even the first three works of his youth which will presently be discussed, he had to wring from a continually failing organism. One will not easily discover elsewhere such an unconditional commitment to the idea, such an ardent intellectual passion, such an immense power of thought.

II.

Through Søren Kierkegaard we are familiar with the notion of "stages on the path through life." According to this notion, the existence of man takes place on the basis of an order structured in levels. A life receives its meaning to the extent that it purely and fully embodies this order. And of course this does not take place in such a way that it simply develops ever further and higher, but rather decides and dares. This order is constituted by levels of existence. It is one and the same man who is to exist on each of these levels, but he does not get from the lower to the higher by simply continuing to live. He does not automatically develop from one level to another; this would only be possible if they differed from one another in a purely quantitative manner. Rather, the difference is qualitative and man attains the higher level—higher in its differentness—only by deciding and daring. It is thus not a matter of approach and transition, but of choice and leap. On his momentary, variously determined level of existence, man comes to a "brink." The level has been

20

lived through to its end. At first dimly, then ever more clearly and urgently, he becomes aware that there is something higher —until he feels himself faced with the decision, whether or not he will take the risk. And not only in such a way that this something higher is "there," lying visible before his eyes, but it is only really "given," visible and subject to evaluation when he ventures upon it. It is given to him to the extent to which he dares. He lives, for example, in the immediacy of enraptured ideality, of sensible communion with the world, of contemplation and creation touched by beauty. Then he becomes aware of what "person" really means, its solitude, its responsibility, its earnestness, and that it is something different, something higher than any immediate structure of life and culture. He thereby comes to the brink of his hitherto existing level of existence; he divines the new level and its demand upon him. In order to satisfy the demand, he must let go of the present level and "leap" to the next. He must leap, because he receives no guarantee from his old position that he will gain a foothold on the new one, for the latter is of a higher kind and thus "other." He must thus take the risk. Between the two levels lies an abyss, an obscurity. Man must, in the earnestness of the decision, gather himself together, raise himself out of himself, and throw himself across. Then he gains a footing and is able to exist on a higher level; his eyes are opened to a new and superior reality; a new power of evaluation awakens, and he is able to appreciate and to love on a higher level. Thus the existence of a truly living man is divided according to existential levels and the risks which lie before each level: according to "stages" which in each case bear their own values within themselves, pose their special problems, and in which corresponding possibilities of the given, concrete man are realized.

The idea is not without danger. It induces one to construct one's life, especially if a fixed order in the succession of levels, and thereby of "leaps," is asserted. The animation of life, in which all rules prove correct only within non-deducible unique events, must be preserved before making use of this or any other doctrinal crutch. Furthermore, the notion easily overlooks the continuity of life, and thus threatens to decompose existence. But it contains a great deal of truth, and there are men for whose existence it furnishes the stylizing element. Pascal belongs among them.

Now, the *Mémorial* informs us about the luminous appearance of the highest existential level in Pascal's life and about the accomplishment of the decisive "leap" with which it was attained.

III.

Blaise Pascal was born June 19, 1623, in Clermont. He lost his mother when he was three and grew up in the company of his two sisters, Gilberte and Jacqueline.[3] His home surrounded him with love, with all the dignity and well-being of a distinguished position and a choice social milieu, as well as with an atmosphere filled with the liveliest intellectual, above all scientifc and mathematical, interests.

When the children were still young, their father moved to Paris. There the Pascals' house formed one of the private centers of scientific endeavor so important at that period. At the same time the family came into contact with the court. The highly gifted brother and sister, Blaise and the charming Jacqueline, made a most favorable impression there, especially with Cardinal Richelieu.

In 1639 the family moved again, this time to Rouen, where the foremost post in the internal revenue department had been entrusted to Pascal's father. There, too, the intellectual life, above all of an artistic, social kind, was very lively. Corneille lived in Rouen and gave the first exhibitions of his creativity there.

The education of the boy lay entirely in the hands of his father. He thought very highly of his son's natural ability, and educated him according to a self-devised system. Thus Blaise grew up with an education which indeed showed many lacunae —he never really became familiar with philosophy, theology, and the entire field of history—and which lacked method; but for this very reason, it was original and absolutely forced him to intellectual independence.

His gift for mathematics developed above all. Gilberte, in her *Vie de Blaise Pascal,* tells the well-known story of how the father withheld mathematics from his son because he feared lest this most splendid of all sciences completely captivate him and not let him come to the necessary absorption in the ancient languages. One day, however, he surprised the twelve-year-old drawing all sorts of figures on the floor-tiles, and took him to task—whereupon it was found that the boy, starting from the elements of geometry, had by himself found the first thirty-two theorems of Euclid. Even if only part of the story were true, that the boy studied and understood Euclid without guidance, that alone would justify the fact that his father, as Gilberte reports, "appalled by the greatness and power of this genius," permitted him the study of mathematics (P. O., p. 6).

Pascal's real life took place in thought. Research and understanding were his life. His thinking, on the other hand, did not take place in unconcerned objectivity; rather, the objects which he contemplated, the problems which he investigated, the way in which he formed his questions, the results which he obtained, were such that they were borne by, and in turn determined, personal conviction. For Pascal, understanding did not mean only confirmation, discovery, or even intellectual breakthrough, but always a general personal attitude as well. And a general attitude not only toward prevalent views, but towards all existence. Again and again it threw him into inner and exterior struggles, which were extremely difficult at times—and not only intellectual but also "political" struggles; indeed in the last years of his life, it was a matter of freedom and prison for him.

The subjects which came freshly before his eyes at the various times of his life and attracted his inquiry; the problems which resulted for him; the values which thereby dawned on him, and

23

what they demanded from his personal attitude—all this determined the "stages of his path through life."

The first was oriented towards nature. In it Pascal became the great mathematician, physician, and engineer.

In his seventeenth year he wrote his "Essai pour les coniques," a study on the theory of the sections of cones, of an admirable rigor in the posing of the problems and of a no less astonishing perfection in their development.[4]

In Rouen he had to help his father in his tax calculations. To facilitate his task, he created, in two years of intensive work—from the age of nineteen to twenty-one—a calculating machine capable of many operations, giving proof of complete mastery in the matter, from the theoretical bases to the technical details of the construction, which was worked out in some fifty different models. It is interesting to note that the industrial impulse, indeed closely linked to technics, was already coming to life: Pascal had precise plans for an industrial-commercial exploitation of his invention, was able to reserve for himself the necessary patents, and worked consciously towards the goal of publicizing his machine (*Oeuvres*, I, pp. 291ff.).

To these accomplishments a third was added: the Italian physicist Torricelli had posed the problem of the vacuum, thus plunging the scientific world of his time into a state of excitement. His experiments seemed to prove the possibility of the vacuum: a glass tube closed at the top had been filled with mercury, and its lower, open end held in a recipient filled with the same liquid. Now if one raised it, without letting the open end leave the surface of the liquid in the recipient, a vacuum seemed to form at the upper end. The news of the experiment came to France incomplete and was received with mistrust, especially since traditional scientific convictions about the impossibility of the vacuum—which was identified with nothingness—were in opposition. Pascal repeated and developed Torricelli's experiment in an exemplary form and thus provided the proof of the possibility of the vacuum. But that is not all: he placed the result thus obtained under a general principle, treated air and liquid as fluid substances, and thus arrived at the theory of hydrostatic equilibrium, as well as its application in a "new machine for the multiplication of forces," in other words the hydraulic press or elevator. His experiments were especially impressive due to the fact that he connected the measuring of the height of the column of mercury with an ascension of the Puy-de-Dôme, a conical mountain near Clermont, thus providing also the experimental proof of the rarefaction of the air (*Oeuvres*, I, pp. 323ff.; II, pp. 3ff.).

These intellectual efforts so shook his health that from 1647 —his twenty-fifth year—on, a continuous intellectual labor became impossible for him. The desire to find better doctors, and at the same time to be near the center of the intellectual life of the times, led him to Paris, accompanied by his sister Jacqueline. Decisive relations were there knotted with Port-Royal, the center of the religious movement of Jansenism. But at the same time Pascal was also received into the most brilliant circles of society. He made the acquaintance of the ingenious Chevalier de Méré, a man of the world filled with both *esprit* and a sense of reality, the arbiter of the refinements of his time. It is probably he who introduced the great observer and analyst of man, Michel de Montaigne, to the young Pascal. Montaigne's *Essais* —next to the *Encheiridion* of Epictetus—were to be from that moment on of the greatest importance for him. Pascal also met the liberal young Duc de Roannez and was soon bound in close friendship with him and his sister.

In the contact with these circles, and above all in the home of the Duc de Roannez, the notion of what "man" really is comes suddenly to the young mathematician: man as specific reality, other than that of mathematics and physics, as a distinct world, filled with special values—embodied in the canon of the "*honnête homme,*" the highly cultured man, open to all the fullness of life, capable of judgment and full of good will. Pascal's eyes are opened to the fact that human things take place differently

25

than those of physics; he sees how human acts and their continuity arise and develop, in which structures human existence is built up, etc. He sees the problems posed by this different reality; he recognizes that in order to do them justice, the mathematical and scientific methods are not appropriate, and creates for himself—utilizing everywhere what Montaigne prepared—the necessary concepts and methods.

In other words: his thinking attains a new qualitative level of reality. When one passes from the Pascal of the mathematical and physical-technical works to the Pascal who stands behind the "Discours sur les passions de l'amour" (P. O., pp. 123ff.), or the first section of the *Pensées,* one is amazed by the force and purity of this "leap." A mathematician and scientist of genius, little more than twenty years of age, is thus here endangered by the temptation to set up the knowledge at work in him as an absolute and to reduce everything to geometry and physics. But Pascal, who would really have been capable of constructing an *"homme-machine,"* does not for an instant fall prey to the danger—which has nonetheless devoured researchers of the highest class—, that of subjugating all reality to a passionately grasped but partial principle. Pascal sees a new reality, man; he recognizes that it is essentially different from that of the world of mere substances. And while mathematics and physics remain as familiar to him as before, so that he continues to accomplish works of the highest class in these fields—we are thinking of his researches in infinitesimal and probability calculus—he grasps man with complete lucidity as a particular problem to be investigated. He establishes the appropriate basic concepts and creates for himself a method for the problems of concrete human existence, the full significance of which will not become clear before the works of the modern psychology of the structure and levels of behavior. His method is indeed ahead of the latter in decisive points, because it works with a more comprehensive consciousness of man.

He created the imperishable concepts of the *"esprit de finesse"* and *"coeur"*—for if they are already present in the general consciousness of the *"honnête homme,"* it is nonetheless Pascal who gives them their true intellectual valence.[5] *"Esprit de finesse"* is the capacity to grasp, in its singularity, the concrete reality of man, differentiated from mere matter which the *"esprit de géométrie"* investigates in mathematics and physics. *"Coeur"* is the unity of the acts which values experience and appropriate. But both are intellectual processes, perceptions which found knowledge. What the *"esprit de finesse"* accomplishes is no anti-rational intuition; there is rather a "logic" attached to it. And even if Pascal modestly declares that he is not in a position to construct it, the *Lettres provinciales,* the "Entretien avec M. de Saci sur Epictète et Montaigne," the essays entitled "De l'esprit géométrique" and "De l'art de persuader" (*Oeuvres,* IV, pp. 107ff. —VII; P. O., pp. 146ff., 164ff., 184ff.), but above all the *Pensées* contain astonishing contributions to the question, with which rational instruments the living, concrete reality of man must be grasped. Likewise, *"coeur"* is not some kind of irrational feeling, but a spiritual value-experience which founds knowledge in the most precise sense of the word, so much so that there is a logic of the heart, of motives, of value-efficacities. In his theory of *"agrément,"* Pascal worked on this question and attempted to construct, from this starting point, a theory of the art of persuasion.[6]

The time during which Pascal lived *"en homme du monde"* was not to last long. Once more his existence entered upon a crisis, provoked by a newly discovered reality, the religious—or more precisely, the Christian—crisis.

The religious sentiment had already become lively in the family at an early date. Pascal's father, as a result of an accident which had condemned him to a long retirement, had come into contact with a recently awakened religious movement, the early Jansenism, which attempted to carry out the primacy of grace with excessive consistency. At that time, Jacqueline was so strongly affected that several years later she entered the Abbey of Port-Royal. Pascal was also touched, but this "first conversion" did not penetrate his innermost being. Science, along with the newly opening "world," was too strong. A letter which he wrote to his sister after the death of his father, and in which he considers the event from the point of view of faith—a sort of long dissertation—is singularly cold; the language of his mathematical writings touches us more personally than what he says on such an occasion which concerns him so intimately. (P. O., pp. 95ff.)

But it is at work within him. He becomes uneasy. The realities which he sees, the values which he knows, and the problems which the known poses for him, are called into question. He feels that there is something higher. He feels himself drawn into the divine sphere. But this feeling is not clear enough, not real enough to be a match for the other reality in this mind which so demands reality.

A period of hard struggle begins, a period full of anguish, because what is pressing for recognition is still obscure and confused. The situation becomes both ever more profound and ever more difficult. His illness is also very oppressive. It is perhaps from this period that the ardent "Prière pour demander à Dieu le bon usage des maladies" (P. O., pp. 56ff.) stems.

The crisis comes to its final climax and at the same time resolves itself in the event of the evening of November 23, 1654, in which God appears to Pascal as the reality of realities, in that it becomes clear to him who the living God is—distinct from man, distinct from nature. It is the event which find its expression in the *Mémorial*.

A new level of existence appears distinctly to Pascal: not the religious, but the Christian, founded by a new reality, God himself, as he appears in the revelation in Christ. He distinctly perceives the summons contained in the revelation of who God is, and which addresses him through the words of this God; and he takes the step which begins to respond to that summons with the proper earnestness.

Pascal is now thirty-one years old, and he begins that life

28

of ardent devotion which made him one of the "great Christians."

Once more his thinking stands before a new reality. Again Pascal is so great that he is not tempted for an instant to grasp it with the conceptions, norms, and methods utilized for those previously encountered. They remain, just as the physical and intellectual levels subsist, and just as before, the work on these levels with the appropriate methods follows its course. But the new level is brought clearly into relief: founded by the new subject, determined by a new value and basic character, attained and affirmed by a specific act. And the task arises: to find the points of departure, the ways of thinking, the methods which belong to this level.

The precision of the qualitative distinction, allied to the most vigorous will to totality; the breadth of intellectual horizon, whose expanse is nonetheless organized with unequivocal clarity: herein lies the secret of the style and greatness of Pascal's thought. The fragment 793 of the *Pensées* is a splendid example:[7]

"The infinite distance between bodies and minds symbolizes the infinitely more infinite distance between minds and charity, for charity is supernatural.

"All the glory of greatness has no lustre for people engaged in intellectual quests.

"The greatness of intellectuals is invisible to kings, to the rich, to captains, to all the great of the flesh.

"The greatness of wisdom, which is nothing if not of God, is invisible to the carnal-minded and to intellectuals. These are three orders differing in kind.

"Great geniuses have their dominion, their splendor, their greatness, their victory, their lustre, and have no need of carnal greatness, which has no relation to their domain. They are seen not by the eyes, but by the minds, that is sufficient.

"The saints have their dominion, their splendor, their greatness, their victory, their lustre, and have no need of carnal or intellectual greatness, which has no relation to their domain,

29

for it neither adds to nor detracts from it. They are seen by God and the angels, not by bodies or curious minds: God suffices them.

"Archimedes, without splendor, would have the same veneration. He fought no battles for the eyes, but he furnished his inventions to all minds. Oh! how brilliant he was to the mind!

"Jesus Christ, without riches, and without any external exhibition of knowledge, is in his order of holiness. He did not make any inventions, he did not reign; but he was humble, patient, holy, holy to God, terrible to demons, without any sin. Oh! in what great pomp and prodigious magnificence he came, to the eyes of the heart which see wisdom!

"It would have been useless for Archimedes to have played the prince in his books on geometry, although he was one.

"It would have been useless for Our Lord, Jesus Christ, to come as a king, in order to shine forth in his kingdom of holiness; but he certainly came with the splendor of his own order!

"It is quite ridiculous to be scandalized by the lowliness of Jesus Christ, as if this lowliness were of the same order as the greatness which he came to manifest. If one considers this greatness in his life, in his passion, in his obscurity, in his death, in the choice of his disciples, in their desertion, in his secret resurrection, and in the rest, then one will see it to be so great that one will have no reason to be scandalized by a lowliness which is not there.

"But there are some who can admire only carnal greatness, as if there were no intellectual greatness; and others who only admire intellectual greatness, as though there were not an infinitely higher greatness in wisdom.

"All bodies, the firmament, the stars, the earth and its kingdoms, are not equal to the least of minds; for it knows all that, and itself; and the bodies, nothing.

"All bodies together, and all minds together, and all their productions, are not equal to the least movement of charity. This is of an order infinitely more exalted.

"From all bodies together, one would not be able to obtain

30

one little thought: this is impossible, and of another order. From all bodies and minds, one would not be able to produce a movement of true charity: this is impossible, and of another, supernatural order."

The text is extraordinary and would deserve a thorough analysis. Three domains of reality separate from one another: *"les corps"*—*"les esprits"*—*"la charité," "la sainteté,"* or *"le surnaturel."* Between them lies a *"distance infinie"*; more than that, a *"différence de genre."* Everything which is material cannot produce the tiniest intellectual act; all material and intellectual realities cannot produce the slightest movement of Christian charity, for between them stands in each case the qualitative difference of the *"autre ordre."* Between the latter two domains the difference is yet more accentuated, that which separates the natural and the supernatural. Each domain has its own type of value, its own *"grandeur"*; but they are qualitatively different, and one valence can no more be derived from the other than one definition of essence from the other. For the comprehension of each domain, specific categories are necessary. These categories must be found in the object itself. But this is impossible without the specific power of sight, the *"vue,"* which must reconstitute itself on each new level. So much so that the *"rois"* (they form the analogy of the *"savants"*: the latter have a perception for the material world, and their royalty consists in the power to engender convictions; the former have a perception for the concreteness of their subjects and of political realities and royalty over their wills[8])—the kings, then, and the rich, and the *"grands de chair"* the intrinsically incapable of seeing the *"grandeurs spirituelles"* at all; and the *"gens d'esprit"* in their turn cannot see the *"grandeurs de la sagesse,"* for which *"charité"* or *"sainteté"* is required. Thus there are *"trois ordres différant de genre."*

It is impossible to be clearer. But it is particularly significant that also the third domain of reality thus attained is not left to some irrational experience or anti-conceptual intuition; it too possesses its rationality and thus remains subject to scientific investigation. Just as nature has its logical structure, which is stressed by the "*sciences abstraites,*" mathematics and physics; just as the human domain has its logic, so that it can be grasped through a rational "*étude de l'homme*"—so also the realm of the wisdom and charity coming from revelation has its own logic. Attempts to disengage this logic can be found in many passages: in the endeavors to elucidate the problem of grace, especially in the first of the *Lettres provinciales,* more profoundly in the last two—the seventeenth and eighteenth—, and in the "Ecrits sur la grâce." The ways of thinking are there sought in a dialectic between freedom and motive, between causality of grace and human initiative. Or in the "Entretien avec M. de Saci sur Epictète et Montaigne," in which possible fundamental human structures—the skeptic and the Stoic, Montaigne and Epictetus—are contrasted in such a way that they criticize one another. But not in order to edify an harmonious, collective humanity, but to prove mere man an impossibility. Between those antithetical structures appears an empty spot; and for whomever can see, it becomes clear that here, in the "*misère de l'homme,*" the love of God searches out and touches him who is lost.[9] Here belong also the essays of the *Pensées* on a dialectic of the sacred history of the Old and New Testaments; on the phenomenon of the miracle[10] and its meaning for the history of the Christian phenomenon, and so on.

Such is the work of the thinker. It is sustained by the struggle of the living Christian. In what remains of his letters to Mlle. de Roannez gleams the majesty of Christian values. The *Lettres provinciales* reveal the combat which he waged for the decisive positions of Christian existence as he understood it. This combat was not pure: Pascal perceived incorrectly certain things of great importance, he simplified what was in reality complicated, and from a certain point on, everything was contaminated by the irresistible power of the struggle itself. But the ardor, the originality, and the courage with which the combat was waged were something of grandeur.

Greater than all else, however, was the inward journey which

32

Pascal now began. His religious life became more and more fervent; it pressed on more and more into the depths, to terminate finally in a sublime silence. Fragments like the remains of letters mentioned, or the wondrous "Mystère de Jesus" from the *Pensées*, inform us about this development.

IV.

After Pascal's death a discovery was made, told of in the following account:

"A few days after the death of Pascal, a domestic of the house noticed by chance that, in the lining of the coat of the famous deceased, there was something which seemed thicker than the rest, and having undone this place to see what it was, he found a small, folded parchment, written in Pascal's hand, and in this parchment, a paper written in the same hand: the one was a faithful copy of the other. The two pieces were immediately placed in the hands of Madame Périer [Pascal's sister], who showed them to several of his special friends. All agreed that this parchment, written with such care and with such remarkable characters, was without a doubt a sort of memorial which he kept very carefully in order to conserve the memory of something which he wanted always present to his eyes and mind, since for eight years he took care to sew it in and remove it whenever he had new clothes made."[11]

At the top of the sheet there is a cross surrounded by rays. Underneath, the following:

The year of grace 1654
Monday, November 23, day of Saint Clement, pope and martyr,
and others in the martyrology.
Vigil of Saint Chrysogonus, martyr, and others.
From about ten-thirty in the evening to about half an hour after
midnight,
Fire.
God of Abraham, God of Isaac, God of Jacob,
not of the philosophers and savants.

33

Certitude, certitude; feeling, joy, peace.
God of Jesus Christ.
Deum meum et Deum vestrum.
"Thy God shall be my God."
Forgetting the world and everything, except God.
He is only found by the paths taught in the Gospel.
Grandeur of the human soul.
"Just Father, the world has not known you, but
I have known you."
Joy, joy, joy, tears of joy.
I separated myself from him:
Dereliquerunt me fontem aquae vivae.
"My God, will you abandon me?"
May I not be eternally separated from him.
"This is eternal life, that they know you, the only true God, and
him whom you have sent, Jesus Christ."
Jesus Christ.
Jesus Christ.
I separated myself from him; I fled him, renounced him,
crucified him.
May I never be separated from him!
He is only kept by the paths taught in the Gospel.
Total and sweet renunciation.
Total submission to Jesus Christ and to my director.
Eternally in joy for a day of trial on earth.
Non obliviscar sermones tuos. Amen.[12]

V.

This is an historical document in the strict sense of the word. It attests an event which separates a before and an after. Not an episodic feeling, a fugitive presentiment, an abstract insight devoid of obligation, which could have ensued at any moment, but rather a turning point and decision which stands in history. And which engenders history: the inner, Christian history of this man, in that it brings to its culmination everything experienced up to this point, and fixes a new beginning. It is the analogy in one man's life of the event which separated human history into an *ante-* and *post-Nativitatem Domini.*

The text thus begins with an exact dating. "1654, Monday, November 23 . . ." But here it is a matter of the history of a Christian existence. The dating is thus sacred, one could say hieratic: "The year of grace 1654 . . ." The day, however, is noted according to the ritual order of the liturgical calendar of saints, the martyrology: "day of Saint Clement, pope and martyr, and others in the martyrology. Vigil of Saint Chrysogonus, martyr, and others."

And even the hour is mentioned, with the care not only of the exact observer, but of one who knows the preciousness of such an inner experience and is anxious to preserve it: "From about ten-thirty in the evening to about half an hour after midnight."

Then comes a series of hastily written words, short sentences, fragments from Holy Scripture, all vibrating with the excitement of a prodigious experience.

The first line is formed by a single word which stands in the middle: *"Feu"*—"Fire."

Two lines below:

"Certitude; certitude; feeling, joy, peace."

And once again, several lines later:

"Joy, joy, joy, tears of joy."

Something colossal has happened here. Pascal has stood in fire. We may not take the word allegorically. If the elect of religious experience speak of inner "light," of inner "glow," they do not intend to use comparisons, but mean real beaming, real burning, . . . coming, of course, from another source than physical nature or psychic consciousness. It is an experience of the spirit; more exactly, of the Holy Spirit, of the *"Pneuma."* There takes place therein an elucidation in certitude, a seizure by glory, a clarification of life, which place man on a new level of existence.

And we should also observe that in the *Mémorial* there stands

35

the phrase: "Grandeur of the human soul." At the heart of Christian experience, in the midst of the experience of the holy "fire," in which God's grandeur and the reality of sin become clear, the fact remains that man is marked by the sign of grandeur.

We have come to know the man who here writes in this manner: a first-class physicist, mathematician, engineer, psychologist, and philosopher of concrete humanity. What makes him stammer so?

"Certitude, certitude; feeling, joy, peace." All this is thus new to him. He had longed for it, but without possessing it. He had thought about God with concepts, but without arriving at any reality. He had exerted himself, but had not gotten off the ground—now he stands before the reality of God.

This reality is luminous and burning. It engenders absolute certitude, abundant peace, and a joy which is independent of the conditions of one's existence.

Pascal, who demands for all knowledge experience—that confirmation which is only possible when one stands before the reality itself—, who has grasped the reality of nature in experiment and calculation, and the reality of man in observation and analysis—this same Pascal now stands before the reality of the living God. He will now be able to speak, also in the religious realm, with that authenticity deriving from the object itself, which he had as a physicist and psychologist. Not always, however—especially not when the demon of polemics lays hold of him—but certainly when he speaks purely of that which is.

Then—and here we come to the essential—the strange phrases:

> "God of Abraham, God of Isaac, God of Jacob,
>   not of the philosophers and savants. . . .
>   God of Jesus Christ."

What does that mean?

One must have thrown oneself with all one's soul into the effort of understanding; one must have been unhappy when one did not understand a philosophical concept, and blissful, when it dawned on one, if one is to be able to judge the significance of these words, spoken by Pascal. It is generally customary these days to emphasize that God, the God of the Christian life, is different than that of philosophy. Since Søren Kierkegaard stated it with such enormous forcefulness; since this man, owing to the collapse of liberal theology and philosophy of religion, was brought into prominence and in a special sense became modern, many people have repeated this affirmation, but one is a little skeptical. It is too easily said. One must be qualified to say such a thing. He who pretends to the right to speak in this way must have exerted himself in honest philosophical labor. He must have worked to attain the clarity and depth of true intellectual understanding, the precision and defensibility of a concept, the pure necessity of real insight into laws and essences; to attain that which Anselm of Canterbury means when he says: to know is "to comprehend that something could not be otherwise than as it is grasped." He must have experienced the intolerance of the passion for knowledge, which admits as knowledge only that of the absolute and eternal. In this disposition—now often rejected with very dubious credibility—lies a great tradition of Western thought. Yes, he must at least have understood how one could be of the belief that mathematics, with its strict necessity, is really the only true knowledge . . . Something of all this must be present for one to be able to judge the enormity of this Christian insight of a philosopher and mathematician: that God is not the God "of the philosophers and savants," but "the God of Abraham, God of Isaac, God of Jacob."

Once more, what does that mean?

What would be, then, the "God of the philosophers"? It is what is meant by the notion of the absolute, as it can be obtained by reflecting on exterior reality, or by analyzing inner experience, or by elaborating the world of logic or values. Thus "the first Cause," "the supreme Being," "the absolute Idea," "the eternal Law," "the absolute Value," etc. The characteristic of this definition of God is that it attempts to grasp him in pure

37

unconditionality, free from everything which could in any way mean limitation, finitization, secularization, anthropomorphism. This God is more absolute than man can conceive him.

And what is now the staggering discovery of Pascal? What is it that makes him stammer with joy? A Pascal knows how to appreciate the significance of the struggle for the pure comprehension of the concept of God. He is a stranger to the modern weak-nervedness which feels that the domain of "the religious" is menaced whenever one works with concepts. His religion is not a vague "religious experience" in the modern sense of the word. But now his own experience has shown him that God is "the God of Abraham, God of Isaac, God of Jacob, not of the philosophers and savants"—that he is the "God of Jesus Christ." This means first of all that God is a person.

But let us be careful here. This word, too, could be meant "philosophically." But this is not the case. It does not in any way mean that God is "the absolute Person," or "Personality," but rather that he is "He," who is so and not otherwise. Here we touch upon the essential.

When a man, hitherto accustomed to the absolute character of thought, declares: "God is This Person," something extraordinary has come about. That which he previously maintained under the protection of the most general concepts, preserved from all finiteness, deriving from the realm of the cosmological, the ontological, or the ideal—he now ventures its entry into the domain of those concepts which stem from finite human activity, from the distinctions of human persons, from the I-Thou relationship, from history. Previously, he would have refused to do so. For it is precisely the scandal of the "philosopher" regarding religious thought, that it operates "anthropomorphically"! For this is why he rejects this way of thought, in the name of the purity of the concepts of the absolute. What has then come about, that Pascal experiences this shattering of the merely philosophical idea of God with such deeply stirring happiness? With the consciousness of standing for the first time before the essential, now that he has entered the realm of "anthropomorphic" concepts? There is only one answer which Pascal himself would acknowledge: he has encountered the living God. This God is precisely the being of whom one must say, if one wishes to speak of him truthfully: he comes, he acts, he speaks . . . God has confronted him as "This Person," and it is only possible to speak of such an encounter with the words found on every page of Holy Scripture.

God is This Person. "I am who I am," he said of himself at a most important moment (Ex. 3, 14). He is he who is sovereignly himself, whose living being can not be derived from anything, not even from a concept of the absolute. All concepts can only express something about him, they can never express him as he is himself. He himself surpasses every concept and only becomes a given when he gives himself. He can only be perceived if he comes towards man. One can only speak about him if one is addressed by him, and by drawing from the Word which he says about himself.

This movement of God towards man does not take place in a generally describable experience nor in an ascent of thought to be attained from within any human domains, but rather through historical revelation: messengers sent, word spoken, event providentially disposed. He is the "God of Abraham, God of Isaac, God of Jacob"; of those men, therefore, who lived at a given time, in a given country, in a definitely localized attitude, in a specifiable historical context. But it is "scandal and folly" for the mind enclosed in its philosophy to be obliged to acquiesce in this apparently arbitrary binding of the absolute to historical contingency.

God is the "God of Jesus Christ." When Philip asks, "Lord, show us the Father," Jesus answers, "Have I been with you so long, and yet you do not know me, Philip? He who has seen me has seen the Father" (Jn. 14, 9). Scandal anew for the mind concerned only with philosophy: instead of conceiving God from the indications of nature, from the necessities of logic, from the structure of the categories of consciousness, from the postulates of action, from the specific contents of religious value-

39

experience, one must receive him from the being, the value, the action of a concrete historical figure, who lived at that time and not earlier or later; in that country and not elsewhere; so constituted and not otherwise. It is the scandal of the philosophical will to absoluteness placed before the irreducibility of the historic fact, which is to be of decisive importance for the definition of God.

The Christian God is the "God of Jesus Christ." He, whom Jesus means when he says, "My Father." He, by whom Jesus is sent. Through whom he lives, and towards whom he is turned. God is he who is "the God and Father of Jesus Christ." It is not possible to detach a "Christian conception of God," a "Christian truth," from the concrete Christ. What is Christian doctrine remains Christian only as long as it is heard as if from the mouth of Christ; as long as it is understood in a living way, drawing its life from him, from his existence and action. There is no "essence of Christianity" separable from him—we repeat, separable from him, and expressible in a free-floating, conceptual scheme.[13] The essence of Christianity is Christ. What he is; whence he comes and towards what he goes; what lives in him and around him—heard living from his mouth, read from his countenance.[14] A demand is here made of the philosophical mind, which is, in reality, a stumbling block for mere philosophy: that the definitive category of Christianity—and "category" means the inescapable condition for all assertions about a given subject matter—is the particular, unique reality of the concrete personality of Jesus of Nazareth.

And once again: the way to this God is not a general religious experience and endeavor, an ethical exertion and penetrating rational interpretation—all of which, in other respects, retain their significance—but rather that way "which is taught in the Gospel." ". . . no one knows the Father except the Son and any one to whom the Son chooses to reveal him" (Mt. 11, 27). "I am the way, and the truth, and the life; no one comes to the Father, but by me."[15] It is the way of faith. Faith is that act of personal adherence, of binding oneself in definitive fidelity, through which Jesus Christ becomes the beginning, out of which something new, a new existence in the fullest sense of the word, arises. The believer puts himself in the place of Jesus. In "rebirth" and "imitation" he sees through Jesus' eyes; he takes Jesus' norms, goals, and estimations as his own. For all merely natural perception, this is walking on the water. But therein begins, for the believer, the "kingdom of God."

Under the title of "Sur la conversion du pécheur" (P. O., pp. 196ff.), a little note has come down to us, which probably stems from the year 1655. It expresses with great power the experience of the newness of life, of the new order of existence attained, in the sense of fragment 793:

"The first thing that God inspires in the soul which he deigns to truly touch is a quite extraordinary knowledge and power of sight (*vue*) through which the soul considers things and itself in a completely new way.

"This new light causes it fear, and brings it an anxiety which traverses the repose which it used to find in the things which delighted it. It can no longer enjoy with tranquillity the things which used to charm it. A continual scruple combats it in this enjoyment . . . But it finds still more bitterness in the exercises of piety than in the vanities of the world. On the one hand, the presence of visible objects affects it more than the hope of invisible ones, and on the other, the solidity of the invisible ones affects it more than the vanity of the visible ones. And thus the presence of the ones and the solidity of the others excite its affection, and the vanity of the ones and the absence of the others excite its aversion, so that there arises within it a disorder and a confusion . . ."

What appears in the experience of the *Mémorial* as a beginning is here already grasped in its development. The old and the new forms of consciousness and evaluation penetrate one another and struggle with one another.

This is also true for the life of understanding and thought. A new reality, a new level, a new power of vision are given. There now begins a difficult and wonderful labor. The general conceptions of God, the universal concepts of him which claimed to be so "pure," and were so in a certain sense, are thrown into this apparent humanization of God. The two worlds of experience and thought, which one could express with the formulas "God is the Absolute" and "God is he, who speaks through Jesus Christ," struggle with one another. There is a tension between them, and often an apparent contradiction, which pervades not only thought, but the whole manner in which the person apprehends himself and the world, in his whole living attitude—yet they are both addressed to the same reality: the Living God. Religious thought endeavors to learn the mode of thinking which corresponds to the living nature of God; it is that of Scripture and the saints. Reason reacts against this; it has the impression that it is losing its footing, but has at the same time the presentiment therein of new problems and new ways of dealing with them. Abstract thought injects its concepts into this concreteness. It cannot reject them, however, for they do indeed contain a truth. Thus it must win them anew—in such a way, that they hold their own in the face of that concreteness.

Everything which honest labor has brought to light as "philosophical knowledge of God" retains its value. Its value is great, despite those who scorn philosophy, in all times as in our own; for the coherence of being as well as the postulates of thought and the power of the mind, whence these concepts were obtained, do not originate just anywhere at all, nor from evil, but from the same God who spoke in Christ. But creation is structured towards grace and can be truly seen only in relation to grace. The anti-philosophical vogue in the religious thinking of our time turns against the "paganism" of ancient philosophy, yet already bears its own paganism in its bosom . . . A thought thus awakens, with a vitality, a concentration, an inner richness, but of course also an exigency, which are not given to and imposed upon merely philosophical thinking. Only from this viewpoint can one understand what is at stake in the struggle of Pascal's *Pensées*.

And the whole world enters into this tension. The world is no longer only "the finite," which is understood in reference to "an absolute," as in mere philosophy; it is rather work of the Living God, object of his Providence, space into which he comes. It is the field and the fullness of the actions and events in which he encounters man.

How is one then to think of the world? If it is all that—and yet neither its scientific exactness, nor its historical objectivity, nor the philosophical categories with which it must be clearly thought, may be destroyed? How, for instance, can the Christian concept of Providence—that is, of the living action of God's love in history—be conceived in a genuine and Christian way? Conceived in such a way that it does not become a rationalistic ordering of the whole world or a system of human welfare, but rather that singular, energetic, unheard of action of God's love which Christ means—and that without abdicating the neatness and exactitude with which science and history have taught us to grasp reality? Thus, the Providence of the Father—not in a world of fantasy, or of children, or of the scope of the Church closed in upon itself, but in the real world, as it is?[16]

Here lie the tasks at hand.

When Pascal lived through that experience, of which the *Mémorial* informs us, he did not cease to be a mathematician, a physicist, an engineer, a psychologist, and a philosopher.

Just as before, he saw the reality corresponding to each of these powers of understanding, and just as before, he was resolved to do them justice. But in addition, a new reality had dawned on him, the Living God. A reality which he could not let be, nor isolate in a special sphere, following, for example, the idealistic method of twofold truth. Rather, this reality was such that it demanded the rethinking of all existence from its standpoint. If a physicist were first to see in the human body only the statics and dynamics of specific organic or energy structures, but one day it were to dawn on him, what life is—then he would not

43

be able to make two separate compartments, one for the physical structure of man, the other for his living nature. He would much rather feel himself called upon to pose the problem of the "physics of life"; a physics in which the physical phenomena would have to undergo a new classification based on the superior phenomena of life. Once more, something analogous would take place were the existence of the intellectual, the personal domain to dawn on our physicist. So, too, it here goes higher—yet not only "higher," but really and definitively "high," before that event which "comes from heaven," "from above." For Pascal, the world remains the world, philosophy remains philosophy. But everything is called into a new coherence, and thought is challenged to a new effort through the discovery that God, grasped by the "philosopher" merely as "the absolute," is in truth the Living God, who enters into history in Jesus Christ; and that the relation of man to him, conceived by the philosophical theory of being as "relation to the absolute," is in truth the very life, oriented towards God, of him who is called by God.

The prodigious ruins which the following creative effort of Pascal has left behind for us, the *Pensées,* bear witness to his struggle to accomplish this task.

CHAPTER II

Man and His Situation in the World

I.

The goal of knowledge is the structure of the whole of being. But this structure is inaccessible to knowledge. Yet knowledge cannot give up its pretension to the whole. The whole is thus replaced by a reduction: a specific but universally fruitful point of view will determine the movement of knowledge, so that its result rounds itself out and despite its partial nature gains a universality of meaning. It gains a relatively universal character and thus becomes a symbol of the inaccessible total universe. The way in which this reduction is carried out, whether it aims for depth or breadth, for plenitude or monumental structure, for the unique or the typical—this way expresses the individuality of the cognizing personality.

There is such a stylizing tendency at work in Pascal's thought. It lies in the effort to unite spontaneous experience of the object with conceptual precision; in a tendency towards construction, whereby, within a strongly emphasized total synthesis, different levels of being and value, no longer derivable from one another, are worked out and set in a dynamic relationship to the totality. And finally, Pascal's basic instinct is tragic-heroic in nature. The charm of existence resides for him in the fact that it is unusual and demanding. Thus, without departing from the strictest scientific will to clarity, he is attracted chiefly by the entangled knots of reality, the points of crisis of existence.

45

We now have to show how Pascal, guided by this tendency, constructs the image of man, and how he places it into the totality of the world.

II.

Pascal's image of man is based on the wealth of phenomena which he had been able to observe during his life *"en homme du monde"*—at the time when the insight into the realm of the specifically human had dawned on the mathematician and physicist. And two masters had taught him to put into practice the *"vue pour les choses humaines"*: Montaigne, whose *Essais* he continually reread, and his friend, the Chevalier de Méré, one of the creators of the canon of the *"honnête homme,"* which was to determine the French conception of the proper man until the Revolution. In this school, Pascal became the greatest of the French *"moralistes"*—those thinkers whose point of departure is not a concept, but the observation, guided by a certain sentiment of values, of man as he is; who do not smooth over complexities and contradictions of this human nature, but see in them the essential, and who assimilate, through dialectical reflexion, what *"vue"* and *"sentiment"* merely perceive.

III.

This image of man is founded on the phenomenon of concretion. Man, as he really is, can thus not be grasped by means of a simple series of concepts, but only by means of a dialectical structure which unites the multiple and the contradictory in a whole, and thus guides the intuition to the point where it can grasp the cohesion of the whole.

The very first fragment of the *Pensées* begins with this problem. The "geometricians"—that is, the logicians of the abstract —have no insight for the concrete, they are not *"fins"* because, "being used to the clear, unadorned principles of geometry and to arguing when they have had a good look at their principles

46

and obtained a firm grasp of them, they become lost among the subtleties when principles cannot be grasped in this way. We can scarcely see them; we feel rather than see them; we have the greatest difficulty in making people feel them who are incapable of feeling them on their own account: these matters are so subtle and so involved that we need a very clear and very delicate sense of perception to feel and to judge them rightly and fairly in accordance with this feeling, usually without being able to give an orderly demonstration of them as in geometry, because we do not perceive the principles governing them, and because the task imposed on us would be endless. What is necessary is to take the matter in at a glance, and not by a process of rational argument, at least up to a certain point" (P. O., p. 318).

The description of the phenomenon is classic. Man exists in a multiplicity of moments, which must not be added up, but rather comprehended as a totality. Pascal now tries to determine the particular nature of this unity from the most varied points of departure.

He repeatedly compares human existence and its contents to the unity of a current, for "our nature lies in movement" (fr. 129, p. 387).

This movement is variously formulated. Thus, for example, as a struggle: "The struggle alone pleases us, but not the victory. We love to see the struggles of animals, not the victor infuriated over the vanquished. What did we want to see but the victorious end; and, as soon as it comes, we are satiated. So it is in play, and so in the search for truth. In disputes we like to see the clash of opinions, but to contemplate truth when found, not at all. To have it observed with pleasure, we have to show it to emerge out of strife. So in the passions, there is pleasure in seeing the collision of two contraries; but when one acquires the mastery, it is but brutality. We never seek things, but the search for things" (fr. 135, p. 389). Or as the succession of different states: "Time heals griefs and quarrels, for one changes, and is no longer the same person. Neither the offender nor the offended are any longer themselves. It is like a nation which one has provoked, and meets again after two generations. They are still Frenchmen, but not the same" (fr. 122, p. 386). Fragment 355 finally associates with continual change the law of contrast and comes thus to the conception of rhythm: "Princes and kings play sometimes. They are not always on their thrones; they become bored there. Grandeur must be abandoned to be appreciated. Continuity in everything satiates. Cold is agreeable that we may get warm. Nature acts by progress, *itus et reditus*. It goes and comes back, then advances further, then twice as much backwards, then further than ever, etc. . . ." (p. 492).

As soon as the movement comes to a stop, life stands still. This leads to *ennui,* at once the great enemy of high culture and its consequence: "Nothing is so insufferable to man as to be in full repose, without passions, without business, without diversion, without study. He then feels his nothingness, his abandonment, his insufficiency, his dependence, his impotence, his emptiness. There will immediately arise from the depth of his soul boredom, gloom, sadness, chagrin, vexation, despair" (fr. 131, p. 388).

This unity in the multiplicity of the "*principes si déliés et en si grand nombre,*" of which fragment 1 spoke, lies here in their succession. It is the task of the "*esprit de finesse*" to grasp it with a "clear view" and a "delicate sense," and to understand it with a "right and just judgment."

In this same context is found the conception of structures, in the modern sense of the word. Thus, for example, different qualities, different attitudes or points of view, etc., are condensed to human types and opposed to one another in conversation or conflict. For example, in the "Entretien avec M. de Saci sur Epictète et Montaigne," in which the rigoristic Stoic and the worldly-wise skeptic confront one another (P. O., pp. 146ff., esp. 160ff.); then again in the first *Lettres provinciales,* in which different conceptions of the problem of grace are opposed as in a spiritual drama.

48

Another way to grasp the concrete character of the human order, by grasping the "many in one," lies in the fact that a moment of existence is determined by its place in the whole. Thus fragment 104 speaks of the positional value of an impression: "When our passion leads us to do something, we forget our duty; when one likes a book, one reads it, when one ought to be doing something else. But, to remind oneself of one's duty, one must set oneself a task one dislikes, one then pleads that one has something else to do, and by this means remembers one's duty" (p. 380; see fr. 105, p. 381). Fragment 263 points out how different the impression produced by an event is, if one anticipates it in imagination, or if one actually experiences it in a concrete situation (p. 454). The treatise "De l'art de persuader" develops in detail the importance of the situational context for the fruitfulness of an idea (P. O., pp. 184ff.), etc.

Here belongs, too, the notion of the *"pensée de derrière la tête,"* which is very important for Pascal: a certain train of thought is carried out as the immediate purpose demands. But if the researcher in question is great enough, he can already, beyond this immediate goal, have a more distant goal of knowledge. If the fruitful instant of perception occurs, then the first train of thought is subordinated to the higher goal of knowledge, and receives a new significance from it.[17] The process can take place among two or more men, for instance in a conversation between a superior and one or more less gifted minds. The former knows that the others are not capable of understanding the true facts of the case. Thus, using their own presuppositions as a point of departure, he says what is false in itself, but which contains the maximum of truth accessible at the moment to his listeners. A very subtle situation, in which the feeling for the differentiations of the function of truth can of course also turn into dishonesty. In this connection one may cite the striking remarks about the significance of error in the general economy of human existence, which already anticipate modern pragmatism: "When the truth of a thing is not known, it is advantageous that

49

there be a common error which determines the mind of man, . . . For the principal malady of man is restless curiosity about things which he cannot know; and it is not as bad for him to be in error as to be curious to no purpose" (fr. 18, p. 327). These propositions contain no simple assertion, but rather the definition of a situation: someone is there who understands the whole. He knows that an error is at hand, but that the insight really required cannot be produced. Thus he lets the error persist, in order that it exert an organizing influence upon the consciousness and the behavior of the others.[18]

Still further examples could be cited. But it has no doubt become clear how Pascal sees the phenomenon of concrete human existence: as a succession of different moments in the flow of the selfsame continuity of life . . . as a constructive coexistence and interpenetration in the simultaneous whole . . . as an inclusion of elements in the total *Gestalt* . . . as a succession of the levels of meaning of a spiritual operation, which reveal themselves to the extent that the perceptive power of the observer is able to push forward. (Perspectivism.)

IV.

Man thus exists in concretion. His reality is composed of multiply entwined moments, partially opposed to one another. A further step leads from this dialectical tension to a state of suspension.

The phenomenon already appears in the analysis of concretion. Since the concrete can only be grasped from the reciprocal determination of contradictory moments, what is really meant remains in suspension between them: "Nature has so well placed us in the middle that if we change one side of the balance, we change the other too." And then, regarding the mechanism of cognition: "That makes me believe that there are springs in our head, which are so disposed that he who touches one, touches also the contrary" (fr. 70, p. 346).

50

If living human existence thus hovers between oppositely arranged moments, the problem of proper proportion acquires a particular significance. In every action, it is a matter of finding the "point indivisible," which determines the proper proportion.

Thus epistemologically: "If one is too young, one does not judge well; so, also, if one is too old. If one does not think enough, or if one thinks too much on any matter, one becomes obstinate and infatuated about it. If one considers one's work immediately after having done it, one is still entirely prepossessed in its favor; if too long afterwards, one can no longer enter into it. So with pictures seen from too far or too near; there is but one indivisibly fine point which is the true place from which to look at them: the others are too near, too far, too high or too low. Perspective determines that point in the art of painting. But who shall determine it in truth and morality?" (fr. 381, p. 502).

To the capacity, in the field of cognition, of finding the "infinitely fine point" of proper perspectives, corresponds, in the ethical realm, the gift of discovering the exact point of reference for the various moments of the concrete demand. "When one wants to pursue virtues to their extremes on either side, vices appear, which insinuate themselves insensibly . . . so that one loses oneself in the vices, and no longer sees the virtues. One is trapped in perfection itself" (fr. 357, p. 492). And fragment 359 explains: "We do not sustain ourselves in virtue by our own strength, but by the balancing of two opposed vices, just as we remain upright between two contrary winds. Remove one of these vices, and we fall into the other" (p. 493; see also fr. 151, p. 401). "*Simplicité*" thus appears as the central moral value, a simplicity in multiplicity, which Pascal only declares possible, indeed, as the "*simplicité de l'évangile*"—a concept to which correspond, in the realm of cognition, those of the "*vue nette*," the "*jugement droit*," and the "*bon goût*."[19] Fragment 353 expresses this ethical suspension in a striking dynamic formula:

51

"One does not display one's greatness by being at one extreme, but by touching both at once and filling all the intervening space. But perhaps this is only a sudden movement of the soul from one to the other extreme, and in fact it is ever at one point only, like the firebrand [which one swings on a string, giving the impression of a continual circular line, whereas in fact it is always at only one point of the circle]" (p. 491).

This concept of the mean to be maintained is associated with that of genuine humanity: "One leaves humanity, if one deviates from the mean. It is the grandeur of the human soul to be able to remain in it." On the other hand, the impossibility of living at the extremes is very strikingly described by the long fragment 72 (pp. 347ff., esp. 353)—with the result, to be sure, that man never succeeds in finding a firm foothold: "This is our true state; this is what makes us incapable of certain knowledge and of absolute ignorance. We sail on a vast milieu, always uncertain and drifting, driven from one end towards the other. Whenever we think we can attach ourselves to any point and hold fast to it, it wavers and abandons us; and if we follow it, it eludes our grasp, slips past us and flees in an eternal flight. Nothing stands firm for us. This is our natural condition, and yet the most contrary to our inclination; we burn with desire to find solid ground and an ultimate lasting foundation, there to build a tower reaching to the infinite. But our whole groundwork cracks, and the earth opens to abysses" (p. 354).

So far the suspension has taken place in the interior of the concrete itself. It receives a new character—as already in the last text cited—as soon as man as a whole becomes aware of his relationship to the poles of the totality of existence, and has to maintain himself between them.

In the same fragment 72 it is stated: ". . . supported in the mass, which nature has given him"—we notice the threatening undertone: "*soutenu dans la masse*"; under him, gaping emptiness!—man hangs "between the two abysses of the infinite and nothingness." Thus he is "a nothing in regard to the infinite, an everything in regard to nothingness, a mean between nothingness and everything."[20] How is man to deal with this situation? He is "infinitely removed from understanding the extremes; the end of things and their beginning are invincibly hidden from him in an impenetrable secret; he is equally incapable of seeing the nothingness from which he was made and the infinite in which he is swallowed up. What will he do, then, but perceive (some) appearance of the middle of things, in an eternal despair of knowing either their beginning or their end?" (p. 350).

The situation takes on a very particular character, as soon as it is no longer a question of suspension between mere points of reference, but rather between positive and negative terms of value, or, as Pascal repeatedly formulates it, between "*grandeur*" and "*misère*" (frs. 400–423 and elsewhere). Thus, for example, fragment 411: "In spite of the sight of all our miseries, which press upon us and hold us by the throat, we have an instinct which we cannot repress which lifts us up" (p. 512).

Pascal's basic conviction appears here: man exists in nobility and misery, in fidelity and defection. This is not a genuine suspension, which always means a dialectical relationship between moments differing in kind but of equal value, but rather a confusion; a tangle of contradictions; an "evil" dialectic opposed to the other good dialectic, constructive in nature. Fragment 346 states: "Thought constitutes the greatness of man"; and fragment 347 confirms: "All our dignity consists in thought" (p. 488). But fragment 83 opposes to the preceding the proposition: "Man is but a subject full of error, natural and ineffaceable without grace. Nothing shows him the truth. Everything deceives him" (p. 369). And fragment 365: "All the dignity of man consists in thought. Thought is therefore by its nature a wonderful and incomparable thing. It would have to have strange defects to be contemptible. But it has such defects that nothing is more ridiculous. How great it is in its nature! How base it is in its defects! But what is this thought? How foolish it is!" (p. 496). The idea could thus be pursued in reference to the

53

various values: moral good and evil, honor and dishonor, wisdom and folly, etc.

"Grandeur" and "misery" are not, however, simply mixed, they do not merely crisscross, mislead and disorder one another, but mutually determine one another as well. The idea is verified by numerous observations; fragment 151, for example: "Admiration spoils everything already in childhood . . . The children of Port-Royal, who are not goaded on by this prick of envy and vainglory, fall into carelessness" (p. 401). The same thought touches on the essential in such formulations as fragment 397: "The greatness of man is great in that he knows himself to be miserable. A tree does not know itself to be miserable" (p. 509). It is precisely his miseries which prove his greatness; they are "*misères d'un roi dépossédé*" (fr. 398, p. 509). ". . . to the extent that men possess light they discover both the greatness and the wretchedness in man." For "wretchedness is deduced from greatness, and greatness from wretchedness" (fr. 416, p. 509). And so on and so forth, until the contradiction takes on such a character that one no longer sees how one is still to bring together "this twofold nature of man," and "some have thought that we had two souls. A single subject seemed to them incapable of such sudden variations from an unmeasured presumption to a horrible dejection of heart" (fr. 417, p. 515).

Man is suspended between angel and beast, "*et le malheur veut, que qui veut faire l'ange, fait la bête*" (fr. 358, p. 493). Fragment 431 asks still more anxiously: "What then will man become? Will he be equal to God or the beasts? What a frightful difference! What then will we be?" (p. 527).[21]

V.

Man thus lives in inner tensions which belong to his own particular existence, and at the same time in suspension between objective points of reference dependent on the exterior universe. The situation acquires a particularly critical character from the relationship, which so very much preoccupied Pascal, between the limited finite and the unlimited infinite.

The treatise "De l'esprit géométrique" develops the concept of a series of numbers which can be prolonged indefinitely, in the direction of larger and smaller numbers, without ever coming to an end. Velocity can likewise be geometrically increased or diminished, without ever coming to an end; so, too, space, time, etc. ". . . in a word: whatever movement, whatever number, whatever space, whatever time it be, there are always a larger and a smaller." Thence the conclusion: "Thus there are properties common to all things, the knowledge of which opens the mind to the greatest wonders of nature." The most important such property includes "the two infinities which meet in all things: one of greatness, the other of smallness." Between them, "between nothingness [the infinitely small] and the infinite [the infinitely great], being always infinitely distant from these extremes," is to be found every concretely definite thing. This state of affairs is at once evident and irreducible. It belongs among the constituent elements of being and human thought; and the fact that it can neither be proved nor derived "is not a defect, but rather a perfection" (pp. 174f.).

Here the finite and the infinite, or more precisely, the limited and the unlimited, are taken purely quantitatively. In the long fragment 72 the subject matter is qualitative. "Let man then contemplate the whole of nature in her full and lofty majesty, and turn his vision from the base objects which surround him. Let him gaze on that brilliant light, set like an eternal lamp to illuminate the universe, let the earth appear to him a point in comparison to the vast circle described by the sun; and let him wonder at the fact that this vast circle is itself but a very fine point in comparison to that described by the stars which revolve in the firmament. But if our view stops there, let our imagination pass beyond; it will sooner tire of conceiving than nature of supplying material for conception. This whole visible world is but an imperceptible dash in the ample bosom of nature. No idea approaches it. We may enlarge our conceptions beyond all imaginable space; we only produce atoms in comparison to the reality of things. It is a sphere, the center of which is everywhere, the circumference nowhere" (p. 347).

The same *processus in infinitum* which so staggers the mind goes also towards smallness. Let us suppose that an observer discover in the tiny body of a mite the "parts incomparably more minute, legs with their joints, veins in the legs, blood in the veins, humors in the blood, drops in the humors, vapors in the drops; that, dividing these last things again, he exhaust his powers in these conceptions, and that the last object at which he can arrive be now that of our discourse. Perhaps he will think that here is the smallest point in nature. I want to make him see therein a new abyss. I want to paint for him not only the visible universe, but the immensity of nature which one can conceive, in the womb of this abridged atom. Let him see in it an infinity of universes, each of which has its firmament, its planets, its earth, in the same proportion as in the visible world; in this earth, animals, and finally mites, in which he will find again what the first had; and finding still in these others the same thing without end and without cessation, let him lose himself in these wonders as amazing in their littleness as the others in their vastness. For who will not be astounded at the fact that our body, which a moment ago was imperceptible in the universe, itself imperceptible in the bosom of the whole, is now a colossus, a world, or rather a whole, in comparison to the nothingness which one cannot attain?" (pp. 349f.).

The same state of affairs recurs in the notion of the chain of causes: "All things proceed from nothingness, and are borne towards the infinite. Who will follow these astonishing processes?" (p. 350). We thus have here a genetic, evolutionary conception: what exists originates in each case from more simple postulates. It integrates itself, as it were, in more and more simple moments in the direction of the causes. On the other hand, it differentiates itself, in the direction of the effects, into more and more complex and extended products. The two inaccessible terminal points are here called "nothingness"—whereby the concept of what does not yet exist unites with that of pure potentiality—and "the infinite." ". . . the end of things and their beginning are invincibly hidden from him in an impenetrable secret; he is equally incapable of seeing the nothingness from which he was made, and the infinite in which he is swallowed up" (p. 350).

The same situation recurs in the axiological realm: "Nature seems to have accomplished the same thing with its two infinites, natural and moral: for there will always be higher and lower, people who are more astute and less astute, more elevated and more wretched, in order to lower our pride and raise up our abjection" (fr. 532, p. 567; see also fr. 525, p. 566). So, too, in the noetic realm: it is impossible to define the limits of knowledge. It is endless in its extension, in the sense of a movement towards what is greater and broader; and endless in its concentration, in the return towards the antecedent, in that principles established in each case are based ever anew on earlier, simpler principles (fr. 72, p. 350f.). This state of affairs "is found in all our faculties" (p. 353).

Both forms of the infinite elude man's power of understanding. They disappear in the same inaccessibility, even if in opposite directions. It is precisely in this that they approach one another and become different modifications of one and the same thing: "and it seems to me that whoever had understood the ultimate principles of things might also come to know the infinite. The one depends on the other, and the one leads to the other. These extremes meet and reunite by dint of having withdrawn from one another . . ." (fr. 72, p. 352).

The inconceivable is thus like the surface of a sphere, upon which straight lines, fleeing one another, join to form a ring. The image joins others, already cited, according to which being has the character of a sphere. To be sure, an infinitely vast sphere, whose center (symbol for the infinitely small) is everywhere and whose surface (symbol for the infinitely great) is nowhere. Here the determinations flow into one another.

What is there behind all this?

First of all, something personal: the fervor of greatness, so strongly felt by Pascal, which suffers no limitation: *"L'homme est fait pour l'infini."* And with it, the will to the highest possible achievement, the goal of which can only lie in the infinite; and finally, the demand of an eternal striving forwards.[22]

But then, this sudden appearance of the consciousness of the infinite indicates the disintegration of the medieval sense of existence. The medieval as well as the ancient view of life was thoroughly and fundamentally limited. This limitation bore, however, the value of unequivocal definiteness and perfect form. The image for it was the figure of the sphere, which had a periphery and a center, and in which each point is determined by the radius and the stratum. Thence stemmed the symbolic figures organized into degrees and hierarchies, sometimes built up in pyramids, sometimes in concentric spheres. The whole was finite, and moreover, clearly "surrounded" by the infinite God, who had created it, who encircles and penetrates it. In this very fact of having been created, however, it was the expression of eternal values and orders. The finiteness thus acquired absolute accents. The finite thing or event had the character of symbol or representation. Man was the synthesis of these symbols, and as such, endowed with all accents of significance. In the fact that the world with its order sustained him, that he formed its center or summit, he had a secure though finite position . . . But now, in the modern consciousness making its appearance, the world begins to expand in all directions into the illimitable; it becomes "infinite." For the immediate consciousness, it hereby rises up abreast of God: he is lessened in importance; the world begins to become the essential, to occupy the whole of consciousness. Thereby, however, man is also lessened in importance. For along with its finiteness, the world loses its form perceptible to immediate consciousness; it no longer has either circumference, or center, or order. Man thus ceases to be its center or its summit. His finiteness is no longer absorbed into symbolic, representative meanings, but appears as such, as if naked, to consciousness. Man loses his foothold, his security, he falls into a state of suspension. He is "equally incapable of seeing the nothingness from which he was made, and the infinite in which he is swallowed up." He is in a *"désespoir éternel de connaître ni leur principe ni leur fin."*

This state of suspension has still an "abode": in the fact that man is capable *"d'apercevoir (quelque) apparence du milieu des choses."* But if the impression produced by those infinities really breaks through, then even that last moment of order disappears: that consciousness of "any appearance at all of the middle." In Pascal one can witness this occurrence with upsetting intensity.

Fragment 205 notes: "When I consider the short duration of my life, absorbed in the eternity preceding and following it; the little space which I fill, and even that I see, engulfed in the infinite immensity of spaces which I do not know, and which do not know me, I am frightened and I am astonished to see myself here rather than there; for there is no reason why here rather than there, why now rather than then" (p. 427). And fragment 206 consists of the famous sentence: *"Le silence éternel de ces espaces infinis m'effraie"* (p. 428).

The mental burden of the quantities, between which man hangs suspended, becomes so enormous that the last stable moment—which Pascal termed "any appearance at all of the middle"—is withdrawn. Indeed, even the clear notions of "here" and "now" lose their meaning. Radical suspension, the indefiniteness of time and space, thus arises, powerfully expressed by the words: "I do not know why," and "the spaces do not know me." Man no longer has a mental abode, where he can feel at home; he no longer knows where he is, nor why he is here. He begins to feel that there is no reason for what exists, for its time and place. Existence slips into fortuitousness.[23] The experience of finiteness reaches its final paroxysm. Tragic finitism: existence feels robbed of all foundation. Man's existence has no resting place. He continually seeks to define himself, without managing to do so in a real and lasting way. Man is "*égaré.*"

Fragment 72 gives the principle behind this process: "In the sight of these infinities, all finites are equal, and I see no reason for fixing one's imagination on one rather than on another" (p. 355). Man has become homeless. He is suspended no matter where. He exists, with his qualities, in no matter what. With his limits, in no matter how much. From the consciousness of his essentialness, he has slipped into that of pure facticity.

There therefore awakens in man an anxiety in the face of the world, a terror in the face of the powers of existence. Not only because they can destroy him exteriorly, but because they lessen the importance of his own being and take away the spiritual place where he stands. Whereas in the symbolic view of the world, the All was felt to be in relation to man, man now becomes aware that it is indifferent. That is worse than the fear in the face of a mysterious, indeed even of a hostilely threatening world. The most terrifying of all is the cold indifference of the infinitely great; the impression of being swallowed, sunk, "*abimé,*" in the "infinite immensity of spaces, which I do not know, and which do not know me." And man cries out, "*Je m'étonne . . . je m'effraie!*"

VI.

This transformation in the experiencing of the world threatens man to the depths of his being. The mutually determining experiences of finiteness and endlessness melt away the substance of his existence, violently shake his standing place, evaporate the why of his destiny, and throw him into mere fortuitousness. How is he to prevail against it?

Materially, he is not capable of doing so. He can not oppose his mass to the masses which face him; nor his force to the cosmic forces; nor his fleeting transitoriness to the immensities of duration. He seems to be able to do it only by finding a footing in something which is other than the power of the world, which he experiences as such a new burden: that is, in the mind.

The famous fragment 347 says: "Man is but a reed, the most feeble thing in nature; but he is a thinking reed. It is not necessary for the entire universe to arm itself in order to crush him. A vapor, a drop of water suffices to kill him. But, if the universe were to crush him, man would still be more noble than that which kills him, because he knows that he dies and the advantage which the universe has over him; the universe knows nothing of this" (p. 488). And fragment 348: "It is not from space that I must seek my dignity, but from the regulation of my thought. I will have no more by possessing lands. By space the universe encompasses and swallows me up like a point; by thought I encompass the world" (p. 488).

We think of that letter, which the young Pascal sent to the Queen of Sweden. It bears witness to the deep impression which human greatness, also and especially that of the ruler, makes on him; but then, it is impressive to read the way in which the young man candidly assumes superiority and declares to the queen that there are two sorts of mastery, the political and the intellectual, but that the latter is superior (P. O., pp. 112f.). Here something similar occurs, but in the face of the world. Aware of his intellectual powers, man assumes a superiority in the face of the overly powerful universe.

It could thus seem as if the solid point of Pascal's anthropology lay therein. According to it, man would be by his body an element of nature, he would stand under its powers and be subject to them. The mind, however, would be rooted in itself and as such would be removed from nature. It could even, by thought, raise itself up in the face of nature and contain it. It would thus be greater than nature. It would find its center and footing in its own essence, and absolutely stated, it would by its own force be able to remain victorious even in its own destruc-

61

tion. The process of transposition of the consciousness of the world would thereby be continued in a positive way: the individual, lost with his smallness in the boundless world, would, by the force of his mind, be a match for this very world. We would have the ethic of heroic finiteness, which does indeed constitute one of the fundamental traits of the modern period at the threshold of its maturity. But Pascal—need it be said?—measured by an ultimate standard, is too great to be satisfied with this formula. Something decisive is lacking in the view of man just sketched, and he would not be willing to let it be taken lightly: evil.

VII.

When Pascal speaks of evil, he means less the particular immoral act than the evil inclination: evil as attitude, state, power. He derives the insight into its strength first of all from the consideration of universally human situations.

In the conceptions of what is just and unjust, Pascal finds such obscurities and contradictions that a valid judgment becomes impossible. "Three degrees of latitude reverse all jurisprudence; a meridian decides the truth. Fundamental laws change within a few years of possession; right has its epochs; the entry of Saturn into the Lion marks to us the origin of such and such a crime . . . Theft, incest, infanticide, parricide, everything has had its place among virtuous actions. Can anything be more ridiculous than that a man should have the right to kill me because he lives on the other side of the water, and because his prince has a quarrel with mine, although I have none with him?" (fr. 294, pp. 465f.).

In the abstract, there would have to be a natural norm for the relations of man to man; a just morality, stemming from the inner essential order of things and from just moral judgment. Instead, good and evil appear inextricably bound together in law and morality; in the judgment of men, truth and error are inseparably blended. Pascal thus comes to a pessimistic conception of social life. He renounces every sociological order which would try to legitimize itself on the basis of intrinsic virtue, and declares that a purely positive social order is the only one possible.

But the fact that things are so is an effect of the power of evil.

In the France of the sixteenth and seventeenth centuries, the frightful barbarity of the civil and religious wars had given birth to the longing for an amiable culture which would embellish life. At the center of this culture was the ideal type of the *"honnête homme,"* oriented towards making life worth living for himself, by being anxious to make it so for others as well. Secure political order, increasing authority and this spirit collaborated to produce a highly refined social culture. Pascal knows it most intimately. He perceives the richness and refinement of its values, but at the same time sees what is hidden behind the brilliant manners of this fleeting life: the urge for *"divertissement,"* the flight from one's self. In a long series of thoughts, from fragment 111 on, he investigates this impulse and its manifestations.

He finds its roots first of all in the ever-changing nature of human life itself. See fragment 135 (p. 389) already cited above.

His gaze then penetrates further and discovers a deeper unrest. Strictly speaking, man should be capable of "sitting quietly in his room," that is, of facing up to what he himself is and what things are. But he is not able to do so, for as soon as he comes to rest he becomes aware of the misery, the torment, the terror of existence. He therefore flees into diversion. Men have "a secret instinct which impels them to seek amusement and occupation abroad, and which comes from the sense of their continual miseries. They have another secret instinct, a remnant of the greatness of our original nature, which teaches them that happiness is in fact found only in rest, and not in tumult. And of these two contrary instincts, there forms within them a confused project, which hides itself from their view in the depths of their soul, exciting them to aim at rest through agitation, and to always imagine that the satisfaction which they do not have will come to them, if, by surmounting whatever difficulties they envisage, they

can thereby open the door to rest . . . and if they have surmounted them, rest becomes insufferable. For one thinks either
of the miseries one has or of those which threaten us. And even
if one should see oneself sufficiently sheltered on all sides, ennui,
by its own authority, would not fail to arise from the depths of
the heart in which it has its natural roots, and to fill the mind
with its poison" (fr. 139, pp. 393f.). When man stands face to
face with himself, he becomes aware of the evil which he is himself: "Hence it is that men so much love noise and stir; hence it
is that prison is so horrible a punishment; hence it is that the
pleasure of solitude is a thing so incomprehensible. And finally,
it is the greatest source of happiness in the condition of kings,
that men constantly try to divert them, and to procure for them
all kinds of pleasures. The king is surrounded by persons whose
only thought is to divert the king, and to prevent him from thinking of himself. For he is unhappy, king though he be, if he
thinks of himself" (fr. 139, pp. 391ff.).

We sense here a profound experience of life, what remains
after all particular experiences, value judgments, and possibilities of pleasure have had their say: not only the insufficiency,
but the intolerability of that which exists. From everything which
is in man and around him arises the feeling: it is evil. Thus begins the chase from one thing to another; but in the end the
ennui remains. How elementary this sentiment is becomes clear
from the bitter tone of words like the following: "*Mais ôtez
leur divertissement, vous les verrez se sécher d'ennui . . .*" (fr.
164, p. 405). "Boredom" becomes an ultimate expression for
the metaphysical condition of man. It is the experience of the
nothingness of existence, of its deception and its "*tristesse in-
supportable.*"

This condition, too, is the expression of evil, and the continual
source of new evil.

The analysis of the human heart penetrates deeper still. The
"Discours sur les passions de l'amour" (P. O., pp. 123ff.) indicates two roots of the life of passion: the "*passion de l'amour*"
and the "*passion de l'orgueil.*" We do not know to what extent

64

Pascal experienced the former. The nature of his relationship to Mlle. de Roannez is still uncertain: a profound spiritual and religious friendship, as the family tradition and its image of an ascetic and spiritual Pascal suppose—or a genuine passion, which left behind deep traces in his experience and thought, and which perhaps ended tragically, as a recent interpretation claims. To be sure, what is reported regarding the strange neurotic states to which Pascal was subject as a child: the darkly threatening passionateness of his entire nature and the brewing melancholy, which repeatedly forces its way through—all this certainly suggests that the ascetic attitude of his later life was bought at the cost, at the very least, of arduous struggles against elementary forces in his own inner self.

The consciousness of the *libido excellendi* or *dominandi* stands out all the more prominently in the *Pensées*. "The two sources of our sins are pride and laziness . . ." (fr. 497, p. 556). "The sweetness of fame is so great, that we love it, no matter to what object it is attached, even death" (fr. 158, p. 403). "Pride, counterbalancing all miseries. It either hides its miseries, or, if it discloses them, prides itself on knowing them" (fr. 405, p. 510). And with ironic bitterness, fragment 150 states: "Vanity is so anchored in the heart of man that a soldier, a hodman, a cook, a porter brags and wishes to have his admirers. Even philosophers desire them. Those who write against it want to have the glory of having written well; and those who read it want to have the glory of having read it. I who write this have perhaps this desire, and perhaps those who will read it . . ." (p. 401).

There was in Pascal a powerful will to domination, the analysis of which leads one into the most dangerous tensions of his existence. Neither his general attitude nor his devoutness can be understood outside of this context. It is characteristic in this regard to observe how deeply the history of his scientific accomplishments is bound up with the struggle for prestige as an inventor—of which, after all, he had so little need, for he was surrounded by respect and soon famous. Another essential trait

65

of Pascal's image is a peculiar violence against his adversaries. This trait appears very early—already in the young opponent of the Sieur Saint-Ange in Clermont, a somewhat confused but basically harmless man, whom Pascal afflicts until he forces him to the most humiliating retraction—and intensifies throughout his entire life. Therein resides Pascal's demon: the demon of combat, which not only incited him to attack the adversary ruthlessly, but to so caricature him, that he becomes the absolute adversary, against whom the absolute, that is, annihilating combat would be possible and invited—the adversary, therefore, who does not uphold something erroneous *bona fide,* but who stands *mala fide* against the truth. In the same context, one may note that Pascal thought very little of the will to truth in men. Not only, following Montaigne, did he show, by a subtle analysis of the presuppositions of thought, how doubtful man's attitude in cognition is and how strong prejudicial motives are, but he expressly declares that man does not want to know the truth; that he deceives himself and the others. "Man is thus nothing but disguise, falsehood, and hypocrisy, both in himself and in regard to others. He does not want to tell him the truth; he avoids telling it to others, and all these dispositions, so far removed from justice and reason, have a natural root in his heart" (fr. 100, p. 379).

Pascal had an intense and lasting experience of evil, and formulates it in gripping terms.

There is the ever recurring cry over the "*misère de l'homme*": the consciousness of pain, misery, evil, weakness, wretchedness; the consciousness of an incapacity which burns, for it is after all accompanied by the sentiment of an unforgettable greatness: "Wretchedness is deduced from greatness, and greatness from wretchedness." Thus arises "an endless circle, it being certain that to the extent that men possess light they discover both the greatness and the wretchedness in man" (fr. 416, pp. 541f.).

There is also the strangely violent explosion about the "pride of reason," which wants to know, to be right, to dominate.

Pascal's antagonism to Descartes follows indeed, at bottom, from the fact that he sees embodied in him an attitude which he experiences in his own inner self as pride and *hubris*. *"Ecrire contre ceux qui approfondissent trop les sciences. Descartes"* (fr. 76, p. 360). And further: *"Je ne puis pardonner à Descartes; il aurait bien voulu, dans toute sa philosophie, pouvoir se passer de Dieu"* (fr. 77, p. 360). Here rumbles an anger which comes from the most profound experience. He hates himself in the other. One feels the same sentiment in the long fragment 434 on dogmatism and skepticism, the two possible standpoints of overbearing reason. He explodes, as it were, in invectives against them: "Know then, pride, what a paradox you are to yourself. Humble yourself, feeble reason; be silent, imbecile nature . . ." (p. 531).

For one who has learned to esteem Pascal's greatness, an ever recurring tone has a staggering effect: the feeling that in human existence there lies something which ultimately leaves him with an impression of humiliation. It so much contradicts his consciousness of nobility that he rages: "What a chimera then is man! What a novelty, what a monster, what a chaos, what a subject of contradiction, what a prodigy! Judge of all things, imbecile worm of the earth; depositary of truth, sink of incertitude and error; the glory and refuse of the universe!" (p. 531).

For Pascal, a very bitter taste lies at the bottom of existence!

The consciousness that man is not as he should be is concentrated in Pascal's experience of the self.

This experience is built up in antitheses. On the one hand, the self is the bearer of the meaning of existence: "Each one is an all to himself; for when he is dead, everything is dead for him. Hence it is that each believes himself to be all to everybody" (fr. 457, pp. 542f.). At the same time, however, man feels that he is not absolute at all, indeed, that he is not even comprehensible as such: "I feel that I might not have been . . . I am not a necessary being" (fr. 469, p. 547).

67

This self becomes very problematical as soon as one wishes to grasp it: "What is the *self*? . . . Does he who loves someone because of his beauty really love him? No; for the small-pox, which will kill beauty without killing the person, will cause him to love him no longer. And if one loves me for my judgment, for my memory, does one love *me*? No; for I can lose these qualities without losing myself. Where, then, is this *self,* if it be neither in the body nor in the soul? And how love the body or the soul, if not for these qualities which do not constitute the self, since they are perishable? For would one love the substance of the soul of a person abstractly, no matter what qualities were in it? That is impossible and would be unjust. One thus never loves a person, but only qualities" (fr. 323, p. 478). Here the self evaporates into the ungraspable.

Its ethically doubtful character is thrown into relief in fragment 455: "In a word, the *self* has two qualities: It is unjust in itself, in that it makes itself the center of everything; it is inconvenient to others, in that it wants to enslave them; for each *self* is the enemy, and would like to be the tyrant of all others. You take away its inconvenience, but not its injustice, and so you do not render it lovable to those who hate its injustice; you render it lovable only to the unjust [who have nothing to object to the ethical defectiveness, if only the agreeable form is preserved] . . ." (p. 542). Thus the famous consequence: "*Le* moi *est haïssable!*" Once more the excessive emotional state, which stems from direct experience and hard struggle.

Or fragment 476: "One must love but God, and hate but self" (p. 549). And thence an ethic in which man must act against the pretention of his self to be the center: give everything to God and serve God with all one's strength. "The true and unique virtue is thus to hate oneself . . . and to seek a truly lovable being, in order to love" (p. 553).

Only through faith does it become clear to what extent the self is menaced by evil, and to what extent its confusion is thus an expression of sin. (See further below.)

68

VIII.

We had come to the problem of evil from the discussion of the act by which Pascal sought, in the face of the power of external forces, to take his stand on the indestructibility and dignity of the mind. But now, through evil, the power of the mind itself becomes dubious. And indeed, not only dialectically, as a thesis is called into question by an antithesis. Evil does not represent a necessary power in the whole of existence, whose reaction would push upwards the movement of life, the mean force of man; rather, it is to be rejected absolutely. It sometimes appears as if evil were necessary as a function in the whole—for example, in the formula about the pedagogical significance of ambition, reprehensible in itself (fr. 151). Yet Pascal sees therein only a sign of the confusion of human existence. This confusion is so great that often good comes out of evil, and the exclusion of an element not good in itself calls into question a good end result. In any case, evil is the absolute menace.

Hence the distressing suspension, or better, the straying of man, as fragment 427, and still more sharply fragment 431, express it: "What, then, will man become? Will he be equal to God or the brutes? What a frightful difference! What, then, shall we be? Who does not see from all this that man has gone astray [*s'est égaré*], that he has fallen from his place, that he anxiously seeks it, that he can no longer find it again? And who shall then direct him to it? The greatest men have not been able to" (p. 527).

The power and the dignity of the mind are deeply experienced, but the mind as such cannot be relied on. In intellectual life and activity, what matters is not only a simple manifestation of force, but a realization of meaning: a realization of truth, goodness, measure, order. Mind is not simply reality, but determined as reality by value. If it falls into contradiction with meaning, then it becomes questionable in its very being. This is precisely what Pascal experienced.

69

He experiences existence not only combatively, as perception of the mind and establishment of its mastery over matter, but tragically: as rising up and tumbling down again, as struggling and being defeated, as winning and losing, And not in such a way that a force united in itself would be shaken by an adversary from without; rather, man himself, in his struggle, is at once great and pitiful, strong and wretched. And his distress not only implies the difficulty of the ascension, but has something confused, broken, humiliating, absurd about it.

Thus for Pascal something remains which oppresses, fetters, dishonors; something which cannot be denied and yet can in no way be accepted, because it goes against the person's innermost feeling of honor.

There is no longer here a simple suspension, nor a mere intensification of the dialectical relationship from which we started out, but rather an entanglement. It is impossible to go further along this path. The image of man breaks up and becomes confused. It becomes clear that an anthropology strictly limited to the world is impossible. It must be continued from the point of view of faith. Philosophical anthropology, in order to find its consummation, must flow into theological anthropology.

The problem of man can only be solved by his relationship with God. Man can extricate himself from the entanglement through evil only if his spirit is embraced by that which lies above the merely worldly intellectual sphere: By the *Pneuma*.

The deep mistrust which Pascal feels for the mind, taken simply as such, and which makes him see in the mind something so doubtful, at once strong and weak, violent and uncertain, pretentious and destructive—this mistrust is justified. The phenomenon of the mind is not autonomous. It cannot be understood by itself, as rationalism and idealism claim—whereby, necessarily, the opposition to the mind of "race" or of "life" or of "soul" arises. Mind exists essentially in relationship to something, which is falsified if one calls it simply "mind" [*Geist*]. To that, which comes from God: the Holy Spirit, the *Pneuma*.

70

When John says that God is "Spirit" [*Geist*], and that worship must take place "in the Spirit" [*im Geiste*], then that is something different than when one speaks of the intellectuality [*Geistigkeit*] of science or of the objective spirit expressing itself in history. When Paul speaks of "spiritual man," he is not thinking of the distinction between mind and body, but rather means that which comes from God, in distinction to everything which stems from the world. Mind and body, the entire man with his science and culture, all this is for Paul "flesh." On the other hand, the entire man, body and soul along with the whole creation, becomes "spirit" in the rebirth which comes from the Holy Spirit. Pascal does not think otherwise.

To that extent, the Living God is not "spirit" at all in the modern sense of the word, but the "Holy-Spiritual One." The mind of man exists in relation to this God and falls into a profound confusion as soon as he is detached from this relationship. Against the detached modern mind, the objections of the nineteenth and twentieth centuries—of Nietzsche, Klages, and others —are justified, even if they misunderstand themselves in the process. After the mind has constituted itself autonomous and self-sufficient, its overestimation as well as its proscription condition one another mutually. They express at bottom the same state of affairs.

How then can man be defined? How can his image come to its completeness?

IX.

In the fine fragment 793, so important for the determination of Pascal's vision of the world—we have already cited it in the first chapter—it is stated: "The infinite distance between body and mind symbolizes the infinitely more infinite distance between mind and charity; for charity is supernatural.

"All the glory of greatness has no lustre for people engaged in intellectual quests.

71

"The greatness of intellectuals is invisible to kings, to the rich, to captains, to all the great of the flesh.

"The greatness of wisdom, which is nothing if not of God, is invisible to the carnal-minded and to intellectuals. These are three orders differing in kind . . .

"But there are some who can only admire carnal greatness, as though there were no intellectual greatness; and others who only admire intellectual greatness, as though there were not an infinitely higher greatness in wisdom.

"All bodies together, and all minds together, and all their productions, are not equal to the least movement of charity. This is of an order infinitely more exalted.

"From all bodies together, one would not be able to obtain one little thought: this is impossible, and of another order. From all bodies and minds, one would not be able to produce a movement of true charity: this is impossible, and of another, supernatural order."

Three spheres of reality here detach themselves from one another: the sphere of "*corps,*" that of "*esprits,*" and that of "*charité.*" Between them lies a "*différence de genre*"; a qualitative gap which cannot be bridged from below. Each sphere has its own kind of value, its "*grandeur.*" Associated with each is a particular cognitive prerequisite and a particular "*vue,*" a view corresponding to the specific object.

Man exists throughout these three orders—it should be so, at least. And indeed, the structure is not determined from below upwards, but from above downwards. It is not the foundation, but the summit which is decisive. In each case, the higher sphere can no doubt be awaited, desired by the lower sphere, but not constructed; it must come forth of itself.

The final trait, which really defines man, stems not from nature but from God. It cannot be derived from the world, but can only be accepted as a gift of grace. Thus the decisive word about the enigma of man comes from revelation; that is, from the revelation of the mystery of original sin and of the solidarity of all men in guilt. The truth about what man is shines forth only from a source to which he cannot gain access by force. The source must open itself, in grace and revelation. Thus it is possible that only a doctrine which, like that of original sin and of the solidarity of all men in it, upsets all merely ethical and sociological norms, represents the key for the understanding of the visible world. "Certainly nothing shocks us more rudely than this doctrine; and yet, without this mystery, the most incomprehensible of all, we are incomprehensible to ourselves. The knot of our condition takes its twists and turns in this abyss, so that man is more inconceivable without this mystery than this mystery is inconceivable to man" (fr. 434, p. 532). The contents of this mystery are expressed as follows: ". . . there are two truths of faith equally constant: the one, that man, in the state of creation, or in that of grace, is elevated above all nature, made like unto God and sharing in his divinity; the other, that in the state of corruption and sin, he is fallen from this state and made like unto the beasts" (p. 533).

For Pascal, the statement is not only dogmatic doctrine. In many *Pensées,* in ever new turns of expression up to the document of his decisive religious experience of November 23, 1654, the sentiments of the *"grandeur et misère de l'homme"* recur. It is precisely these basic elements of his self-experience which the doctrine of original sin and its consequences makes clear to him.

If we are not mistaken, Pascal's thought is the following: man, as he is today, is something which cannot be understood by itself. He cannot be reduced to the limit of the natural world or the human order. He is by nature *ad Deum creatus,* ordained to be laid hold of by the encounter with God and drawn into a living participation in the divine nature.

Man is not a self-sufficient being, nor is he thus confined within himself. He is a "being above and beyond himself," as fragment 434 magnificently formulates it with the expression: *"l'homme passe infiniment l'homme"* (p. 531). For his nature does not realize itself in the development of a predisposition

73

closed in upon itself, but in that it is drawn above and beyond itself into a communion of life with God.

The necessity of transcending oneself—this, precisely, is the most profound nature of man! The refusal of this self-transcendence, as expressed in the idea of a self-sufficient nature—the ultimate formula of every bourgeois view of man, whether naturalistic or humanistic, individualistic or collectivistic—thus means precisely the destruction of man's most essential nature. This nature is intrinsically based on risk, and thus exposed from the outset to tragic possibilities. The "first nature" of man was no simple state of nature, but a life in the divine sphere. Precisely therein appeared what is most characteristic in human "naturalness"—conforming, indeed, to the fundamental laws of this conception of being, that the essential of a level of existence becomes free only if it opens itself to what is higher than it, and independent of it, and is embraced by it. Through sin man fell out of that union with God. But he did not thereby come to be situated in that, which he was of himself, in a simple "naturalness." Man had but two possibilities: to exist above or below himself. If sin means that he tumbled down from the communion of grace with God, then it also means that he fell below what is truly human. "Nature" in man is not that which it is thought to be in modern times; it is not a self-sufficient notion, intelligible of itself. It needs an ultimate determination, which ensues in the attitude to God. As soon as it is simply considered as a primary, self-determined category, intelligible by itself, it becomes ambiguous, misleading, even demonic. Human nature can only be elevated above itself or precipitated below itself. What is now in man is nature thrown into confusion: a subnature, that "similarity to the beasts" and at the same time that "greatness" reminiscent of man's original vocation, of which Pascal speaks.[24] The long fragment 430 gives a sort of synthesis of this whole state of affairs. Divine wisdom speaks: " 'Expect neither truth nor consolation from men. I am she who formed you, and who alone can teach you what you are. But you are now no longer in the state in which I formed you. I created man holy, innocent,

74

perfect. I filled him with light and intelligence. I communicated to him my glory and my wonders. The eye of man saw then the majesty of God . . . But he was not able to sustain so much glory without falling into presumption. He wanted to make himself the center of himself, and independent of my help. He withdrew himself from my domination; and, making himself equal to me by the desire to find his happiness in himself, I abandoned him to himself. And stirring to revolt the creatures which were subject to him, I made them his enemies; so that today man has become like the beasts, and so estranged from me that he scarcely retains a dim vision of his author. So far has all his knowledge been extinguished and disturbed!' " (pp. 522ff.).

What a difference between this conception of man and the naturalistic and autonomistic conception of modern times![25] For Pascal, such a man does not exist. The claim that there is such a man has only been able to be maintained through a tacit agreement of general self-deception; through a demonically consistent renunciation of the real greatness of man. In the full sense, man can only be man if he dares to be more than "man"—but turned towards God: *"L'homme passe infiniment l'homme."*

Here we have a new tension in which Pascal's man exists. But the mind, of which we were speaking earlier and on which man sought to base himself in the distress of suspension, is drawn into it. The opposition of good and evil is not such that the mind would be the good, and the body the evil; rather, evil penetrates the entire man. It is not only the body which has fallen into sin, become doubtful, and gone astray, but the mind as well. Indeed, it is first and strictly speaking the mind, for sin stems from the mind, even the sin of sensuality. The original sin was arrogance, pride.

If, therefore, man tries to lift himself out of the devaluation by the powers of the world with the force of mind, then he cannot succeed, for this mind is itself called into question by evil: "Man does not know in what rank to place himself. He has plainly gone astray, and fallen from his true place without being able to

75

find it again. He seeks it everywhere, anxiously and without success in impenetrable darkness" (fr. 427, p. 521).

X.

The structure of human existence thus passes into the theological sphere. But this is no illicit passage into an unfamiliar field—no more so for Pascal than for a Thomas Aquinas or Augustine. For this new domain is just as real as the preceding—indeed, more eminently real because of its higher existential significance —and the total image of human reality is determined from this realm of the greatest height, not from that of the lower beginning.

Fragment 693 takes up again the notion of "*égarement*": "When I see the blindness and the wretchedness of man, when I regard the whole silent universe, and man without light, abandoned to himself, and lost, as it were, in this corner of the universe, without knowing who put him there, what he came to do, what he will become when he dies, and incapable of all knowledge, I become terrified, like a man who had been carried in his sleep to a desert island, and awoke without knowing where he was, and without means of escape. And thereupon I wonder how one does not fall into despair over such a miserable state. I see other persons around me of a like nature: I ask them if they are better informed than I am, they tell me they are not. And thereupon these wretched and lost beings, having looked around them and seen some pleasing objects, have abandoned and attached themselves to them. For my own part, I have not been able to attach myself to them, and, considering how strongly it appears that there is something else than what I see, I have investigated whether this God has not left some sign of himself" (p. 646).

Even the hint of a higher life coming from God is not unequivocal: "If man is not made for God, why is he only happy in God? If man is made for God, why is he so contrary to God?" (fr. 438, p. 536). It is the "yes" and "no" which form the

76

characteristic of the new level of existence announcing itself, and which one surmounts not by simply going forward, but only by decision and leap. But this level is not objectively necessary, it is not in the nature of things, as it is in the nature of things that above the physical level lies that of life, above the biophysical level that of the mind, above the cultural level that of the person. It is not simply "higher," but is only made accessible by the free initiative of God, by the action of his grace. It is not universally "there," through the necessary effect of an "absolute being," but is given, bestowed, brought in the coming of the Living God.

This coming, however, takes place in "Abraham, Isaac, Jacob"; in Jesus Christ. Men are "incapable of going to God," and "if God does not come to them, they can have no communion with him." Thus "God made himself to unite himself to us" (fr. 286, p. 461).[26] Only in Christ is man given a canon, by which his existence can be interpreted, the reconstruction of his disrupted form begun anew, and the force for its realization found. This cannot be done in continuity to worldly human existence, for it is indeed a question of communion with God. And this communion is given *"par grâce, non par nature"*; it is adopted *"par pénitence, non par nature."* The canon which Christ brings is sovereign and overturns our own. "Let us change the rule which we have taken till now for judging what is good. We had our own will as our rule. Let us now take the will of him [God]; all that he wills is good and right for us, all that he does not will is [bad]" (fr. 668, p. 631).

This canon has its own order of value. We have already encountered it in fragment 793: it is the "greatness" of Christ, which consists in "holiness" and "charity." It is not the general religious quality of "the sacred" or "the numinous," but rather the holiness of the living God as it appears in revelation. It is bound to historical revelation. It is reserved to God, and can only be accepted.[27] This canon is all-inclusive. It is directed to human existence in all its breadth. In very impressive lines Pascal says: "I consider Jesus Christ in all persons and in ourselves . . . He is by his glory all that is great, being God, and by his mortal life, all that is poor and abject. For that he took this unhappy condition, in order to be in all persons, and the model of all conditions" (fr. 785, p. 694). All that is human is laid hold of and receives its place and measure from the "*sainteté*" of Christ.

Only in this canon does the possibility open itself, that the destructive powers be overcome and the unity of the living image be obtained.

In general terms of forceful terseness, fragment 556 states: "Let one examine the order of the world in this regard, and see if all things do not tend to establish the two chief points of this religion: Jesus Christ is the end of all, and the center to which all tends. Whoever knows him knows the reason of everything. Those who go astray only go astray through failure to see one of these two things. One can thus have an excellent knowledge of God without that of his own wretchedness, or of his own wretchedness without that of God. But one cannot know Jesus Christ without knowing at the same time both God and one's own wretchedness" (p. 580). And still more: "Without Jesus Christ the world would not subsist; for it would of necessity either be destroyed or be like a hell" (p. 582).

Christ is the foundation of creation: the Logos. He is the canon of true existence. He is the key to the questions which it poses. In him is the point of convergence of elements which, taken alone, stand in insoluble contradictions: "In Jesus Christ all contradictions are reconciled" (fr. 684, p. 639). He, who brings the revelation of original sin and of the redemptive love of God, is the "imperceptible point," not only above reason, but against mere autonomous reason, and on which the condition, the measure, and the order of real human existence depend.

The notion is no pious exuberance. Pascal knows exactly what he intends, and pursues the thought into its details.

Christ, with his figure, his life, his words, is in an absolute sense he who indicates the direction to follow: he is the "way," "the way of willing what God wills." What God wills becomes known through revelation: "Jesus Christ alone leads to it: *Via, Veritas*" (fr. 466, p. 546).

He heals the blindness of the mind in face of God: "God is a hidden God, and . . . since the corruption of nature, he has left men in a darkness from which they can escape only through Jesus Christ, without whom all communion with God is cut off" (fr. 242, p. 446). The eyes of the man who believes in Christ are opened. He sees how things really are.

Of itself, the mind slides into evil. It speaks about the good and the sublime, and "does not know its own corruption." Even its ideal striving becomes an instrument of induration. (fr. 463, p. 545). Indeed, "The place specific to pride is [philosophical] wisdom" (fr. 460, p. 544). God alone can give that wisdom which bestows the superior clarity of knowledge and at the same time opens the soul in humility (*ibid.*). "The knowledge of God without that of one's misery causes pride. The knowledge of one's misery without that of God causes despair. The knowledge of Jesus Christ constitutes the mean, for in him we find both God and our misery" (fr. 527, p. 567).

The knowledge of God is existential, or it does not exist. Man knows God to the extent that he understands his existential condition. "We can know God well only by knowing our iniquities" (fr. 547, p. 572). Jesus Christ has opened men's eyes about themselves; he has made them aware that they are turned in upon themselves, hardened in their own will, and thus blind for God. As soon as they acquiesce in this, realize it, convert themselves by participating in Christ's orientation of being, their eyes are opened for God. "We know God only through Jesus Christ. Without this mediator, all communion with God is taken away" (*ibid.*, p. 571). Thus it holds good universally: "Not only do we know God only by Jesus Christ, but we know ourselves only by Jesus Christ. We know life and death only through Jesus Christ. Apart from Jesus Christ, we do not know what is our life, nor our death, nor God, nor ourselves . . . We know

79

nothing, and see but darkness and confusion in the nature of God, and in our own nature" (fr. 548, p. 572).

There thus results the phenomenon of mediatory knowledge: that of the living God and of the real self by means of the Mediator. It is objective, in so far as Christ brings man the image of the living God and the image of man as God intends him. It is subjective, in that he gives to the man who opens himself to him the fulcrum, from which the arc of existence closes itself; in that he brings him into the open and loving attitude which opens his eyes: "All who seek God without Jesus Christ, . . . or come to form for themselves a means of knowing God and serving him without a mediator, . . . fall either into atheism, or into deism, two things which the Christian religion abhors almost equally" (fr. 556, p. 581). The idea that the "god of the philosophers" and the godlessness of the atheists should be "almost the same" is naturally exaggerated, but gains in significance the longer one reflects and sees the profound tendencies of human thought.

It is the Mediator as well who teaches us to love God, for the love of which Christianity speaks is not the love found in the world, be it even the numinous love of natural religion. Christian love is participation in the love of God revealed in Christ (fr. 607, p. 600). "Our prayers and our virtues are abominable before God, if they are not the prayers and the virtues of Jesus Christ. And our sins will never be the object of it [mercy], but of the justice of God, if they are not [those of] Jesus Christ" (fr. 668, p. 630).

"Let us change the rule which we have taken till now for judging what is good. We had our own will as our rule. Let us now take the will of him [God]; all that he wills is good and right for us, all that he does not will is (bad)" (*ibid.,* p. 631).

Pascal's thoughts are only sketched, scanty memory aids for the definitive version. In the latter, the audacious construction

80

and at the same time the profound significance of this image of man would have had a completely different appearance. But even so, enough of the great over-all context is clear: through sin, the orientation of human existence towards God was lost, and with it the aiming point, the total tension, the measure, the agreement. What remained was an unintelligible, half-formed figure, a confusion hinting at but never realizing the true image, a struggle for form and meaning which never succeeded. Now a new image rises resplendent, in which God comes to meet us in Christ. Christ is really "the" man—he who is also God. Only he who is more than man, who truly and by nature "*passe infiniment l'homme,*" is at once perfectly and archetypally man. His personality, his life, his way of thinking, his destiny are the canon of the humanity intended by God. To believe means to acknowledge this and to enter with one's own existence into the sphere of influence of this canon. Christ, without sin himself, took sin upon himself—see the wonderful "*mystère de Jésus*" discussed in the last chapter (fr. 553, p. 574)—and atoned for it out of the purity of his love, at once divine and human. Now sin is in his existence, but as something surmounted: not simply repulsed, not simply left beneath his loftiness in sublime righteousness, but assumed in love, atoned for and surmounted in love. The image of man in Christ is not that of paradise, before all guilt, but ours with the guilt surmounted. It is realistic, not idealistic. In it there is room for man as he really is, not as someone dreams him.

In faith, man enters into the space, the norm, the living force of this image: what Paul calls "being in Christ." Here man does not only think of this image, understand it, assent to it, but enters into it in a living way. It is *dynamis*. It acts and creates. Living in faith, man stands in that image, and the image, which is indeed the living "pneumatic" Christ himself, acts in him.

A series of fragments, however, hints at a very impressive theory, with which Pascal shifts from the individual existence of the individual believer to a total existence: "If the foot had always been ignorant that it belonged to the body, and that there

81

was a body on which it depended, if it had only had the knowledge and the love of self, and if it came to know that it belonged to a body on which it depended, what regret, what shame for its past life . . . And with what submission it would allow itself to be governed by the will which rules the body, even to consenting, if necessary, to be cut off, or it would lose its character as a member! For it is necessary for each member to be quite willing to perish for the body, for which alone the whole exists" (fr. 476, p. 549).

This train of thought is based on Pauline and stoic ideas, but in the context of Pascal's anthropology it takes on a new and stimulating character. Pascal starts from the concept of the member in its relationship to the total organism. Man is such a member, but does not know it. His consciousness thus has the cramped, unnatural, constricted character, which a foot would have, if it could as such think and—apparently—exist for itself. It is self-love, the root of sin, which so confines it in itself; its result is at once crime, nonsense, destruction, and death. If, however, the consciousness of the whole dawns on him, then he recognizes the evil cramp; "hating" himself in his obduracy, he enters into the context and, broadening and giving himself in love, he experiences the total form and the fullness of its life and meaning—so much so that he would be prepared, in the truth of love, to be sacrificed if the will guiding the whole should demand it.

Is there such a situation? Certainly, already in the relationship of the individual to the "*communautés naturelles et civiles*" (fr. 477, p. 550). But above and beyond all sociological contexts, and different from them, there is a totality which comes from above, from God. It consists in the fact that all things, related to God, governed by his will, standing in his service, are his kingdom. In it, everything froms a body, and God's will, in a certain way, its soul, the "universal soul" (fr. 482, p. 552). Even this unity is shattered; every man takes himself as the center of everything. Here, too, therefore, the redemptive approach of God had to take place: the new total body is the "*corpus Christi*," of which Paul speaks. In it the "*moi haïssable*" is abolished; all are submitted to the whole, and each belongs to each other: "We love one another, because we are members of Jesus Christ. We love Jesus Christ, because he is the body of which we are members. All is one, one is in the other,"—and here the thought, in the Johannine manner, goes back to the divine community in the Trinity—"like the Three Persons" (fr. 483, p. 553).

Here the totality of mankind stands in an orientation towards God, and receives through Christ its form, the Church, which was for Augustine, under whose forceful influence Pascal stands, above all the *Corpus Christi mysticum*.

But Pascal, following Paul—see the letters to the Colossians and Ephesians—broadens the concept of totality once more. The formula "If there is a sole principle of everything, a sole end of everything, everything for him, everything through him" (fr. 489, p. 554) has an absolutely universal application. Fragment 482 thus develops the imposing notion of a "*corps de membres pensants*" (p. 552). Our members do not "think"; they thus have no consciousness of the "happiness of their union, of their wonderful intelligence,[28] of the care which nature has taken to infuse minds into them, and to make them grow and endure." For this they would have to have "intelligence to know it and good will to consent to that of the universal soul." The situation is analogous with "heaven and earth, which God created, and which do not feel the happiness of their being." Thus God "has willed to make beings who should know him, and who should compose a body of thinking members." This is the "Mystical Body of Christ," formed of men who believe, but who—so we may interpret the comparisons used—in their consciousness of the relationship of the totality to God, also assimilate "heaven and earth": the Pauline concept of the New Creation, which is an extension of the concept of the Church.

Here something decisive takes place. The relationship of the believing individual to God in Christ has reformed the figure of man, and given new light and power to human existence. In the same relation to the "God of Jesus Christ" arises the figure of a world in relationship with God. The merely scientific universe once more becomes the authentic world—for the "world" does not exist of and in itself, but in orientation towards God. In a new order of a universal corporality, in which the merely natural orders are assumed into that of an all-embracing personal life— which, of course, does not stem from the world itself, which would make it phantastic or mythological, but from God, in Christ who is the Logos.

There man's straying, his "*égarement*," is abolished. Not through a limitation of the endlessness, but through the clear appearance of a new relationship of the natural world—which may in other respects be as science ascertains it—to God in grace.

Now man has once more a place to stand: his place, his sense, his task in the "*ordre de la charité, de la sagesse, de la sainteté.*"

The consciousness of this new state cannot be expressed more powerfully than with the image of the place of the organ of the body. This consciousness is so powerful that, as fragment 476 (p. 550) cited above states, the member is even agreed "*à être retranché s'il le faut!*" So much a "member," so much in agreement with "the will which rules the body," that it is willing to be cut off and to die, if the will and the destination of the body demand it. Here something very profound is hinted at: the acceptance of predestination out of loving oneness with the will of God. The "*égarement*" is thereby surmounted, even in its most extreme depths. Even the possibility of condemnation is assumed in the conditionless "yes" of this love, in the absolute "consciousness of place" of this confidence—as the borderline case of the complete freedom which God's love must have, in order to be perfect love. And thereby, to be sure, as far as it is permissible to speak in this way, predestination is itself "surmounted."

How little the whole is self-evident, how much it contradicts what is usual and generally intelligible, is underlined by frag-

84

ment 618: "This is positive. While all philosophers separate into different sects, there is found in one corner of the world the most ancient people in it, declaring that all the world is in error, that God has revealed to them the truth, that it will always exist on the earth. In fact, all other sects come to an end, this one still endures, and that for four thousand years. They declare that they hold from their ancestors that man has fallen from communication with God, into an entire estrangement from God, but that he has promised to redeem them; that this doctrine shall always exist on the earth; that their law has a double meaning; that during sixteen hundred years they had people, whom they believed prophets, who foretold the time and the manner; that four hundred years later they were scattered everywhere, because Jesus Christ was to be announced everywhere; that Jesus Christ came in the manner and at the time foretold; that the Jews have since been scattered abroad under a curse, and nevertheless subsist" (pp. 607f.).

The strange tension of Christian consciousness is here forcefully expressed. "Strange thing, the Christian condition!", Pascal says elsewhere. A consciousness of the highest, most ancient, indestructible, absolute significance—and at the same time a questionableness in face of all otherwise valid standards, so much so that the former claim seems nonsensical or—sometimes even to him who advances it—intolerable, and yet ineffaceable.

XI.

At the beginning of this chapter, the search for the complicated spots in reality was indicated as a basic tendency of Pascal's thought. We have seen how forcefully this tendency asserts itself in the construction of his anthropology. The most significant points of human existence lie in its points of crisis.

This existence, as we have seen, is constructed according to levels and stages, whose unity must be accomplished ever anew in tension. This tension, seemingly only constructive in the beginning, then becomes a real menace. The fulfillment of existence becomes ever more difficult, and finally impossible.

We then saw how the human predicament, without remedy within the world, finds its answer in the redemption, and how man, by turning towards the God manifested by the Redeemer, obtains for the first time hope-giving stability and the possibility of genuine self-realization and thus of genuine self-definition.

Strictly speaking, that should be sufficient. This human existence is already inconceivable enough. Still, the last word is not yet spoken. That last summit, with which human existence seems to find stability in the redeeming God, and to receive from him fulfillment and definition of his endless danger, is once more called into question.

Wherever Pascal deals with the knowledge of God, he shows, with the passion of genuine experience, how the "yes" is always combated by the "no," certainty traversed by uncertainty, clarity invaded by obscurity. He shows how the real reason for this "*ambiguité*" is found in sin, and that therefore only redemption can bring light. Only in Christ does it become clear who God is and how things appear seen by God. But although sin is atoned for through the Redeemer, it continues to have an effect as real derangement and confusion. The disguising, bewildering, distorting powers of inner disorder are never completely overcome on earth. They thus assert themselves even in face of the redemptive self-revelation of God. Precisely that which reveals God, the incarnation, threatens to become another concealment. The fact that God thereby translates himself, as it were, into human terms, and that he can thus be contemplated and perceived, reveals him; but the human aspect of the incarnation becomes at the same time an objection, that God could not really be here, and threatens to hide him. The evil in man has an interest, that God not be revealed; it thus summons forth from revelation itself a new ambiguity. And it belongs to the mystery of grace and of the ultimate freedom of the heart, whether that clarity is won and this final doubting overcome.

Thus the summit of the total figure of man—already so

86

infinitely under tension, shaken in so many places, struggling upwards over abysses and through ruins—stands once more in an ultimate obscurity.

This final problem of the relationship between God and man in the Christian perspective is to be discussed, in a particular context, in our fourth chapter.

CHAPTER III

Nature and the Artificial

I.

In sketching Pascal's image of man, we have left out of consideration an element which is of great importance in the dawning modern consciousness and in that of Pascal himself: nature. Taking nature as a point of departure, the following question could have been asked: the same nature which surrounds man is nonetheless also in him himself; does "nature" not then mean a primary given, reliable and intelligible by itself, on which man can stand with assurance? Does not Pascal himself seem to suggest this thought, when in fragment 434 he states: "Nature sustains our feeble reason and prevents it from talking nonsense to this extent" (p. 530)? We want to make up for what we have neglected. We want to investigate Pascal's concept of nature. We will find some very remarkable relationships in the process.

II.

The phenomenon of nature is constructed in different layers. The first of them corresponds to that reality which was the object of the natural sciences, extremely flourishing in Pascal's time, especially of physics and astronomy. This realm has its own essence, independent of man and his will. What is scientifically established and understood within it stands firm as "fact" and "law."

It forms the foundation and content of reliable insight. It also provides the means of exercising control over things, of obtaining power and pleasure. It is the realm of the *"ordre des éléments"* and of the *"vérités géométriques"* (fr. 556, p. 581). Its exploration is called *"l'étude des sciences abstraites,"* as opposed to the *"étude de l'homme,"* that is, to the investigation of living man, of his nature, of his existence, of the values, goals, and tasks which concern him (fr. 144, p. 399).

Above this conceptual layer, which is the narrowest, lies a broader one. There "nature" designates the sum total of the conditions of existence; that which is not willed or done, but which is given from the outset.

Of this first existence of things, Pascal asserts that it is in harmony with itself. The principles which hold good in the various realms of things form analogies to one another. One can recognize one realm in another, because one and the same fundamental reality is "nature." Fragment 119 states: "Nature imitates herself. A seed sown in good ground brings forth fruit. A principle sown in a good mind brings forth fruit. Numbers imitate space, which is so different in nature. All is made and guided by one and the same master: root, branches, and fruits; principles and consequences" (p. 385). And again, very ingeniously: "There is a certain model of grace and beauty which consists in a certain relation between our nature, such as it is, weak or strong, and the thing which pleases us. Whatever is formed according to this model pleases us, be it house, song, discourse, verse, prose, woman, birds, rivers, trees, rooms, dress, etc. . . . And as there is a perfect relation between a song and a house which are made on a good model, because they resemble this single good model, though each according to its kind; so, too, there is a perfect relation between things made on a bad model. Not that the bad model is unique, for there is an infinite number of them; but each bad sonnet, for example, on whatever false model it is formed, is just like a woman dressed on that model. Nothing makes us understand better how ridiculous a false sonnet is than to consider nature and the model, and then to imagine a woman or a house made on that model" (fr. 32, p. 331). The same phenomenon which in fragment 119 was considered from a scientific point of view is here transposed into the aesthetic realm (similarly also in fr. 33, p. 332).

This pervasive reality, this norm which asserts itself throughout all the variety of things, this fundamental unity which is expressed in the multiplicity of realities objectively irreducible to one another, this is "nature."

Here the word designates no longer only a concept of existence, but also of value. "Nature" here means as much as "naturalness," and stands in opposition to that which is distorted, false, artificial, in other words to what is unnatural. This concept includes also man and his world. "When one sees a natural style, one is astonished and delighted; for one expected to find an author and one finds a man. Whereas those who have good taste, and who upon seeing a book expect to find a man, are quite surprised to find an author . . . Those honor nature well, who teach her that she can speak of everything, even of theology" (fr. 29, 330). The natural is a universal standard of what is properly formed and precious; to spoil or distort nature is a sign of artificiality and false sense of value. Nature placed everything in its proper place, man included. *"La nature nous a bien mis au milieu"* (fr. 70, p. 346), so that from this standpoint, we acquire the proper relationship to everything. And while the systematics of scientific thought forcibly splits apart domains, things, and elements of reality and arranges them in artificial classifications, nature has characterized each thing in itself and at the same time brought it into a total interrelation; she has divided, yet not torn apart (fr. 20, p. 328). In the cultural domain, situation and profession absorb man; they make of men masons or soldiers, and thus destroy the living existence. Nature, on the contrary, is spontaneous and strong—so much so, that it "sometimes overcomes custom, and retains man in his instinct, in spite of all custom, good or bad" (fr. 97, p. 374).

Thus the best bases for a fruitful striving for knowledge are the natural sense, the natural attitude to things, the natural feeling for what is important and for what is not: *"les premières vues du sens commun et . . . les sentiments de la nature"* (fr. 195, p. 424). The reflections in "De l'esprit géométrique" see the superiority of mathematics in the fact that it has the greatest natural clarity. "De l'art de persuader" makes the natural impression the basis for every influence on the persuasion of men; and the natural style seems the best and most adapted to this purpose (fr. 14, p. 325). The same standard of naturalness holds good also for the moral life: "Nature seems to have done the same thing by her two infinities, natural and moral" (fr. 532, p. 567). The foundation of genuine morality is natural moderation, equilibrium true to nature, and obedience to the laws of respect and sincerity of heart.

We have already seen that fragment 29 declares naturalness a standard even for theology. Fragment 81 states: "The mind believes naturally, and the will loves naturally; so that, for want of true objects, they must attach themselves to false" (p. 362). Fragment 425 speaks of the *"gouffre infini"* in man, which wants to be filled, so that God is, so to speak, naturally ordained to him. The longing for God is "natural to man, since it is necessarily in all, and it is impossible not to have it . . ." (pp. 519ff.). And fragment 521 states: "Grace will always be in the world, and nature, too; so that the former is in some way natural" (p. 565). What is Christian is not thereby declared natural; it rather means that there are primitive elements of Christian existence which provide ultimate standards of conformity to nature.[29]

The organ, however, destined to receive the norms of this naturalness and to hold to them, is the *"première vue du sens commun,"* the *"sentiment de la nature,"* the *"vue droite"* or *"vue nette,"* the pure and clear perception of the heart, of instinct, etc.

These norms of value, the corresponding attitude of mind and heart, the resulting view of the proper man and the proper existence, consolidated into a canon of which we have already spoken, that of the "*honnête homme*." From this point of view, it is the opposite of the coarse, violent man of club law, troublesome or fearful to his neighbor. The "*honnête homme*" possesses a high culture, a lively and sure sense for human values, and refined taste. Pascal's friend, the Chevalier de Méré, one of the creators of this canon, defines the "*honnêtes gens*" as "*des esprits doux et des coeurs tendres; des gens fiers et civils, hardis et modestes qui ne sont ni avares, ni ambitieux.*" They do not force themselves upon one. "They have hardly any goal but to bring joy everywhere, and their great care seeks but to merit esteem and to make themselves loved." In their whole being they have "*je ne sais quoi de juste et d'insinuant.*"[30] The extent to which this feeling for existence penetrated Pascal is shown by his letter to the mathematician Fermat, dating from the last years of his life. It begins with the words, "You are '*le plus galant homme du monde*' and I am certainly one of those who know best how to recognize these qualities and to infinitely admire them, above all when they are joined to the talents which are found singularly in you . . . I will tell you also that, although you are the man whom I consider the greatest geometrician [mathematician] in all Europe, it is not this quality which would have attracted me; rather I imagine '*tant d'esprit et d'honnêteté en votre conversation,*' that it is for this reason that I would seek you out" (P. O., pp. 228f.). This entire culture has the character of "naturalness," not in the sense of primitiveness, but of an inner genuineness of thought, feeling, and expression. So much so that on a higher level, as it were, it loses its character as culture—which always has an aspect of difficult achievement about it—and becomes self-evident. It obtains a perfect assurance and ease, in which everything seems to work of itself; perfect, without willing anything particular; beneficent to all precisely because one has the impression that it is completely disinterested.

92

III.

A stable position in a clear system of norms, attitudes, and forms here seems to become possible. But let us hear what fragment 93, prepared by fragment 92, says: "Fathers fear lest the natural love of their children fade away. What is then this nature, subject to decay? Custom is a second nature which destroys the first. But what is nature? Why is custom not natural? I am much afraid that nature is itself but a first custom, as custom is a second nature" (p. 372). If nature and naturalness are to be that which was claimed, then there must be above all something inherent in them: something unequivocal and self-evident, which enables one to be immediately sure of it and to base oneself upon it to approach everything else. But precisely this becomes doubtful for Pascal: "There is nothing one may not make natural; there is nothing natural one may not lose" (fr. 94, p. 375). Nature in man is certainly nothing constant. It can change. And indeed, man himself, everything which makes up human existence: education, work, culture, brings about this change. How can this be? Fragment 426 gives the formula: "True nature being lost, everything becomes its own nature; just as, the true good being lost, everything becomes its own true good" (p. 520). Fragment 425 expresses the same idea more sharply: God alone "is man's true good, and since man has forsaken him . . . everything can equally appear such to him, even his own destruction, though so contrary to God, to reason, and to the whole of nature" (p. 519). What was said in the preceding chapter about sin here flows into the train of thought.

Nature is in man something other than in the animal. In the animal, it is the aggregate of all the animal's simply inherited conditions: of its substances, energies, instincts, etc. They operate reliably; they form a whole closed in upon itself and intelligible of itself—because in them, there is no mind, no freedom. Mind, however, is not something which exists simply, mechanically, naturally, but rather based on value. More correctly stated: Mind is intrinsically based on that which is above the mind, the "Holy Spiritual," the Holy and Living God. Man was once faced with the decision, whether he wanted to live in obedience, turned towards God and existing through God, or not. He refused to do so; he sinned. This was not only an offense, but a catastrophe. Man is not a complete being, to which would then be added, as intentional characterization, the ethical or religious decision; rather, he is only defined in his being by his religious decision, by his relationship to the Holy God. The existence of man is constructed with the relationship to God in view; thus, through the destruction of this relationship, it too is destroyed. Through sin, man became a confused fragment, which nevertheless claims to be complete and to have a clear meaning; a disordered assemblage of substances, energies, attitudes, dispositions, elements of form, value, and perception, which—convinced in its delusion—claims to be a sufficient and authentic image, a being, a "nature."

In truth, man is not nature at all in the real sense of the word. The animal, on its level, is one. The free man, determined by mind, called by God, would have been a nature, if he had remained true to God in obedience and love. The fact of being a nature would have been for man the ultimate fruit of self-transcendence towards God, and a gift of God. His naturalness would not have been "natural," but the fruit of grace and freedom; not the starting point of biophysical, human, cultural development, but a gift coming from the mystery of divine favor; not the presupposition at the beginning, but the end incommensurable with every merely human beginning. Only in the holy self-evidence of the *charis* would the value of naturalness have been realized for man. Now man has lost grace, and with it his real nature. He henceforth stands in a fundamental obscurity, and to speak now of a norm of naturalness is an illusion. So much so that the nature of the first man has become a mystery. "We understand neither the glorious state of Adam, nor the nature of his sin, nor the transmission of it to us. These are things which took place in the state of a nature altogether different from our own, and which transcend the state of our present understanding" (fr. 560, p. 583).

The "*première nature*" is thus lost. That profound disorder, of which we have often spoken already, has resulted. In order to be able to exist, man must create a status, a *modus vivendi* in the literal sense, an emergency order. And this is indeed what happens. Man, become unsure of his existence, adopts—we will see later how—a second order, line of action, form, stemming not from his genuine nature but from secondary factors. This "*seconde nature*" has a strange double character. On the one hand, there arises in it ill-will stemming from the first fall, original sin, a system of motives, justifications, disguises, in order to prove itself reasonable and legitimate. There thereby arises a culture of non-value, an order of nonsense, a logic of fallen being, behind whose endless display of power, achievement, and glitter gapes an ultimate absurdity. "Lust has become natural to us, and has made our second nature. Thus there are two natures in us—the one good, the other evil" (fr. 660, p. 628). We continually become aware of this absurdity in all that Pascal characterizes with such forcefulness as the experience of the "*misère de l'homme*," as boredom, satiety, despair. It is the vengeance of the possibility of genuine human nature on him who has destroyed it. Fragment 109 sums up concisely: "Nature makes us always unhappy in all our states" (p. 383). But on the other hand, there is always good in us too: the responsibility we feel for our being, which despite all devastation has remained somehow godlike. Armed with this feeling, man takes his fallen condition in hand and establishes on it that emergency order. The latter repeatedly reveals the character of confusion; yet it is something courageous and noble, similar to the act of a man who accepts a hopeless situation which he cannot fundamentally change, and creates out of it, as it were, a desperate order. The "*grandeur de l'homme*" here becomes clear.

It is in this perspective that Pascal's concept of culture and education—or more exactly, its second component—has its roots. The first is based on naturalness, conformity to nature, harmony in existence; the second on a grim necessity, on the insight into the desperate situation of man. It is dis-illusioned, hard, somber, but grand.

It is thus the sharpest antithesis to every optimistically humanistic conception of man. There is not a trace in it of confidence in human nature, nor in the presence in man of good potentialities which can be developed. To be man is an uncertain, evil, sorrowful thing—and yet full of grandeur.

IV.

In the preceding we spoke of the lack of direction to which man fell prey after he had lost his constructive vertex. In this naturelessness, there arose, in order that life might go on, a makeshift nature. How did this take place?

The question leads us to a concept, already touched upon briefly, which is fundamental for Pascal's philosophy of culture: *"la coutume,"* custom.

Fragment 252 states: "For we must not misunderstand ourselves; we are as much automaton as mind; and hence it is that the instrument by which conviction is attained is not demonstration alone. How few things are demonstrated! Proofs convince but the mind. Custom provides our strongest and most believed proofs. It inclines the automaton, which sweeps along the mind without its thinking about the matter. Who has demonstrated that there will be a tomorrow, and that we will die? And what is more believed? It is thus custom which persuades us of it; it is custom that makes so many men Christians; custom that makes Turks, heathens, artisans, soldiers, etc. . . . . Finally, one must have recourse to it when once the mind has seen where the truth is, in order to quench our thirst, and steep ourselves in that belief, which escapes us at every hour; for always to have proofs at hand is too much trouble. We must acquire an easier belief, which is that of habit, which, without violence, without art, without argument, makes us believe things, and inclines all our powers to this belief, so that our soul falls naturally into it. It is not enough when one believes only by force of conviction, and when the automaton is inclined to believe the contrary. Both our parts must be made to believe, the mind by reasons which it is sufficient to have seen once in one's life, and the automaton by custom, and by not allowing it to incline to the contrary . . . The reason acts slowly, with so many views and on so many principles, which must always be present, that at every hour it falls asleep, or wanders, for want of having all its principles present. Feeling does not act in this way; it acts in a moment, and is always ready to act. We must thus put our faith in feeling; otherwise it will be always vacillating" (pp. 449ff.).

This is a very far-reaching text. Pascal sees the "esprit" in man, that is, the capacity of realizing, in a living act, truth and value, validity and meaning. This takes place through *"raison"* and *"coeur"*: the grasping of truth and the experience of value. But then there is also the *"automate,"* the ensemble of the spontaneous attitudes and associations of ideas: preferences, aversions, motives, and so on which are always operative—thus the mechanisms of the acts realizing value. For example, how does conviction come about? What takes place, that a given, concrete man is convinced and remains so? The heart of the whole process is the realization of truth, the certainty of what?, why?, and wherefore? But this certainly is not suspended in a vacuum; it is embedded in a living act, which itself unrolls according to a series of structures. These structures are not the essence of the phenomenon, but only the form of its execution. They prolong this execution into mechanical, biological, psychological, and sociological domains, anchor it there, and support it from there. In them the mechanization, vitalization, socialization of the mind takes place. This is the "automaton" of which Pascal speaks.[31]

What is the importance of this automatism in the whole of human existence? First of all, it has an unburdening effect. The real intellectual act is tiring; the more it is supported by such

97

autonomously working mechanisms, the more easily it proceeds
. . . But the intellectual act is not only laborious, it can also
miscarry. The necessary postulates can be lacking, for example
the inner alertness, the receptivity, the knowledge of the different factors to be considered for the full knowledge of the
object, etc. The more reliably the mechanism works, the more
easily the truly intellectual element can get into action, or be
replaced, if it cannot get into action. In case it were now to be
objected that this is a very unintellectual conception, Pascal
would probably reply that one must live; and since the nature
of man finds itself in such a questionable condition, an expedient
is necessary. To fail to recognize this would by no means be an
authentic intellectuality, but an irrealism, which would infallibly
lead to the downgrading of precisely that, in behalf of which
the protest was entered, namely, the mind. The "pure" intellectuality demanded, because it is not based on real man but
on a phantom, would unavoidably fall prey to materialism.

But then, and here we strike more profoundly: even the mind
itself is indeed questionable. One cannot count on its will to
truth, nor on its readiness for effort, risk, and inner freedom,
nor on the trustworthiness of its work. For intellectual work
does not take place mechanically, but rather out of an inner
relationship to value and meaning. And this relationship stems
from freedom. In freedom, for its part, motives of the most
varied kind come into play, bad as well as good: cowardice,
laziness, revolt, egotism in all their forms. So that often there,
where apparently pure intellectuality, pledged to truth, seems
to be operative, the most questionable impulses are at work.
But if the genuine intellectual attitude, based on a just understanding—one's own or another's—is vitalized and transposed
into automatisms, then these automatisms come to the aid of the
mind, and form, indeed, a counter-weight against its own un-
trustworthiness.

Now what creates such mechanisms? What transposes the
truth, the good, the just intellectual attitude into the domain of
the spontaneous, the instinctive, the functional? What vitalizes,

"biologizes," socializes the mind? *"La coutume,"* custom. And here we stand before the pedagogical problem in the broadest sense of the word.

V.

Yet let us stop for a moment. What an image of man! We are first of all struck by its density of reality. No one will claim that Pascal did not know what mind is, or that he materialized the mind. It would be difficult to find a greater clarity, force, or ardor of intellectual experience in a thinker. And yet this mind does not for a moment evaporate into the ideal realm. In its definition, the ancient and medieval concept of man is still operative, according to which the mind is *forma corporis,* presses towards incarnation, and expresses itself in the body. This mind is transposable into corporal reality; inversely, the body is not only something material or biological, but thoroughly determined by the mind.

But what pessimism! A pessimism, to be sure, of the highest order, which abandons neither the truth nor man; which does not let itself subside either tragically or lyrically, but holds fast the meaning of existence and wants to realize it, even if the way be difficult.

There is a skepticism here regarding the mind itself. Not romantic skepticism, however, but one bound up with the most intensive intellectual will. It stems from the insight that a good part of what is called conviction, knowledge, moral action, is in truth the execution of mechanized individual and social attitudes.[32] These mechanisms are not exactly highly valued, but are accepted and put into use without any illusion, with even a grim cynicism.[33] Pascal knows what creative stimulations, what experiences of grandeur lie in the mind; yet he does not trust it. He knows that the intellectual life is determined by motives. In regard to these motives, he abandons himself to no illusion. He thus confides the surveillance and security of the mind to something which is in truth far inferior to it: these very mechanisms.

99

There is no materialism, no mechanization as a negation of the mind. On the contrary, one is almost tempted to say that there is here something at work which is not only transbiological, but even transintellectual. In any case, it is an intellectuality of a very advanced and very exacting kind. It is at such a high level, and of such a freedom of disposition, that it becomes capable of placing the mind itself in distrust. An altitude in very rarefied air is here manifest; a will to domination of great freedom, of dangerous detachment—dangerous, because it is indeed very much a matter of doubt, whether a man can bear such sovereignty.

In any case—and to come back to our point of departure: it is no longer a question here of "nature" and "naturalness." Nature and her inner security as life, psyche, and spirituality have been replaced by reflection, conscious will, free disposition —in short, "culture" in the most extreme sense of the word.

In Pascal's thought, the whole is suspended from an Archimedean point above immediate existence: faith. He places the whole construction in the service of the summons which God addresses to man—about which man and which summons the revelation of this same God instructs him. Knowledge, valuation, and will are enlisted into the service of revelation; it is later to be shown how intensively Pascal was conscious of carrying out a mission conferred by God. This attitude is thus firmly bound; yet it is more than dangerous. One must only ask oneself what must happen when it detaches itself from faith and becomes autonomous; when it is placed in the service of a will to power which no longer has a light above it, nor a responsibility before God, nor a footing in grace. It then becomes an intellectual despotism suspended in nothingness and working in fortuitousness.

Here is the foundation of Pascal's pedagogy. Education is the art of developing habits, of creating the proper automatisms through constant influence. That is not to say that there would be no striving for "conviction," for one must ceaselessly attempt

100

to lead man to authentic realization of values. But one must recognize that this is only possible to a very limited degree, and that education can by no means be based on the ideal of intellectual spontaneity. Rather, it is necessary to develop a system of correctly working forms of conduct, determined by divine revelation and the knowledge of educators, which sustain human existence.

We certainly do not go wrong when we see in the "Règlement pour les enfants, composé pour Port-Royal" (*Oeuvres*, VII, p. 83), a statute of education drawn up by Pascal's sister, Jacqueline, for the boarding school of the abbey, the expression of this intention. It is cruder, to be sure, as generally happens, when an idea passes from the creative domain of a great mind to that of a lesser. This method of education is vigorous, strict, and has one major feature. It starts from the conviction that man is evil; that he is inclined to falsehood and revolt, and resists work and duty. Authority is therefore stressed throughout, and a system of surveillance and the most austere discipline is carried out.

Yet for all that, no false tone is to creep in. Man is never seen as canaille, as an obtuse, malicious, vulgar mass. The grandeur of man is repeatedly stressed. He is a fallen king. But really fallen. Skepticism is thus joined to a sense of grandeur, lack of illusion to a sense of the highest responsibility.

VI.

The same character is to be found also in Pascal's views on the nature and formation of the social life of man.

Pascal had a strong sense for human relationships. Richly developed relations of men among themselves, social intercourse noble in substance and refined in form, good regulation of public life, law, power, and political grandeur—all these are high values for him.

The realm in which they would have to develop would be "human nature." The latter would theoretically have to have

101

an effect in the relations of individual men as well as in the order of public life. The manifestations and ordonnances of the social life would then be just so many expressions of human nature. The standard for the validity of a social form would lie in the question, to what extent that nature asserts itself therein, to what extent it is "natural." In fact, things are quite different.

The fifth section of the *Pensées* treats the sociological problem. Fragment 294 (p. 465) is particularly striking. It deals with the legal order as the backbone of the sociological whole. On what is it based?

A first answer could be the following: It is based on the general feeling of what is right, on the continuity of tradition and general usage. Reply: Three degrees of latitude reverse all jurisprudence; a meridian decides the truth; after a few years the most fundamental laws change. Everything changes. A new answer: It is based not on usage and general feeling, but on natural law, the *"lois naturelles."* To this, the further reply: That could be, if "reckless chance, which has distributed human laws, had encountered even one which was universal." In fact, every injustice, every crime, every act against nature, has already been accepted somewhere as legal. "Doubtless there are natural laws; but beautiful, corrupted reason has corrupted everything." And now the relentless consequence: "The result of this confusion is that one states that the essence of justice is the authority of the legislator; another, the convenience of the sovereign; another, present custom, and this is the most sure. Nothing, according to reason alone, is just of itself; everything changes with time." Thence the lapidary conclusion: *"La coutume fait toute l'equité, par cette seule raison qu'elle est reçue; c'est le fondement mystique de son autorité"* (fr. 294, pp. 464–466).

There may be a natural law, but one cannot find it. The current law may thus not be established on the idea of what is just and in conformity with nature, but on its diametrical opposite: pure facticity, the fact that it is established. "This is the mystical foundation of its authority." The mysterious ground for the majesty of the law and of earthly authority is—that there are none intrinsically. Knowing about human things means knowing that, behind the noble image, there is nothing, and yet maintaining the image. This is complete disillusionment, form for form's sake, stemming purely from the recognition that the chaos is only to be mastered in this way.[34]

The following sentences are even clearer: "Whoever carries it [the law] back to its principle destroys it. Nothing is as faulty as those laws which correct faults. Whoever obeys them because they are just, obeys the justice which he imagines, and not the essence of the law; it is quite self-contained, it is law and nothing more. Whoever will examine its motive will find it so feeble and trifling that if he is not accustomed to contemplate the wonders of human imagination, he will marvel that one century has gained for it so much pomp and reverence." And still clearer: "The art of opposition, of upsetting states, is to unsettle established customs, probing them even to their source, to point out their lack of authority and justice." The effort to go back to the foundations of a natural law, and to oppose this natural law to what is established, to custom, is *"un jeu sûr pour tout perdre."* There is no true law, there is only positive law. To seek after true law brings, in reality, the unsettling of all law. All law is then revealed as injustice, and the advantage falls only to those who want chaos. Indeed, Pascal's skepticism becomes even cynical; referring to Plato, he says that "it is often necessary to deceive men for their own good." And again: "Since man does not know the truth, through which he could be freed, he must be deceived. He must not sense the truth of the usurpation; law was once introduced without reason, and has become reasonable. One must make it regarded as authentic, eternal, and conceal its beginning, if one does not wish it soon to come to an end." It is impossible to anchor legal order into nature, for there is no such nature really capable of supporting it. The recourse to it is already the beginning of the overthrow of law. One must therefore base order on facticity. But what historically

103

establishes the fact is on the one hand power. Fragment 297 thus states: "*C'est là que ne pouvant trouver le juste, on a trouvé le fort*" (p. 469). On the other, it is chance; thus, with a slight tone of disdain, fragment 309 declares: "As fashion determines what is agreeable, so too it determines justice" (p. 474).

What thus, through a combination of chance and power, of occurrence and efficacious coining, becomes reality, then passes over into the different structures of social processes, takes on the character of "what has always been," of inviolability, of "*authenticité*" and "*raison*," and becomes "law."

From the intellectual point of view, this is bad, but there is no other solution. Pascal sees the contradiction, but also, that it is hopeless, and decides: "Justice is subject to dispute; power is quite recognizable and not disputed. One was thus not able to give power to justice, because power contradicted justice and said that it was she herself who was just. And thus being unable to make what is just strong, one has made what is strong just" (fr. 298, p. 470).

In other words: the world of "nature," in which the phenomenon would be in harmony with the essence of things and with "what should be," and everything could therefore be judged according to the norms of the true and the just—this world no longer exists. One can neither go back to a hidden "essence" from what one can experience, nor gain norms for what is from that which should be. Thus, between the now inaccessible "*première nature*" on the one hand—which now only exists in the claim, in the feeling of lost possession, of fundamental privation—and the individual manifestation, the concrete attitude of the individual and of society on the other, a peculiar intermediate level has inserted itself: the "*seconde nature*." It has the character of mere facticity, of fortuitousness, of artificiality.

It consists, from the point of view which occupies us here, of the world of forms, orders, institutions. It is not the expression of nature; it cannot be measured with the norms of absolute justice. It is ossified chance, arbitrary will laid down in rules, usurpation which has become a *de facto* state of affairs. It cannot legitimate itself, except by the insight—accessible to few men—that it cannot be otherwise. It lives of itself, from the pure act of its establishment, from the efficacious event, from the autonomy of power. It is mere artifact. It has various names, in which the fundamental conceptions and the sentiments of value which support them are expressed: *"coutume," "mode," "imagination," "apparence," "fantaisie"* (fr. 82, p. 362, *et al.*). One feels in them the protest of the natural will, the longing for "naturalness," the demand for justice; but at the same time, also the bitter insight of one who sees through things, and the resolution with which he accepts what he really despises, but recognizes as unavoidable.

Thus Pascal, further developing a thought of his master, writes in fragment 325: "Montaigne is wrong. Custom should be followed only because it is custom, and not because it is reasonable or just. But the common people follow it for this reason alone, that they think it just. Otherwise they will follow it no longer, although it were the custom; for one will submit only to reason or justice. Custom without this would pass for tyranny." Here the mass of men, who remain naïvely on the standpoint of a nature which in fact no longer exists, the common people, separates itself from the savants, who see how things really are. "It would therefore be good that one obey laws and customs, because they are laws; that one know that there is no true or just law to introduce, that we know nothing of these, and that thus it is necessary to simply follow those which are received . . . But the common people cannot accept this doctrine" (p. 480).

There is thus a class of initiates, who know about the true state of affairs; but who also know that it cannot be generally explained, and who thus, renouncing all illusion, decide to adopt the attitude and technique of a cynical and yet ultimately conscientious realism. "It is dangerous to tell the common people

105

that the laws are not just; for they obey them only because they think them just. Therefore it is necessary to tell them at the same time that they must obey them because they are laws, just as they must obey superiors, not because they are just, but because they are superiors. In this way all sedition is prevented, if one can make this understood, and what is the proper definition of justice" (fr. 326, p. 480). Still more radically, fragment 336 states: "*Il faut avoir une pensée de derrière (la tête) et juger de tout par là, en parlant cependant comme le peuple*" (p. 484). We sense the danger, that this enlightened realism lose altogether the norm of true and false, just and unjust, and become a pure Machiavellism which, if it had grandeur in its first representative, must become in the second or even third an unscrupulous technique of expediency.

Fragment 327 describes in a very interesting way the different kinds of men which can be distinguished from this point of view. "The sciences have two extremes which meet. The first is the pure natural ignorance in which all men find themselves at birth. The other extreme is that reached by great souls, who, having run through all that men can know, find they know nothing, and come back again to that same ignorance from which they set out; but this is a learned ignorance which is conscious of itself. Those between the two, who have departed from natural ignorance and not been able to reach the other, have some smattering of this sufficient knowledge, and pretend to be wise. These trouble the world and judge poorly of everything." Thence the conclusion: "*Le peuple et les habiles composent le train du monde*": "the common people and the wise make up the course of the world" (p. 480). The affective situation of Pascal's pessimistic, aristocratic, and conservative turn of mind appears clearly here. The naïve common people and the disillusioned wise—the "*gens habiles*" corresponding to the "*honnêtes hommes*"—think correctly, for they do not pose the question about the nature of things. The common people do not, because they are convinced that the laws in vigor are at the same time in conformity to nature; the initiated do not, because they know how things are in fact. Only the people between the two are destructive: the half educated. They have neither naïve faith, nor the bitter knowledge ruled by an ethos of renunciation and responsibility. They are the true destroyers. The real policy to follow will thus come down to keeping the common people in this naïve ignorance, but at the same time, educating a class of "*gens habiles*" in the strict ethos of their responsibility. To what extent can this be realized? What happens if the initiated are not "*grandes âmes*," or detach themselves from the discipline of great souls? What happens, if the common people no longer believe naïvely, but become either foolish or suspicious? Pascal does not ask these questions.

Fragments 330 and 331 show how audacious the construction is. The first even states explicitly: "The power of kings is founded on reason and on the folly of the people, and to the greater extent on the folly. The greatest and most important thing in the world has weakness for its foundation, and this foundation is admirably sure; for there is nothing more sure than this, that the common people will be weak. What is founded on sound reason is very ill founded, such as the esteem of wisdom" (p. 482). The other fragment, however, seems like a grotesque: "One imagines Plato and Aristotle only in grand academic robes. They were '*honnêtes gens*,' and, like others, laughing with their friends, and when they diverted themselves with writing their *Laws* and *Politics,* they did it as an amusement. That was the least philosophic and the least serious part of their life; the most philosophic was to live simply and quietly. If they wrote on politics, it was as if to govern a lunatic asylum; and if they pretended to speak of it as of a great matter, it was because they knew that the madmen to whom they were speaking thought themselves kings and emperors. They entered into their principles in order to make their madness as little harmful as possible" (p. 483). One can certainly not speak more skeptically about the "greatest and most important thing in the world"—and yet the greatness of man is shown "even in his lust, to have known how to extract from it an admirable code,

107

and to have made of it a picture of charity" (fr. 402, p. 509). Fragment 82 expresses the belief that the "imagination"—that is, the phantasy working without any connection with the truth of nature—, a "*faculté trompeuse*," seems to have been expressly given to man in order to lead him into necessary error about his own situation (p. 367).[35]

VII.

What Pascal says about law, he thinks also about the remaining forms of human life in society: the social stratifications, the manners of social intercourse, the professions, etc. Using Montaigne's and his own observations, he brings forth details in abundance to support his thesis. He shows how all these formations claim to be in conformity with nature, and yet are in fact fictitious, accidental, and often meaningless; but how they must remain in force, because otherwise chaos sets in.

A peculiar intermediary domain arises in this way: suspended between reality and irreality; fortuitous, artificial, and yet indispensable for life; questionable, false, and yet, when one sees into the heart of man's situation, truer than the unfounded demand for a form of life conformable to nature, and for a naturalness which does not exist, the supposition of which must therefore lead to devastation and unnaturalness. The abyss above which human existence is suspended here becomes manifest; but also, the tenacity with which it asserts itself, and the responsibility which thence accrues to the knowing man.

There thence arises an ethos and a pedagogy of form—of form existing purely in itself, supported by no intrinsic evidence: of pure authority. It is a cultivation of the capacity to be in suspension; it is necessary, because if this force fails, everything immediately totters. This attitude is only possible if a strong will to live and a high intellectuality are joined to the insight that the human situation is really desperate. It is very mature, capable of looking deeply and holding out tenaciously, of renunciation and discipline; capable at the same time of willing and enjoying with ultimate refinement this state, out of which must come a subtle and strong form of existence, an existential tension between the most urgent danger of destruction and the most intensive presence of life. The situation becomes clear if we consider the *ancien régime* and the French Revolution together, for they do indeed belong together. Their sentimental and intellectual essence has exercised a very profound influence on Nietzsche's idea of the good European, of the free mind, of the political philosopher, and of the educator of ever more superior men.

This way of thinking, precisely because it is very profound, has a high estimation for what is external. Its "profoundness" consists in the fact that it does not measure externals against a criterion of foundation in nature and then condemn them, but takes them purely as form, as mere facticity. We have here a mind so knowing and practiced in the evil depth of existence, that it knows how to accept externals in the *pathos* of their mere exteriority.

There are various statements along these lines, for example fragments 316, 319, 320, *et al.* Fragment 324 is representative: "The common people have very sound opinions, for example: 1. Having preferred diversion and hunting to poetry. The half learned make fun of it, and glory in pointing out in this regard the folly of the world; but for a reason which they do not fathom, the people are right. 2. Having distinguished men by externals, such as birth or wealth. The world again exults in showing how unreasonable this is; but it is very reasonable. (Cannibals laugh at an infant king.)[36] 3. Being offended by a slap in the face, or in so desiring glory. But it is very desirable on account of the other essential goods which are joined to it; and a man who has received a slap without resenting it is overwhelmed with insults and oppressions. 4. Working for the uncertain; sailing on the sea; walking over a plank" (p. 479). All this means: one is wise, and approaches existence correctly, if one sets up the norms for judging it not in the essential, but in the factual, not in the inner being, but in externals. What is apparently second-rate is in fact appropriate. To see and to understand this is genuine culture. Whoever, on the contrary, takes only essence, subjectivity, etc., as his point of departure, is no better off than the cannibals, who are able to assess only the actual. The subtle fiction of seeing the king in a child, in which a victory over raw reality—that is, culture—is expressed, is inaccessible to them. A thought-provoking paradox: it is a sign of profoundness to be able to place in externals the things which determine the social life of men. Elsewhere Pascal speaks of how right it is to regulate one's precedence through doors according to whether one has servants and thus possesses a certain social position—for what would happen, if one were to say: He should go through the door first, who is inwardly better? A wild chaos would be the result (fr. 319, p. 477).

If, then, the forms, manners, and classifications of existence rise out of nothingness; if they may not be tested against an essence without breaking down; if they must simply be obeyed, since it is otherwise impossible to set up anything valid, —do they not then have something rigid, mask-like, lifeless about them?

Something rigid, mask-like, to be sure—something lifeless, certainly not! Pascal would say it were naturalistic superstition, the business of "cannibals," to believe that existence must proceed from the immediate development of life. He would say that even pure form, the artificial, has a life, namely, a purely cultural life. He would perhaps declare such a concept of "life," in the immediate biological or emotional sense, altogether barbarous, and say that there lies in this apparent lack of life a much greater intensity, a completely different *pathos,* than in that "naturalistic" existence.

It is very instructive to note that the most important statement about the structure of the human personality stands in this context, in fragment 323, which begins with the question: "What is the *self?*" There the apparently solid substance of the self is peeled away piece by piece, until the whole ends with the

110

paradox: "Where, then, is this *self,* if it be neither in the body nor in the soul? And how love the body or the soul, except for these qualities which do not constitute the self, since they are perishable? . . . One thus never loves a person himself, but only qualities. Let us, then, jeer no more at those who are honored on account of rank and office; for we love a person only on account of borrowed qualities" (p. 478). Here the mask emerges at the very center of our existence, in the self. That which appears to be the opposite of a mask; what I am myself, and to which I refer when I seek not only what I support or mean, but what I really and essentially am—even this is a mask! And what is behind it? The incomprehensibility of the disrupted "first nature"!

Also, in Pascal's thought, the image of society is the objectivized form of the personality. Sociology is the reduplication of anthropology. And the same bitter tone which came out in the final result of the theory of the self: *"Le moi est haïssable,"* also becomes audible in the almost cynical realism of this theory of society.

Man, whether individual or society, is a dangerous quantity which does not tolerate the confident bliss of the optimistic attitude. As soon as the regulations of existence are erected on nature and conformity to nature, the true forces of nature erupt; and the result is chaos.

Pascal's gaze is penetrating here, all too penetrating. All illusions have disappeared. The will, however, does not give up, but stands firm. According to the inner state of affairs, everything would have to sink into destruction. There is thus need of auxiliary constructions, intermediary formations which remain freely suspended: forms supported only through necessity and the will to live. They can only be inadequately justified, and ultimately cannot be justified at all. Thus culture consists in the last analysis in seeing the sense of what is in itself indefensible, and in standing up for it. Existence is endangered. Everything apparently stable totters, because it rests on laboriously mastered, half-slumbering, titanic powers. One must see

111

it and persevere. Indeed, a certain wild joy greets this dangerousness, which confers on existence a particular intensity, preciousness, delicacy. A mask is also a liberation. Pure form is in suspension, mere construction has an austere beauty. In the "Discours sur les passions d'amour" there are very profound things said on this subject.

"*Raison*" and "*coeur*"—perhaps their greatest accomplishment would be in upholding that which cannot be justified either by reason or natural feeling, but only by the distress of a life at once so endangered and yet so precious, and in fulfilling it with an affirmation proceeding through "yes" and "no" and "nevertheless." The courage of this experience of culture is in the lucid struggle against the powers of destruction rising from within, against "*ennui*" and "*dégoût*." It is classical culture at its most advanced posts.

112

CHAPTER IV

The Hidden God and the Heart

I.

The end of the second chapter left a question unanswered. We now take it up again. Pascal is a scientist: a mathematician, a logician, a psychologist. He has the most intense experience and the highest opinion of the power of reason—what does he think about the possibility of knowing God through this reason?

The fragment 543 of the *Pensées*—it is the note for a "*préface,*" and was thus to occupy an important place—states: "The metaphysical proofs of God are so remote from the reasoning of men, and so complicated, that they make little impression; and if they should be of service to some, it would only be during the moment in which they see such demonstration; but an hour later they fear they have been mistaken" (p. 570). It is thus possible, in itself, to infer the existence of God from the givens of the world. But it is laborious. The rational arguments are understood by few. Even for them, they produce no real, and above all, no lasting conviction. Fragment 242 gives the reason for it: these considerations would make an impression on "the faithful; for it is certain that those who have the living faith in their heart see at once that all existence is none other than the work of the God whom they adore." But whoever examines the sensible world with mere reason, without faith or the readiness for faith, will "find only obscurity and darkness" (p. 445). Pascal does not at all deny, then, the abstract,

113

theoretical possibility of knowing the Creator through creation. What interests him is the concrete persuasive effect of such a proof. This effect does not as a rule take place. If one places before nature a man who does not believe, or is not at least ready to believe, he sees nothing other than just "nature." The abstract possibility is not realized. The proofs remain "*des preuves impuissantes.*" Pascal says elsewhere that, from the consideration "of the elements of nature," one could only come to know a "God of geometry." Here the persuasive effect of the proof is presupposed; but its result is only the colorless "absolute being" of metaphysics—the "God of the philosophers" of the *Mémorial.*

According to all this, then, there is a logical path from the world to God. But in order for it to be correctly perceived and to yield the correct understanding, it must be seen by the proper eye. To each particular object of knowledge there corresponds a particular "*vue.*" The mere contemplation of nature discovers at best an absolute metaphysical being. If more is to be seen, namely, the living God—he whom the soul of man, longing for salvation, addresses—then a new situation must arise, above mere nature, a new form of given: God must reveal himself. A new "*vue*" must open up: the pneumatic illumination of the mind and heart in faith. A new sphere must open, in which this God stands: that of the word of prophecy, of the divine message, ultimately the "Church." Then, in this new situation, the natural means of revelation of God in creation are also liberated and display their real significance. It is the old Augustinian standpoint. And just as Augustine only became clearly aware of this state of affairs when he had found the faith, and was in a position to judge from this higher level of knowledge the possibilities of the lower level, so it was the event of the *Mémorial* which gave Pascal, along with the experience of the state of spiritual knowledge, also the judgment about the accomplishment and limitation of the earlier kind of knowledge. The state of affairs often referred to already recurs: existence is constructed in levels. The significance and possi-

114

bilities of the lower disclose themselves fully only on the higher level. Life cannot be understood from the bottom up, that is, in a naturalistic way or according to a theory of evolution, but only from the top down, that is, hierarchically.

It would now be natural, and would be conformable to Pascal's theory of knowledge, to ask to what extent the "concrete" cognition of fragment 1, the *"esprit de finesse,"* is capable of apprehending God from the evidence of natural existence. Thus not through simple inferences, but through the combination of many indications, probabilities, correlations; through the symbolic effect of many expressional relationships; through the convergence of many lines of meaning in structure and process, etc. To our knowledge, Pascal does not discuss this question. He does not distinguish this possibility of knowledge, which plays such a large role, for example, in Newman's thought, from the knowledge truly conferred by faith.

Now it is the living God who created everything. All things come from him, and are his images. All happenings come from him, and are his messengers. His power holds sway everywhere, everywhere his wisdom is at work. The fourth of the still extant letters to Mlle. de Roannez speaks of the "veil of nature" which hides God, and the beautiful conclusion states: *"Toutes choses couvrent quelques mystères; toutes choses sont des voiles, qui couvrent Dieu"* (p. 215). Why is God not grasped in nature?

There is a power there which veils the gaze. For Pascal, man does not form a self-sufficient unity, himself the source of what he is, but is essentially oriented towards something else. In the second chapter we discussed this in detail. Man is a being drawn upwards, who only reaches his genuine fulfillment if he encounters him who comes from above to meet him, God, and enters into a living relationship with him. Only from God does man receive what makes him really man, in the sense which revelation gives to this word. Only from above himself, and indeed from the absolute "above"—not from metaphysics, but from the Living God—does man get his genuine nature, or more exactly, it is given to him. But this also holds true for knowl-

115

edge. The entire man is present in the act of cognition. Knowledge is wholly itself only when it is spanned towards God and from God, like an arc of fire. Only then is it equal to the full reality. Only then can it clearly know God as he reveals himself in the world. But sin has disrupted this relation, it has interrupted the arc of fire. Now the energy shoots out from one of the poles, that of the world, without being able to realize the arc, or it relapses. It no longer grasps existence in its full sense. . . . But there is a yet more fundamental difficulty! Sin is absolutely opposed to the knowledge of God. It thus uses the destruction of the total figure, of the "arc," in order to safeguard itself. The beam of knowledge is deflected, the true state of affairs concealed, the indications veiled, the meanings falsified.

All things no doubt point above and beyond themselves— but the essence of sin is selfishness, the will to not depend on God, but to exist in oneself. Man loves himself; he makes himself and his world the center of existence. The things, then, which stand in the service of the Creator, reply, in the consciousness of man and to his misfortune, by changing their real center and closing up within themselves. Their indications pointing above and beyond themselves no longer come into play. "It is an incomprehensible enchantment, and a supernatural slumber, which indicates as its cause an all-powerful force." This is the Biblical notion of the wrath of God, into whose service reality itself enters. (See the long fragment 430, pp. 521ff.)

Fragment 242 thus states: "It is not after this manner [of the philosophers] that Scripture speaks, which has a better knowledge of the things that are of God. It says, on the contrary, that God is a hidden God, and that, since the corruption of nature, he has left men in a blindness . . . *Vere tu es Deus absconditus*" (p. 446; see Is. 45, 15).

We sense the significance of these statements. It is not a matter here of a mere theory of knowledge, but of a religious dynamism, of a state of affairs ordained by God. It is no mere theorist of knowledge who here states that reason, for one cause or another, cannot go beyond a certain limit; rather, the limit in question is seen by a believer as the effect of an action of God. That this is so is not a logically self-evident conclusion, but the effect of sin; it is not the nature of things, but a constant judgment of God on men. It is the wrath of God the Judge which brings this about, the force of repulsion of the holy God, who does not allow sinful reason to approach him. And it is folly before this God and before every mind enlightened by him, when philosophical "autonomy" makes a scientific theory out of it.

But because God is hidden—we will come back to this later—, the true self of man is also hidden. The same limit which obstructs the knowledge of God also arrests the knowledge of the self. For if the summit of human nature lies in the relationship to God, then the same veil which covers God covers it too.

A weighty earnestness lies over the doctrine of the hiddenness of God; the same profound pessimism which we find so often in Pascal.

We must here make a distinction, however. This concept of the hiddenness or obscurity of God has nothing to do with that developed, for example, by dialectical theology. It is absolutely misleading to interpret Pascal from the point of view of Kierkegaard. Pascal knows nothing about the absolute incommensurability which Kierkegaard erects between God's holiness and man who is not only a "sinner," but "sin." Fragment 557 thus states: "It is not true that everything reveals God, and it is not true that everything conceals God. But it is at the same time true that he hides himself from those who tempt him, and that he reveals himself to those who seek him, because men are both unworthy and capable of God ["*capables de Dieu*"— the Augustinian "*capax Dei*"]; unworthy by their corruption, capable by their first nature" (p. 582). This is thus something quite different than radical incomparability. To be sure, the "first nature," that is, the openness of vision of the original

117

relationship with God before sin, is disrupted; so much so that man no longer even understands his own first state: "We do not understand the glorious state of Adam, nor the nature of his sin, nor the transmission of it to us. These are matters which took place under conditions of a nature altogether different from our own, and which transcend our present understanding" (fr. 560, p. 583). Yet that which is lost has an after-effect. It is not simply gone; it is disrupted, but not completely obliterated; it is poisoned by evil, but has not become evil itself. Man is today a sinner, but to be man is not immediately sinfulness. Those are exaggerations of the Biblical notion, which can be justified neither in Saint Paul nor elsewhere. They are based on transparent structural motives, on a very determined tendency to a tragic view of existence, and not least on a specifiable experience of the way body and soul are related to one another. The New Testament does not think in this way. According to it, man is indeed a sinner, but God is still given to him as his end. His incommensurability with God is not absolute, but relative; the hiddenness of God is not complete impossibility of knowledge, but a veiling. This is also the thought of Pascal: "If there had never been any appearance of God, this eternal deprivation would have been equivocal, and might as well have corresponded to the absence of all divinity, as to the unworthiness of men to know him; but his occasional, though not continual, appearances remove the ambiguity" (fr. 559, p. 583). This speaks clearly. So, too, other passages, above all the fourth letter to Mlle. de Roannez, in which it is expressly stated that pagans do not apprehend God in his hiddenness in the world, whereas Christians do so; that Protestants do not perceive God veiled in the sacraments, whereas Catholics do so; and at the end, that, where "the others" do not recognize him, "he has revealed himself in all things for us" (p. 215).

Yet what Pascal, following the Augustinian tradition, says about the situation of man in the face of the truth of God is grave enough. Fragment 843 begins with the words: "Here is not the country of truth. She wanders unknown amongst men.

118

God has covered her with a veil" (p. 718). According to fragment 194, Christianity teaches that "men are in darkness and estranged from God, that he has hidden himself from their knowledge, that this is in fact the name which he gives himself in the Scriptures, *Deus absconditus*" (p. 415). A God who, in spite of the blindness of the mind and the contamination of the heart, would be readily comprehensible would not be the holy God. The very fact that he becomes hidden through sin is a sign of his truth and holiness. As soon as man becomes a sinner, hiddenness becomes, in relation to him, the locus conformable to the essence of God.

But for the same reason, man is also hidden from himself: "He has so little knowledge of what God is that he does not know what he himself is" (fr. 430, p. 525). And still more pointedly: "We do not know what is our life, nor our death, nor God, nor ourselves" (fr. 548, p. 572). Our real state of nature intended by God has escaped us: "by ourselves, we are incapable of judging what is possible for God in respect to us, and what is not. In reality, not only *Deus,* but *homo absconditus,* and the latter because of the former."

II.

What could pierce through the veil? Pascal repeatedly answers: if our entire being took the direction opposed to sin. Sin is self-love, pride, the pretension of the self to be the center of existence. An about-face is thus required: hatred of self, self-conquest, humility, submission to God. "*Le* moi *est haïssable*" was the last word of the analysis of the self (fr. 455, p. 541). Thus only the heart "which really hates itself" is capable of this inner purification, of this reversal of the orientation of existence, of this fundamental transformation, which is necessary.

But this is not possible on one's own. It is indeed not a matter of a mere ethical self-knowledge and change of disposition, but of a decision which takes God as rule and standpoint, of an alignment which is determined by God, of a movement which can

119

only be initiated by him. It is a matter of a new arching of the arc, of a new restoration of the outward orientation. What is demanded of the heart is the love, the *"charité,"* which does not spring from human sources alone. It is a new level of action and existence which cannot be attained from the natural order, and above all not from the natural order tainted by sin. The long fragment 793, already cited in the first chapter, also belongs here: "All bodies together, and all minds together, and all their productions, are not equal to the least movement of charity. This is of an order infinitely more exalted . . . From all bodies and minds, one would not be able to produce a movement of true charity: this is impossible, and of another, supernatural order." There is a specific order of reality, a specific zone of value, a specific *"grandeur"*; between this order and the rest, there is a *"différence de genre"*—all the energy of the Kierkegaardian concept of qualitative differentiation is here at work. A specific *"vue"* is necessary, a specific way of being given. Only thereby become possible that distance from oneself, that view of oneself, that detachment from oneself, which bring about not a mere ethical judgment, not a mere existential desperation, but salutary hate of self and love of God. But this is grace, and God alone can give it.

Now here enters in that decisive knowledge, which the analysis of the *Mémorial* yields: grace does not come in religious experience detached from all contingency, but is bound to certain historical figures: to the precursory messengers of the Old Testament, "Abraham, Isaac, Jacob," representative for the whole lineage of heralds of the Covenant and prophets; it is bound in a definitive way to the Mediator, Jesus Christ.

Fragment 556 summarizes: "The God of Christians is not a God who is simply the author of mathematical truths, or of the order of the elements . . . He is not merely a God who exercises his providence over the life and fortunes of men, to bestow on those who worship him a long and happy life . . . But the God of Abraham, the God of Isaac, the God of Jacob, the God of Christians, is a God of love and comfort, a God who fills the soul

120

and heart of those whom he possesses, a God who makes them conscious of their inward wretchedness and his infinite mercy, who unites himself to their inmost soul, who fills it with humility and joy, with confidence and love, who renders them incapable of any other end than himself" (p. 581).

The presence of God is thus historical; it is bound to a definite figure. In it, God reveals himself; in it, he comes. In it, the new order of love, of grace, is established. It is in the relationship to it that there awakens the new "*vue,*" the regard and the certitude of faith.

Fragment 547 thus expressly states: "We know God only through Jesus Christ. Without this mediator all communion with God is taken away; through Jesus Christ we know God. All those who have claimed to know God and to prove him without Jesus Christ, have had only weak proofs" (p. 571). And fragment 548: "Not only do we know God through Jesus Christ alone, but we know ourselves only through Jesus Christ. We know life and death only through Jesus Christ. Apart from Jesus Christ, we do not know what is our life, nor our death, nor God, nor ourselves. Thus without the Scripture, which has Jesus Christ alone for its object, we know nothing, and see only darkness and confusion in the nature of God and in our own nature" (p. 572). And fragment 547 concludes quite definitively: "We know at the same time our wretchedness; for this God is none other than the Saviour of our wretchedness. So we can only know God well by knowing our iniquities." The whole forms a single ensemble, in which one moment is clarified by another.

The manifestation of God in the things and events of the world was a universal given: the transparency of creatures for the Creator. Here, in Christ, is a special form of given: an advance, a coming, an acting, a speaking of God. An explicit form of given, the historical. The Holy Scripture of the Old and New Testaments prepares for Christ, and radiates from him. It explains his place in history. The Church, however, to mention this here in passing, stands for Pascal in the most intimate relationship with Christ. ". . . *l'Eglise . . . avec Jésus-Christ qui en est inséparable*," he says in the sixth letter to Mlle. de Roannez (p. 218). The formula is followed by an ardent profession of faith in the Church, echoing that of the seventeenth of the *Lettres provinciales*. Fragment 858 concisely declares: "The history of the Church ought properly to be called the history of the truth" (p. 728). And fragment 850: "It is impossible that those who love God with all their heart should fail to recognize the Church" (p. 724). The history of the Church is continuous with the history of salvation of the Old and New Testament. The Holy Scripture does not form an isolated phenomenon, thrown by God, as it were, into the indifferentiated sphere of history, but is related to a plane; it is entrusted to a reality situated in history, and which is precisely the Church; it is presented by her and can only be properly heard in her sphere. In the final sections of the *Pensées* Pascal has applied himself to constructing a theory of this historical continuity of significant figures in which the freedom of God binds itself to a reality situated in history.

III.

How, then, are we to think of this revelation of God? Does he really come out into the open? The fourth letter to Mlle. de Roannez says: "This great secrecy into which God has withdrawn, impenetrable to the gaze of men, is a great lesson for us . . . He remained hidden, under the veil of nature which hides him from us, until the incarnation; and when it was necessary for him to appear, he hid himself even more by covering himself with humanity. He was much more recognizable when he was invisible than after he made himself visible. And finally, when he wanted to keep the promise he made to his apostles to remain with man until his final advent, he chose to remain in the strangest and most obscure secrecy of all, the species of the Eucharist. It is this sacrament which Saint John calls, in the Apocalypse, a hidden manna; and I believe that Isaiah saw him in this state when he said in the spirit of prophecy: Truly you are a hidden God. This is the ultimate secrecy in which he can be . . . One can add to these considerations the secrecy of the mind of God still hidden in the Scripture. For there are two perfect meanings, the literal and the mystical" (p. 214).

God is thus at once revealed and hidden. That which translates him into human terms veils him at the same time. Pascal calls this situation the "*ambiguité*" of the divine manifestation. It places man before a specific decision, puts him into a specific danger, demands a specific attitude, and is satisfied by a specific act. Thus fragment 430 states: "It was not then right that he [God] should appear in a manner manifestly divine, and completely capable of convincing all men; but it was also not right that he should come in so hidden a manner that he could not be known by those who should sincerely seek him. He has willed to make himself quite recognizable by the latter; and thus, willing to appear openly to those who seek him with all their heart, he so regulates the knowledge of himself that he has given signs of himself visible to those who seek him, and not to those who seek him not. There is enough light for those who only desire to see, and enough obscurity for those who have a contrary disposition" (p. 526).[37]

The revealed God is at once "visible" and "invisible." There are reasons which speak for him and reasons which speak against him. He attracts and repulses. He gives motives for affirmation, but also others for rejecting him. To be sure, he is prepared through prophecy—Pascal occupied himself thoroughly with the phenomenon and problem of prophecy, which made a strong and evident impression upon him—, but the prophetic figure of the Messiah is itself seen ambiguously. "What do the prophets say of Jesus Christ? That he will be clearly God? No; but that he is a God truly hidden; that he will be slighted; that none will think that it is he; that he will be a stumbling block, upon which many will stumble, etc." (fr. 751, p. 683). Besides, the prophetic word, as the word of the Spirit of God, stands in the same ambiguity. It is clear and obscure at the same time. That is part of its nature, of its intention: "without that, no one would have stumbled over Jesus Christ, and this is one of the

123

formal intentions of the prophets" (*ibid.*). Fragment 727 cites a profusion of texts and individual passages from the prophets which show already present in prophecy the situation which then reaches its culminating point with the entrance of the Messiah into time. It is into this situation that, from then on, every man comes who is confronted with the testimony of Christ (p. 673). It is the specific situation of revelation: the possibility of scandal.

This situation has its analogy within the world. As soon as a higher reality—an idea, a challenge, a personality—enters into a closed sphere of life, this sphere is disturbed. That which enters gives it the possibility of existential elevation; but at the same time, and for that very reason, it shakes its self-sufficiency, its tranquility in its own disposition. Examples abound everywhere: let us think, for example, of a social reformer or innovator who makes his appearance in a social situation which is already developed. He points out the possibility of ascending to a better form of existence; by this very fact, however, he disturbs the old status quo and all those who are intimately bound up with it. If the latter hold firm, the establishment remains fixed in its own disposition, and can then, on the basis of the disturbances of its present structure of existence and value, urge all kinds of reasons against the intruder. The latter will hardly be in a position to refute them convincingly, for he is on a level which is not admitted by the established order. It will always be so when the man of genius enters the realm of ordinary existence. So it happens already wherever mind emerges in the realm of merely biological existence. But the situation attains its specific acuteness when it is the Living God who bears witness to himself in the existential domain of the man intimately bound up with the world. The sacred forces and values, which appear in the prophets or in the Messiah himself, speak for him; but on the other hand, it is precisely the divine elevation of these values and dispositions which makes him unable to gain acceptance for them in a resisting world. This world will feel itself threatened and will use this threat as an argument against the revelation. Before a world

124

which asserts itself, God is really—to put it expressively—the big trouble-maker. "I did not come to bring peace, but the sword," Jesus clearly states.

A final trait still remains to be noted: the mysteriously irritating effect which the sacred as such has on man—and all the more so, the more purely it stems from God. It is not true, that man reacts towards God in a merely positive way. To be sure, man is "*ad Deum creatus,*" as Augustine says, and Pascal also emphasizes that we "love God naturally"; but man, at the root of his being, also stands in the state of revolt—and not only certain men, but all men. The sacred is provoking. This troubling effect manifests itself in the most varied forms, from the simplest embarrassment and discomfort to antipathy, to the explosion of hate and the paroxysm of destruction (see the event, fundamentally so incomprehensible, reported by Lk. 4, 16–30). This is one of the most profound approaches to the understanding of history. All forms of reaction can arise against the sacred. And not for any special reason: the reasons only come afterwards, or form a disguise, or are the cause, since something must indeed give them rise. In reality, the reaction is something immediate, stemming from the roots of human nature, directed against the quality of the sacred, against the character of God as such. Because he "goes against taste," as Nietzsche says; because he "goes against nature," as Pascal would say with the most profound ambiguity. Yet this attitude is adopted with reasons. The rejection of the sacred, or the attack against it, has always had reasons; indeed, very important and very illuminating reasons. Now whether they stem from the all too human nature of the messengers of revelation—nothing is more provocative than the weaknesses of man pledged to God!—or from the obliquities of the situation—and the situation of revelation is always "oblique"; for it can hardly be "straight," man being what he is!—or from the petrifications of historical conditions—, for there is always a great deal of evil for which "religion" is to blame . . . And then there is that strange phenomenon, in which the aberrance of human existence is so dishearteningly expressed:

125

each value in itself is clear; but as soon as it passes into the concrete sphere of man's life, into his heart, into his thoughts, into the relationships of men with one another, into the mesh of causes and effects of history, something remarkable takes place with it: it is as if the value attracted evil opposition to itself, from the ever waiting evil tendency at the bottom of the human heart. Thence come the most serious arguments against the messenger of God, which are the most difficult to shake off, since they arise from the very corruption of existence. We all react from this point of departure . . . There will thus always be reasons. And the people who come forward against revelation will always give the impression of moderation and wisdom; they will always appear as the advocates of life, as the guardians of the world and its value. Indeed, there will even appear the paradox, that man will pretend to defend God against the prophet, to defend God against the Son of God, as Jesus indeed said: "Those who kill you will be convinced that they are doing God a service!" The rejector will defend the "pure" concept of God as the absolute being, the mystery of the profound divinity which calms the heart, the creative foundation of the world and the infinitely operative universal life, against the God of revelation, who is "anthropomorphic" or "inhuman" or "barbarous." He will intercede in favor of the "God of the philosophers," of the "God of the poets," against the "God of Abraham, of Isaac, and of Jacob," against the "God of Jesus Christ." And indeed, with excellent, though less than decisive reasons, which are very impressive as long as the heart shuts itself to the genuine, ultimate, and really decisive reasons, which speak for the Living God of the Christian message.

Pascal's "ambiguity" is the fundamental Biblical phenomenon of the possibility of scandal, which is inseparably bound up with revelation. It goes throughout the entire history of the Old Testament, and becomes especially clear in the figures of the prophets. In the presence of Christ, it breaks through violently and becomes a power which brings about his earthly destiny. It takes on a particularly violent form in Christ's contemporaries; but it also manifests itself, appropriately transformed, in every encounter with the testimony for the revelation which took place in him.

This ambiguity determines the situation in which the risk of the decision must take place. Logical evidence leaves no room for decision: one cannot decide for nonsense. Clarity of value leaves just as little: no one wills manifest worthlessness. The essence of the situation of revelation consists in the fact that it brings about a possibility of hesitation. It gives certainty, only to call it immediately into question. It motivates "for," but also "against." Thus arises the psychological and intellectual sphere which is necessary in order for freedom to enter into the possibility of choice. It is the sphere in which man stands before the living God and submits to his sovereignty. In which the person accomplishes, from his own power of initiative, the movement of passage to the beyond, the self-surrender to the divine Thou, and thus, in faith, completes the arc of flame of the human existence tending towards God. Or in which, on the other hand, faith is rejected, the person turns in upon himself in his earthly self-assertion, becomes entangled in doubt, and collapses in the weariness of skepticism.

But God does not only summon, he also gives the ears to hear, the force to follow: in short, grace. And God is so free, so above the human norms of justice and good sense, that he is sovereign in the granting of this grace.

Here the impenetrability of the situation, the ambiguity, thickens: It is the mystery of predestination. Fragment 578 states: "There is sufficient clarity to enlighten the elect, and sufficient obscurity to humble them. There is sufficient obscurity to blind the reprobate, and sufficient clarity to condemn them and make them inexcusable" (p. 590). And fragment 575: "All things turn to good for the elect, even the obscurities of Scripture; for they honor them for what is divinely clear. And all things turn to evil for the others, even what is clear; for they revile what is clear, because of the obscurities which they do not understand" (p. 590).

It is in the ambiguity of revelation that Pascal carried on the struggle of his religious life. He could exist in it alone, for it contained the tensions which he needed. He fought for it against the rationalizing and harmonizing tendencies of the time, because he saw in it the sphere of the freedom and splendor of the divine movement, and at the same time, the sphere of the freedom and grandeur of faith. But here, too, he succumbed to his demon: the demon of combat, the will to the absolute at any price. We will come back to this in another context.

IV.

The innermost starting point of initiative, the center from which the arc of flame shoots out to the other side or is held back, that ultimate, which gives itself or does not, and which is truly called upon in the situation of ambiguity, is the "*heart.*"

"*Le coeur*" is in a certain sense the central reality of Pascal's image of man. The great mathematician, scientist, and designer thereby stands in the noblest tradition which the Christian Occident knows, and which finds its theoretical expression in the "*philosophia*" and the "*theologia cordis.*" As in a sort of Advent, it is prepared by Plato. It appears in Saint Paul. It is lived by Ignatius of Antioch, developed with wonderful vigor by Augustine, powerfully experienced by Bernard of Clairvaux, then again, and completely anew, by Saint Francis, not to forget Gertrude the Great, Elizabeth of Thuringia, and Catherine of Sienna. Saint Bonaventure creates its system, Dante makes it into poetry. At the time of the Renaissance it slips back into a purely metaphysical and aesthetic Neoplatonism, but is immediately lived anew by Saint Theresa of Avila, thought over carefully by Francis de Sales and the theologians of the Oratory, by a Condren and a Bérulle. In the eighteenth century, it seems to trickle away, or only to continue in a practical, bourgeois form.

128

In the nineteenth, it is once more the Oratorians who carry it on: Gratry, Rosmini, and above all the great Newman. At the same time, Eastern philosophers and theologians: Vladimir Soloviev, Khomyakov, Florensky. But it is alive in Kierkegaard as well, in a strange Nordic modification. It is also—as has perhaps not yet been seen—the essential force in Nietzsche's thought, even if it is turned by him against Christ and the Living God.

It is not possible to develop fully here Pascal's concept of the heart. A special essay would be necessary. The reader must thus have recourse to the texts himself, to the "Discours sur les passions de l'amour," the essay "De l'art d'agréer," and the chaos of the *Pensées*.

"C'est le coeur, qui sent Dieu, et non la raison," states fragment 278: *"Voilà ce que c'est que la foi, Dieu sensible au coeur, non à la raison"* (p. 458). And the neighboring fragment 277: *"Le coeur a ses raisons, que la raison ne connaît point; on le sait en mille choses. Je dis, que le coeur aime l'être universel naturellement, et soi-même naturellement, selon qu'il s'y adonne; et il se durcit contre l'un ou l'autre, à son choix"* (p. 458). What is the heart in the Pascalian sense?

One thing above all: It is not the expression of the emotional in opposition to the logical, not feeling in opposition to the intellect, not "soul" in opposition to "mind." *"Coeur"* is itself mind: a manifestation of the mind. The act of the heart is an act productive for knowledge. Certain objects only become given in the act of the heart. But they do not remain there in a-rational intuition, but are accessible to intellectual and rational penetration.

We are here before a basic human structure, which seems at first to be at home in the south, where it sustains the classical, as well as the medieval and more recent neo-Latin culture. But it also reaches out towards the north, either directly or by the detour of "longing" [*Sehnsucht*]. We already said that Nietzsche is a proof for this; so too, although more difficult to understand,

129

is Kierkegaard. The phenomenon depends on the interrelationship between knowledge and will, apprehension of truth and love—objectively expressed, between essence and value. "Value" is the character of preciousness of things: that which makes them worthy of being. To it corresponds the experience of value: that specific, irreducible sensibility, the vibration of the mind at the contact of value. But not of the theoretical mind, of the reason, but of the mind which appreciates and values, that is, of the heart. "Heart" is the mind, so far as it gets into proximity of the blood, into the feeling, living fibre of the body—yet without becoming torpid. Heart is the mind rendered ardent and sensitive by the blood, but which at the same time ascends into the clarity of contemplation, the distinctness of form, the precision of judgment. Heart is the organ of love—of that love from which arose Platonic philosophy, and then, newly fructified by Christian faith, the *Divine Comedy*. This love implies, namely, the relationship of the center of man's desires and feelings to the idea; the movement from the blood to the mind, from the presence of the body to the eternity of the mind. It is what is experienced in the heart.

Let us listen to the following phrases from the "Discours": *"La netteté d'esprit cause aussi la netteté de la passion; c'est pourquoi un esprit grand et net aime avec ardeur, et il voit distinctement ce qu'il aime"* (P. O. 125). In this concept of "neatness" we must include the moment of clarity, but also that of purity; "neatness" is here a value of a superior order, not merely of propriety—"and it causes also the neatness of passion; that is why a great and neat mind loves with ardor, and sees distinctly what it loves." And further: "In proportion as one has more mind, the passions are greater; for since the passions are but sentiments and ideas"—note the unusualness of this association, as of the following—, "which belong exclusively to the mind, although they are occasioned by the body, it is clear that they are nothing but the mind itself, and that they thus employ all its capacity. I am only speaking of the burning passions [*des passions de feu*]; for as far as the others are concerned, they

130

often mingle together, and cause a very inconvenient confusion; but this is never so in those which have mind" (p. 124). And once again: "One has inappropriately taken the name of reason from love, and opposed them to one another without a good foundation, for love and reason are one and the same thing" (p. 133). The idea should come from Dante,[38] just as well as from Augustine, and yet again from Plato. Pascal elsewhere expresses the same idea differently: "*Nous naissons avec un caractère d'amour dans nos coeurs*"—the source of *eros,* the origin of the movement of love—"*qui se développe à mesure que l'esprit se perfectionne* . . . who doubts after this whether we are in the world for something other than to love? Indeed, one may well hide it from oneself, one always loves. Even in the things in which one seems to have excluded love, it is there secretly and in hiding, and it is impossible that man could live a moment without that" (pp. 125ff.).

The heart responds to value. Value is being's inner movement of meaning. Value is the self-justification of what is, that it is worthy of its existence. This *dynamis* summons the movement of the heart, love. Thus the "*coeur,*" for Pascal, is the organ which grasps the value of being; the value of all that exists, even of that apparently the most distant, because there is no being which would not have some value, and thereby be capable of that inner contact which brings about the vibration of appreciation. But the heart grasps especially the value of that which is living, and particularly that of man. Finally, and in a definitive way, the heart is the organ for grasping that value which only manifests itself from above, from revelation: that of the holiness of God, which brings man his fulfillment and his salvation.

But in order not to slip into something merely emotional, let us now listen to Pascal's most astounding statements. "*Coeur*" is the organ of the "*esprit de finesse.*" "There are two kinds of minds: the one, geometrical"—that is, abstractly logical—, "the other which one can call '*de finesse.*' The first has views which are slow, hard and inflexible; but the second has a flexibility of thought which it applies at the same time to the diverse lovable

131

parts of that which it loves. From the eyes, it penetrates to the heart, and by the movement of the exterior, it knows what is taking place within. When one has the one mind and the other at the same time, how great is then the pleasure of love! For one possesses at once the force and the flexibility of mind, which are both very necessary for eloquence [the possibility of expression] between two persons" (p. 125). We will certainly not go wrong in here conjecturing an experience of Pascal himself. He is evidently describing himself. Still more unusual, however, and more shocking for any emotionalist, is the role which is attributed to the heart in the following sentences . . . and we want to remain aware that it is not some sentimental dreamer who is speaking here, but rather the author of the essay on conical sections, one of the founders of the theory of probabilities, and the designer of the calculating machine! Pascal declares that the first axioms of thought are perceived in the heart; that it is the heart which actualizes the prerequisites of all possible knowledge. Fragment 282 states: "We know truth not only by the reason, but by the heart; it is in this latter way that we know first principles, and it is in vain that reasoning, which has no part in it, tries to combat them. The skeptics, who have only this for their object, labor to no purpose . . . For the knowledge of first principles, as space, time, motion, number, is as sure as any of those which we get from reasoning. And reason must trust these knowledges of the heart and of instinct, and base all its arguments on them. (The heart feels that there are three dimensions in space, and that numbers are infinite; and reason then demonstrates that there are no two square numbers, one of which is double the other. Principles are intuited, propositions are inferred, all with certainty, though in different ways.) And it is as useless and absurd for reason to demand from the heart proofs of her first principles, before admitting them, as it would be for the heart to demand from reason an intuition of all the demonstrated propositions before accepting them" (pp. 459ff.).[39]

It would be a fine task to analyze these texts more closely, but it would lead us too far afield. Besides, they speak for themselves. One thing above all follows from them: genuine knowledge of the theoretical mind is not possible, if it is not supported by the movement of the appreciating mind. Knowledge presupposes love. One will know the truth—really know it, in the most profound sense, with the passion of appropriation—to the extent that one is loving. Again the figure of Dante rises up behind Pascal, and once more that of Augustine; and at the beginning stands Plato.

But now: love does not only mean reacting to value, but becoming active towards it. Love is not only a movement of reaction, but also one of initiative. Love is freedom. Every value calls forth an attitude, which in turn determines the character taken on by the influence of the value in the sphere of existence of the man affected by it—its existential significance, whether it has a constructive or destructive effect.

One can attempt to define this attitude from different sides. It lies above all in the choice of value: everything is endowed with value, but every value is not urgent. All values as such have validity, but only a certain one is ever appropriate. A wrongly chosen value is good in itself, but has a harmful effect, or at least represses the appropriate value . . . Then there is the matter of the extent of submission, the degree, in which power over one's own life is conferred on a value. Therein is decided whether the value leads to freedom or to slavery . . . There is in addition the inner release: whether the will of the heart permits the value or the image of the value to develop purely out of itself, which at the same time means that this heart must rise above and beyond itself; or whether the heart subordinates what it encounters to its own volition, makes it subservient to itself—which can already lie in the way in which man looks at it . . . And finally, whether the value is kept pure or perverted into evil. Whether the heart manages to prevent the rise of the evil opposition, the distortion into evil already mentioned . . . It is thus a matter of whether the heart

133

is fundamentally vigilant, obedient to the summons, selfless, generous, pure—pure in the spiritual sense.

But the problem of man's existence thereby comes in again: sin. Sin means that man wants to stand in himself, that he is arrogant, selfish, impure in mind, that is, he endeavors to subordinate by force the freedom of what is valid to his own volition. This sin, which exercises its influence everywhere, above all in the mind, and thus also in the depths of the heart, threatens to become an evil prior decision which precedes all individual decisions. It strives to confer autonomy on values, and in this way to make them instruments of the revolt against God. It influences the force of the heart and seeks thus to falsify the true image of things. It troubles the view for value, misleads the value sentiment, diverts the judgment of value—and the danger is all the greater as the heart, in the characteristic immediacy of its act, feels so sure of itself and is not willing to believe in the possibility of an error. In reality, nothing can err in a way as profound, as fateful, and as difficult to set right as the heart.

What does all this signify for our question?

In his analysis of the religious decision, Pascal has in view above all the aspect of value in religious reality. When he says of God that he is *"sensible au coeur, non à la raison,"* he evidently means the element of value in the divine: the "highest good"; that which, in the nearness of God, is unique, inwardly stirring, which gives meaning, which fulfills. That, in other words, which modern philosophy of religion calls the quality of the "numinous," the value of the "sacred"; that which leads Pascal to say that Christ and Saint Paul "wanted to inflame, not instruct" (fr. 283, p. 460); that which inwardly consoles, that which fundamentally fulfills, illuminates, protects, purifies, strengthens the heart.

Now one could ask whether Pascal knows the natural religious experience, the contact with the "numinous," as it occurs in detached religious experience—which would then lead to the further question of the relationship between this experience and faith. As far as I can see, he did not pose this problem. Probably, he did not at all seriously envisage a genuine religious experience outside the realm of Christian faith, although it could have been suggested to him by the interests of his time; certainly, his master, Montaigne, could have showed it to him. The religious sensitivity of the heart, of which Pascal speaks, is still always situated in the sphere of revelation.

The holiness which he means is the character of the God who reveals himself in the Old and New Testaments. The "*sainteté*" he speaks of is no universal religious holiness, but the definite Biblical holiness. It is this which comes to meet man, ready to "fill the soul and heart" (fr. 556, p. 581), which nothing else can fill; to be the "*véritable bien*," which alone is capable of satisfying the hunger for value which is in man's nature. From here opens up the "*ordre de la sainteté*," of which the long fragment 793 speaks; the "*ordre de la charité*," which has its own "*grandeur*," its own "splendor," that is, its specific plenitude of value; an order essentially different and situated unattainably higher than the order of the "flesh" as well as that of the "mind," to which also the natural heart belongs. It is the plenitude of value not of the "God of the philosophers," but of the "God of Jesus Christ."

Now it is precisely these values which are situated in ambiguity. The heart is summoned by them and placed before the decision, whether or not to recognize them for what they are and accord them the sovereignty which they demand.

But the option of the heart itself stands under the falsifying influence of sin! It is thus logical when Pascal speaks with such emphasis of the proper inner attitude: of humility, of unselfishness, of good will—various designations for the fact that the heart loosens its constriction within itself, gives itself up as the center of existence, and becomes ready to accept that which is summoning it as the real point of reference. It is fundamentally what is meant by the saying of the Gospel: "He who keeps his soul will lose it; but he who loses his soul will win it."

The purer this readiness, the more perfect this detachment, the greater the chance of penetrating the ambiguity; the clearer the view for that, which here speaks; the surer the response to the value; the stronger the movement, by which the ascension towards the divine is realized and the genuine structure of man regained: the arc of flame across towards God.

What happens then? Then "*amour*" becomes "*charité*." "*Amour*" in the sense employed above is simply the force of the heart: the natural response to the value which vibrates everywhere. This force of the heart is itself "natural," that is, everything which was said of the problem of nature, applies to it. It stands itself in the state of fall, in ambiguity. In it, too, is chaos, illusion, quasi-nothingness. If the heart yields to the call, then something happens to it. For the first time appears the genuine center, the counterpart of the divine center which is calling. For the first time awakens the genuine, God-intended self, the real self, not that ghost-like self of the "*moi haïssable*." And in it awakens a new love, a new faculty of appreciation, with a new inner certainty and freedom. It is what theology calls the "divine virtue" of love, which consists in a sharing in the love of God, and is thus a grace.

The God who reveals himself and comes to meet man is love, as Saint John says. We can unfortunately not go into what this would mean in the framework of the thought developed above; it would yield something very profound about the God of the Christians. Now, the decisive event consists in the fact that He, substantial and holy love, comes into contact with the "*fonds du coeur*"; that the "fundus of the heart"—we see how the concept of heart is here prolonged into the mystical sphere—surrenders to him, and that therein the new love of "*charité*" awakens.

One can say a great deal which is true and ingenious about the ambiguity of revelation, as well about the reality of the God who reveals himself as about that of man. About the problem of scandal as the critical point of this ambiguity, one can also say a great deal—more than we can find valuable. But one cannot say much about how the possibility of scandal is overcome, about how the chiaroscuro of revelation is traversed. What takes place here disappears at both extremities into mystery: into the mystery of that absolute initiative, by which God reveals himself, gives light, touches the bottom of the heart so effectively that it unbinds itself, opens, recovers sight and freedom . . . And into the mystery of the human heart, of its finite initiative, in which the power of sin remains, and by which it opens itself and abandons itself, in order to share in God's nature. It is the mystery of grace and freedom.

How they come together, how they are twofold and yet one, about that one can say nothing more. But that they can come together Pascal experienced in that event reported by the *Mémorial*.

CHAPTER V

The Argument of the Wager. An Historical Correlation

I.

History is built up in various continuities. One cuts across the instant and consists in the way in which one stratum of happening is supported, developed or obstructed, revealed or veiled by another; how its motives are structured, deepened, or traversed. Another goes into the past and the future and consists in the way in which what is happening at the moment is determined by what has preceded it, and in turn prepares what is to come.

The preceding inquiries several times provided the occasion to point out Pascal's position in the history of modern intellectual life. For the rest, they had to limit themselves, in conformity to their intention, to a systematic analysis. The present chapter is now to trace an historical continuity, and indeed, one of a special kind. It is not established by tangible dependencies, but by the fact that a given motif, a given element of personal intellectual existence emerges in various historical epochs and thus, connecting similarity and mutation, a line of movement becomes clear. We believe Pascal to be situated in such a series of intellectual manifestations, independent from one another but inviting correlation by dint of their inner affinity. And we are thinking especially of that singular train of thought, which under the title "Argument du pari"—the proof of God from the

138

chances of a wager concerning the meaning of existence—has met with more attention than understanding. Its real meaning seems to disclose itself more easily if it is taken together with two other no less individualistic and no better understood ideas or attempts: the so-called "ontological proof of God" of the old master of Augustinian theology, Anselm of Canterbury, and again with the "absolute paradox," thought out about seven hundred years later by Søren Kierkegaard.

II.

THE ONTOLOGICAL PROOF OF GOD

The first of the three trains of thought occupying us is developed by Anselm of Canterbury in his little treatise, *Proslogion seu alloquium de Dei existentia.*[40] Gaunilon, a monk of the abbey of Marmoutiers, attacked him with his *Liber pro insipiente,* to which Anselm replied by a *Liber apologeticus contra Gaunilonem.*

The train of thought which concerns us here is as follows:
(Ch. II) "And so, Lord, do thou, who dost give understanding to faith, give me, so far as thou knowest it to be profitable, to understand that thou art as we believe; and that thou art that which we believe. And, indeed, we believe that thou art a being than which nothing greater can be conceived. Or is there no such nature, since the fool has said in his heart, there is no God? (Ps. 14, 1). But, at any rate, this very fool, when he hears of this being of which I speak—a being than which nothing greater can be conceived—understands what he hears, and what he understands is in his understanding; although he does not understand it to exist.

"For it is one thing for the object to be in the understanding, and another to understand[41] that the object exists. When a painter first conceives of what he will afterwards perform, he has it in his understanding, but he does not yet understand it to

139

be, because he has not yet performed it. But after he has made the painting, he both has it in his understanding, and he understands that it exists, because he has made it . . . And whatever is understood exists in the understanding. And assuredly that, than which nothing greater can be conceived, cannot exist in the understanding alone. For, suppose it exists in the understanding alone: then it can be conceived to exist in reality; which is greater.

"Therefore, if that, than which nothing greater can be conceived, exists in the understanding alone, the very being, than which nothing greater can be conceived, is one, than which a greater can be conceived. But obviously this is impossible . . ."

(Ch. III) "And it assuredly exists so truly, that it cannot be conceived not to exist. For, it is possible to conceive of a being which cannot be conceived not to exist; and this is greater than one which can be conceived not to exist. Hence, if that, than which nothing greater can be conceived, can be conceived not to exist, it is not that, than which nothing greater can be conceived. But this is an irreconcilable contradiction. There is, then, so truly a being than which nothing greater can be conceived to exist, that it cannot even be conceived not to exist; and this being thou art, O Lord, our God . . . And, indeed, whatever else there is, except thee alone, can be conceived not to exist. To thee alone, therefore, it belongs to exist more truly than all other beings, and hence in a higher degree than all others. For, whatever else exists does not exist so truly, and hence in a less degree it belongs to it to exist . . ."

Chapter V turns the concept into the axiological domain: "What art thou, then, Lord God, than whom nothing greater can be conceived? But what art thou, except that which, as the highest of all beings, alone exists through itself, and creates all other things from nothing? For, whatever is not this is less than a thing which can be conceived of. But this cannot be conceived of thee. What good, therefore, does the supreme Good lack, through which every good is? Therefore, thou art just, truthful, blessed, and whatever it is better to be than not to be . . ."

The following chapters develop the formal definition of God

140

thus obtained by examining the individual elements of the concept of God.

Chapters XIV and XV seek to express the incomprehensibility of God: "Hast thou found what thou didst seek, my soul? Thou didst seek God. Thou hast found him to be a being which is the highest of all beings, a being than which nothing better can be conceived; that this being is life itself, light, wisdom, goodness, eternal blessedness and blessed eternity; and that it is everywhere and always . . .

"But, if thou hast found him, why is it that thou dost not feel thou hast found him? Why, O Lord, our God, does not my soul feel thee, if it hath found thee? Or, has it not found him whom it found to be light and truth? For how did it understand this, except by seeing light and truth? Or, could it understand anything at all of thee, except through thy light and thy truth?

"Hence, if it has seen light and truth, it has seen thee; if it has not seen thee, it has not seen light and truth . . .

"Lord, my God, my creator, and renewer, speak to the desire of my soul, what thou art other than it has seen, that it may clearly see what it desires. It strains to see thee more; and sees nothing beyond this which it hath seen, except darkness. Nay, it does not see darkness, of which there is none in thee; but it sees that it cannot see farther, because of its own darkness . . .

"Surely it is both darkened in itself, and dazzled by thee. Doubtless it is both obscured by its own insignificance, and overwhelmed by thy infinity. Truly, it is both contracted by its own narrowness and overcome by thy greatness.

"For how great is that light from which shines every truth that gives light to the rational mind? How great is that truth in which is everything that is true, and outside which is only nothingness and the false? How boundless is the truth which sees at one glance whatsoever has been made, and by whom, and through whom, and how it has been made from nothing? What purity, what certainty, what splendor where it is? Assuredly more than a creature can conceive."

(Ch. XV) "Therefore, O Lord, thou art not only that than

141

which a greater cannot be conceived, but thou art a being greater than can be conceived. For, since it can be conceived that there is such a being, if thou art not this very being, a greater than thou can be conceived. But this is impossible."

Chapter XVI finally draws the final conclusion and shows that the definition thus obtained constitutes precisely the mystery of God: the "inaccessible light" in which he dwells.

Let us disengage the logical structure of this train of thought:

I find myself in possession of the concept of God as the Supreme Being. This concept is in my consciousness; it has a "being" "in me." "Being" means more than a mere noetic given; for the moment, let us put "energy of significance" [*Bedeutungsenergie*].

The concept of God is then more precisely defined: as the concept of that being, above and beyond which nothing greater can be conceived. To the definitions of this "greatness," of its content of essence and value, belongs that, that it really exist. The concept "existing in me" of the highest conceivable being thus contains also the moment of being objectively real.

Now the "energy of significance" spoken of above said in regard to the definitions of essence in the concept of God: they are true, valid, in themselves and apart from the question of their reality. In regard to the definition of real existence, however, this same energy of significance says: What is meant by that definition of essence is objective reality. Thus as soon as I correctly conceive the concept of God, it follows from the content of this thought, that what is conceived, namely, God, must necessarily also be objectively real.

Where the logical "mistake" lies is immediately clear. Gaunilo has already stated it in his *Liber pro insipiente*—standing up for the "fool" who cannot understand Anselm's train of thought. In his answer, Anselm merely repeated the first thesis. The logical impossibility has since been repeatedly pointed out. From Kant on, it has become customary to reduce every proof of God to the

142

schema of the ontological proof and generally to invalidate every attempt at proof through the latter's logical "impossibility." But this in no way does justice to the matter.

The ontological argument is based upon a particular way in which thinking experiences itself.

The process of understanding culminates in the illumination of the evidence. It becomes clear to me therein, "what" it is, that I have there before me; and furthermore, I see clearly that what I conceive is free of inner impossibility and deception and realizes that fundamental and irreducible meaning which is called "truth." Now the process, in the final culmination of which evidence dawns on one, is experienced by the thinking here under discussion in a particular way. It would not be sufficiently characterized by the concepts of "earnestness" or "concern." One no doubt expresses the intention of this thought experience most correctly when one says: knowing is a "touching." First of all, a living "touching," a "contact" with the concrete object of knowledge itself—an exact analysis of the appropriate sense experience would ascertain the consciousness of a continuity from the organ to the thing—; then a touching of the intellectually intrinsic element of the thing, of its "idea." This idea is not experienced as "content of consciousness," or as a concept standing in the merely logical sphere, but as something intellectually real. It is valid and real at once. Indeed, more real than the empirical thing. The Platonic conviction that the idea is more real than the thing is based on this same cognitive experience. Fortified through the meditative training of the Christian's, the monk's life of prayer, it is also at the root of Anselm's train of thought.

This "ontic"[41] character of cognitive experience is linked with a further one: knowing is a "movement." This structure thereby sharply differentiates itself from another, for which the cognitive process takes place in the separated vis-à-vis of subject and object. Between the two, an essential cleavage is felt; the grasping of the object is structured as if at a distance—a qualitative and thus irreducible distance, not merely an interval subject to diminution—, so that it is expressed with the image of "reflection," and its elements, such as "perceiving subject," "perceived object," "perceiving act," etc., tend to be transformed into purely logical values. In the thought experience here under consideration, on the contrary, the cognitive subject has a decided "ontic" character, as does the object. The accomplishment of understanding is experienced as a real process, as an act, as an intellectual movement of the subject towards the object. So much so that the illumination of certainty is experienced not only as a touching of the object—the *attingere regulas aeternas* of Augustine!—, but as a fusion of the knowing with the known. In it, the living man can be passionately concerned to the extreme. The longing for knowledge can be expressed with the most central vital drives, the most energetic impulses towards the grasping of and fusion with the object: hunger and *eros*. Knowing is then an "eating," a "marrying."

For the distanced cognitive experience, the concrete accomplishment of understanding falls basically out of the realm of the essential. It is experienced merely as the necessary way in which the noetic vis-à-vis of subject and object is brought about. Here, on the contrary, the living process belongs absolutely to the core of knowledge. Its realization is experienced not only in the vis-à-vis of the correct view of the object, but just as much, if not even more, in the special nature of this touching of the object, of this living fusion with the substantially existant.

This "kinetic" character of thought is especially strong in the Anselmian argument. It expresses a cognitive movement of the highest intensity and tension towards its goal.

The same is true of the "ontic" character: thinking is experienced as a touching of the idea intended by the thought. The idea in turn as something not only valid but existing. Ideas are existing entities, to think them means: in intellectual movement, *intendere in eas,* touch them, take one's stand on them, unite oneself with them.[42]

The idea of God, however, of which it is here a question, is a special case among ideas—as is, indeed, the idea of the Good in Plato. It is essentially not only the idea of God, but he himself. To conceive the concept of God is, from a strictly noetic point of view, something unique.[43] It means to be in movement towards God himself.

But the motive which bears the process of thought is the particular emotional state which one might call "idealistic," taking this word in its pure meaning, as the expression of a disposition, not of a philosophical theory; that is, the high-mindedness, which considers the intellectual-ideal, the truth, as the essential; as more essential, more important, more real than external reality. This disposition does not mean merely the decision in favor of the idea, but something far more noble: gallantry in regard to the intellectual sphere of ideas. The external things want to represent this sphere as impotent, the fidelity to it as foolish. But he who is so minded decides to attest to the idea as the essential by literally founding his living inner being on it, in the realization of the movement described above. He dares to address the idea as really capable of supporting his inner being, and to step onto it—at the risk of losing the reality of the external world and of obtaining no other in return.

THE ARGUMENT OF THE WAGER

Among Pascal's *Pensées* is found a fragment entitled: *"infini— rien"* (fr. 233, pp. 434–442). It contains a dialogue between the writer and an adversary, the *"libertin."* The parts of the text essential for our purpose read as follows:

(Pascal:) "A unit joined to infinity does not increase it by anything, any more than a foot added to an infinite measure. The finite is annihilated in the presence of the infinite, and becomes a pure nothing. Thus our mind before God; thus our justice before divine justice . . .

"We know that there is an infinite,[44] and ignore its nature. Since we know that it is false that numbers are finite, thus it is true that there is an infinite in number. But we do not know what it is: it is false that it is even, it is false that it is odd. For when one adds a unit, it does not change in nature; yet it is a number, and every number is even or odd . . . Thus one can know that there is a God without knowing what he is . . .

"If there is a God, he is infinitely incomprehensible, since, having neither parts nor limits, he has nothing in common with us . . .

"Let us examine then this point, and say: 'God exists, or he does not exist.' But to which side shall we incline? Reason can determine nothing here: There is an infinite chaos [between God and us] which operates us. A game is being played at the extremity of this infinite distance, where heads or tails will turn up. What will you wager? By reason, you can do neither one nor the other [that is, that God exists or that he does not exist]; by reason, you can defend neither of the two. Do not therefore reprove for error those who have made a choice [that is, decided for belief or disbelief in the existence of God]; for you know nothing about it."

(The partner:) "No, but I will blame them for having made, not this choice, but any choice; . . . they are both in error: the right thing would be not to wager at all."

(Pascal:) "Yes, but one must wager; it is not voluntary, you are embarked. Which will you then take? . . . You have two things to lose: the true and the good, and two things to stake: your reason and your will, your knowledge and your happiness . . . Your reason is not more hurt in choosing one than the other, since one must necessarily choose. That is one point settled. But your happiness? Let us weigh the gain and the loss of wagering that God exists. Let us estimate these two cases: if you win, you win all; if you lose, you lose nothing.[45] Wager then that he exists, without hesitating."

(The partner:) "That is admirable. Yes, one must wager; but I perhaps wager too much."

(Pascal:) "Let me see. Since there is equal risk of gain and of loss, if you had but to gain two lives for one, you could still wager; but if there were three to gain, you would have to gamble (since you are under the necessity of gambling), and you would be imprudent, when you are forced to gamble, not to risk your life in order to win three, at a game where there is equal risk of loss and of gain. But there is an eternity of life and of happiness. And this being so, if there were an infinity of risks, a single one of which were for you, you would still be right to wager one in order to win two; and you would act unreasonably, being obliged to gamble, by refusing to wager one life against three . . . But there is here an infinitity of infinitely happy life to win, and that which you gamble is finite. That eliminates all choice: wherever the infinite is, and where there is not an infinity of chances of loss against that of gain, there is no hesitating, one must give everything. And thus, when one is forced to gamble, one must renounce reason in order to preserve life, rather than risk it for the infinite gain just as likely to occur as the loss of nothingness . . ."

There follows a long analysis of the situation from the point of view of probability; then a conclusion, to be discussed below, concerning Christian practice and custom.

(The partner:) "Oh! this discourse transports me, charms me, etc."

The reader will hopefully not have become indignant over the almost cynical rationality with which these things are here discussed. That would be to forget that it is Pascal who is speaking here. What was fair for him should be reasonable for us . . . Let us disengage once more the logical structure from the train of thought:

First of all, Pascal gives way to every objection of skepticism. Psychologically, inasmuch as he reckons with a man who does not see anywhere a way to God. Theoretically, inasmuch as he renounces that which the skeptic rejects above all; the possibility of exact advancement from the finite to the Living Absolute. The thought starts, namely, from the opposition of the mathematic infinite and the finite, and from the depreciation which the latter undergoes through the former—thus from the insight into the incommensurability of these two "*grandeurs.*"[46] Thus room is cleared for the skeptical "I don't know." Not, however, in a tired, negative form, but rather in a powerful form laden with will to knowledge. We recall, for example, the emphasis, that one can comprehend that something exists, without knowing what it is; so that the establishment of a fact goes beyond the possibility of its intellectual penetration.

The argument itself runs as follows:

If there is a God, then he is, as God, incommensurable with us finite beings. We can thus not decide conclusively either if, nor what, he is. The possibilities: "He is—he is not; he is that which faith indicates—he is not" are thus mutually equivalent for the logical judgment. This theoretical incommensurability therefore has for the understanding the same significance as the impenetrability of effective causes, that is, "chance," for the decision in the game of chance. It thus becomes possible to translate the theoretical situation of the judgment before the problem of the existence of God into the practical situation of the risk before the hazards of the game of chance, and to use those concepts for their elucidation, with which the logical penetration of the gambling situation is attempted, namely those of the theory of probabilities—of which Pascal was indeed one of the creators. Thus:

Here I stand, man, with my judgment: "God exists," or else: "God does not exist." Yonder, separated from me by the "*chaos infini*" of incommensurability, the "objective state of affairs." Each of the two judgments has chances for and chances against it.

The believer wagers "for"; one cannot reproach him, for in regard to logical defensibility, the "for" and "against" are equivalent.

148

With more reason, however, one can reproach him for something else: it is not the fact that you wager this way or that way which is wrong, but the fact that you wager at all; that is, that you do not draw from the impossibility of rational demonstration the appropriate conclusion and abstain from the decision.

Answer: You are not at all free to abstain from judgment. The life of man is by nature such that it forces you to a decision. If you abstain, you have nonetheless, in truth, made a decision; a bad one, to be sure, namely, not to decide. Thus not whether, but how you want to decide, is left up to you.

And now, from the nature of the opposing "*grandeurs*" and from the importance of the matter at hand, and according to the rules of the theory of probability, Pascal shows that the chances "for" are more favorable than those "against"; indeed, that in the last analysis they stand in the relationship of infinity to nothing.

It is thus reasonable to go beyond the limits of reason. The only reasonable thing is the risk "for."

It is clear that there is no question of a "proof," in the real sense of the word, in this train of thought. But it is also clear that we are here dealing with something serious.

The presuppositions of this train of thought lie in Pascal's view of the world, in his conviction of the complex, indeed tragically impenetrable nature of being. As we have already seen, this being is under tension, at once coherent and split apart. Indeed, it is ambiguous, contradictory, misleading, alienating man from his own consciousness of meaning. But it is just this character which also establishes his greatness, or is at least inextricably connected with it. In such a world, no simple movement, but only a likewise complex movement is possible. Its structure is between simple transition and radical leap. This movement cannot confidently receive certainty and direction from being; it must rather bring the dangerous, indeed evil ambiguity of being to a halt and confer on it a character through responsible decision. To this attitude corresponds a particular

149

kind of thinking: dialectical thinking, in which every certainty is called into question and every uncertainty has its logic; "defining" thinking, in which the decision component, present in every judgment, becomes the determining character of the entire way of thinking.

The cognitive act, with which the world is grasped, and on the basis of which the living personality moves in the world, is very complex. In it there is the concept and the intuition, the realization of the general and the sensing of the unique, the permeation of the norm and the participation in the creative emergence, the comprehension of the logical process and the leap over the abyss between one quality and another, between one particular thing and another, between one realm of being and another. It has contact with the constancy of being, but also with its change, its incoherence, ambiguity, abruptness. But the second term in each of these antitheses does not form, as in the rationalistic view of the world, the unrefined preliminary stage of the first, nor the negligible interruption of the essential. Both moments are, rather, equal factors in the concrete cognitive act, and coördinated to being as it is. They sustain one another mutually. They also endanger one another. There is even a moment in their relationship which cannot be reduced to the concept of a merely dialectical system: evil, deception. But only that thought which takes all this into account is human thinking.

The consciousness of an intellectual movement is also at the root of Pascal's thought experience. It has the character of risk, of audacity, indeed of an ultimate *va banque!* Its process is thus of another kind than the peacefully composed pressings forward, the pure and daring flight of Anselmian contemplation. It is more restless, repeatedly forced by being and its disunity to endanger itself. It is of such a kind that the game of chance, with its risk, can become its expression.

With this way of thinking, it seems as if first of all a logical scaffolding were built in the direction of the object, which stands on the other side of the abyss; it would then be pushed up to the edge—and at a certain, exactly calculated instant the leap would take place, and the mind would gain a footing . . . This having a footing is established as a result in the final judgment.

If one goes deeper into the meaning of the whole, one there discovers, developed to representative form, that moment which is contained in every cognitive act and is expressed, significantly, with a term borrowed from judicial language: the "judgment." All determination of an object, after the subject's accuracy of comprehension and assimilation has done all it can, is menaced by an ultimate possibility of doubt. This possibility stems no longer from unmastered elements of the problem, but from an ultimate inadequacy between the subject and his act, which are relative, and the truth, which is absolute. This ultimate suspension is no longer overcome by an intrinsic clarity which the object forces upon one, but by an act of decision, in which the person stakes his honor on the affirmation that this is truth. This state of affairs, which is openly or secretly involved in every judgment—and which, moreover, for the sake of clarification, has nothing to do with subjectivism—is expressed with the utmost sharpness in the Pascalian argument: the real significance of the cognitive process lies here in the act of definition. First an extreme of logical scaffolding; then the leap through the logically no longer penetrable sphere—the "*chaos infini*"—and finally the gaining of a footing and the establishment of what has been comprehended in the judgment.

Also of special importance here is the value factor. The movement of Anselm's thought was borne by the force of attraction of the "greatest possible being," that is, of the absolute value. The movement is thereby revealed as a movement towards this value. So here too: it is a question of "salvation," of the infinite plenitude of value of eternal life in union with the absolute God.

This longing for value receives its color from the particular nature of Pascal's sentiment of value. It is heroic. Pascal disdains security. The greatness of the risk is for him the norm; not only

151

for the order of the man who assumes it, but also for the relative value of the thing which demands it. The higher the value, the less security. The greater the truth, the greater the risk by means of which it must be realized. Thus, where it is a question of the salvation-bringing truth *per se,* a maximum of risk will be demanded. Inversely: where the highest (not accidental, but meaningful) measure of risk is demanded, there is the highest truth.

The particular character of this movement is thus audacity. The risk commanded by meaning characterizes the sphere of genuine existence. And in spite of all foundations laid by the theory of probabilities, the decision made on the basis of the "Argument du pari" remains a risk.

If we become aware of the path of this movement, it leads to the point at which the ontological proof began. The latter took the first step into the reality of God, in that it took possession of its fullness of essence: an *intelligere,* then, in *credere,* a gnosis ($\gamma\nu\hat{\omega}\sigma\iota\varsigma$) in *pistis* ($\pi\iota\sigma\tau\iota\varsigma$). The Pascalian argument in the strict sense attains only to the gaining of a first footing on the reality of God; it does not speak about his essence.

THE ABSOLUTE PARADOX

We now come to the third train of thought, contained in the work which Søren Kierkegaard regarded as the cardinal point of his theoretical production, the *Philosophical Fragments,* published in 1844.[47] It attempts to characterize the essence of the Christian phenomenon in its radical difference from all inner-worldly spheres of being.

The third chapter is entitled "The Absolute Paradox: A Metaphysical Crotchet." The passages in it which concern us read as follows:

". . . However, one should not think slightingly of the paradoxical; for the paradox is the source of the thinker's passion, and the thinker without a paradox is like a lover without feeling: a paltry mediocrity. But the highest pitch of every passion

152

is always to will its own downfall; and so it is also the supreme passion of the Reason to seek a collision,[48] though this collision must in one way or another prove its undoing. The supreme paradox of all thought is the attempt to discover something that thought cannot think . . .

"But what is this unknown something with which the Reason collides when inspired by its paradoxical passion. . . ? It is the Unknown. It is not a human being, insofar as we know what man is; nor is it any other known thing. So let us call this unknown something: *the God*. It is nothing more than a name we assign to it. The idea of demonstrating that this unknown something [the God] exists, could scarcely suggest itself to Reason. For if the God does not exist it would of course be impossible to prove it; and if he does exist it would be folly to attempt it . . .

"And how does God's existence emerge from the proof? Does it follow straightway, without any breach of continuity? Or have we not here an analogy to the behavior of the little Cartesian dolls? As soon as I let go of the doll it stands on its head. As soon as I let it go—I must therefore let it go. So also with the proof. As long as I keep my hold on the proof, i.e., continue to demonstrate, the existence does not come out, if for no other reason than that I am engaged in proving it; but when I let the proof go, the existence is there. But this act of letting go is surely also something; it is indeed a contribution of mine. Must not this also be taken into the account, this little moment, brief as it may be—it need not be long, for it is a *leap* . . .

"The paradoxical passion of the Reason thus comes repeatedly into collision with this Unknown, which does indeed exist, but is unknown, and insofar does not exist. The Reason cannot advance beyond this point, and yet it cannot refrain in its paradoxicalness from arriving at this limit and occupying itself therewith . . .

"What then is the Unknown? It is the limit to which the Reason repeatedly comes, and insofar, substituting a static form of conception for the dynamic, it is the different, the absolutely

153

different. But because it is absolutely different, there is no mark by which it could be distinguished . . .

"But can such a paradox be conceived? . . . The Reason will doubtless find it impossible to conceive it, could not of itself have discovered it, and when it hears it announced will not be able to understand it, sensing merely that its downfall is threatened. Insofar the Reason will have much to urge against it; and yet we have on the other hand seen that the Reason, in its paradoxical passion, precisely desires its own downfall. This is what the Paradox also desires, and thus they are at bottom linked in understanding; but this understanding is present only in the moment of passion."[49]

This passion is faith.

Kierkegaard rejects the "proof." Nonetheless, there is in his thought a structure of proof, namely, the following:

Every intellectually determined species of act possesses a form of meaning. Apart from the more precise, value-giving determinations—for example, the knowledge of truth, the production of the beautiful, the realization of order, etc.—, this meaning signifies that the act strives towards the absolute. In negative terms: the act wants to attain, along the line of its specific value, to an object which contains that value in such a form that the act can no longer master it. This form would signify the really infinite plenitude of the value ordained to the act—which, however, precisely because it is infinite plenitude, could not be mastered by the human, and therefore finite, act. The act would thus be annihilated by the excess of the fulfillment of its meaning. To desire precisely that is its highest intensity: its "passion."[50]

It is here a question of thought. Thought thus wants to attain to an object which—although in it the fulfillment of the meaning of thought, namely, absolute truth is contained—can no longer be mastered by thought.

An object of this kind, however, will not be able to become an "object" in the strict sense at all; it will not afford thought any point of reference at all. Otherwise, thought would assert itself in the face of it, and not "be annihilated." What must the object be like? Completely other; unknown.

Indeed, the next chapter will find the concept not yet sharp enough and say: The decisive otherness is only guaranteed if the object under consideration is "completely other" vis-à-vis man in such a way, that it is not only different from him, but stands in contradiction to him. And indeed, in the most radical contradiction, namely, that of holiness to sin. The being who is for me "wholly Other" possesses this absolute differentness not only because I commit sin against him, but because, with my entire being, I am "sin." (The pessimistic doctrine of redemption and grace of the Reformation here enters into the train of thought.)

This wholly Other, wholly Unknown is the absolute negation of everything that I am. For my being, the limit; for my value, judgment, and condemnation.

But how does cognition become aware of this wholly Other, for which the word "God" is not an expression of a known essence, but only a name? Not by grasping it directly, but by the radically opposite process: the thought seeking comprehension is annihilated; it experiences its absolute noetic incapacity; it sees itself sentenced as human thought—in that it realizes and admits that man and everything he has is "sin," that his will to knowledge and his achievement of knowledge are thus "untruth." But God—who, if he exists, must be the Holy One—could then in no way enter into this thought.

If this annihilation is accepted and realized, then, in the letting go and downfall into one's own nothingness—elsewhere, Kierkegaard will say: in the meaningful passage through "despair"—God is there: in the abandonment of all proof, in the "leap": as the wholly Other.

The intellectual atmosphere for this train of thought is the radically tragic conception of being. It is based on the qualitative vision of being pushed to its ultimate extreme; on the

155

passion of discrimination, which violently separates one quality from another, one thing from another, one realm of being from another, and places incommensurabilities between all determinations, things, and realms of being. The higher the reality, the further it is removed from comprehension, and the more inconceivable it is, how it could be comprehended. It is the pessimistic experience of life and of religion, which finds no relationship in good conscience to the world. Either it seizes upon it titanically, and, precisely when it perceives its questionableness, sets it up—in defiance of God's claim—as the unique reality; or it experiences the world as something of which, in the last analysis, it is ashamed; it feels itself contaminated in its contact with the world; it finds everything corporal contrary to the mind and distressing. At the root of this attitude lies the experience of "*Weltangst*": either surpassed by an affirmation accomplished in defiance and thus with bad conscience—or else suffered in self-sacrifice, in such a way that everything worldly, especially everything sensual and corporal, is experienced as "sin." If this is the case, then the supreme, saving reality must remain uncontaminated from everything which is called "world." This is guaranteed by the thesis of incommensurability. The concept of the wholly Other, which attempts to fulfill this demand, originates in an ultimate religious will to purity—which has, indeed, proved to be impossible.

If there is nevertheless to be a way to the supreme being—and the whole argument wills indeed to open such a way: for the basic intention of this tragic negativity is a positive one—then it likewise can only be absolutely tragic. It goes through the annihilation of everything which is called "world"—but "world" is first of all man himself. The creature must desire its own annihilation, because otherwise it cannot attain to salvation. And it must desire this, its annihilation, in the line of his meaning. In our case: in the line of knowledge. The romantic definition of life through death, of the absolute through the sacrifice, is underlined by the tragic, Nordic Protestant impulse to honor God in that the creature acknowledge himself, in his entire finite existence, as sin and thus as something which must be annihilated.

The decisive process is a letting oneself go into one's annihilation. Thus once more "movement": a movement which has a particular interiority which violently shakes the living being, namely, "passion." Its intensity is defined by the fact that it goes from the brink of being into nothingness. Something Dionysiac is alive in this movement, something which is connected with the mystery of death and rebirth.

What guides it is once more the longing for the absolute value. But the guarantee that it is really the absolute value is seen in a particular sense with which the "world"—thus also man in his immediacy—responds to it: in the sense of the absurd.

We have already spoken about this in the discussion about scandal: as soon as a higher reality comes into play in a lower, it occurs in such a way that it appears questionable from the point of view of this lower reality. We do not have before us a harmonious evolutionary view, in which the inferior develops into the superior, but rather a tragic and aristocratic view. The superior cannot justify itself before the standards and classifications of the inferior; rather, it upsets them. But there is a disposition which does not acknowledge this, which holds fast the inferior realm of meaning in face of the superior, measures the latter against the former, judges it questionable, and rejects it—to be sure, with the secret bad conscience, that it is nonetheless the superior: this is *ressentiment*. The higher the reality in question, the less successful the legitimation before the inferior, the greater the danger of resentment, the worse the possible hate. The absolutely High, in regard to everything worldly the wholly Other, can no longer justify itself before

157

the world in any way. It thus appears as the absolutely questionable, as nonsense, destruction, evil folly.

This state of affairs: that the supreme reality, measured by the standards of the world, appears foolish, is the absolute paradox. It is given in the existence of God incarnate, Jesus Christ.[51]

Now if I hold the world fast as the essential, if I demand that the supreme reality legitimate itself by the world's standards—then a particular form of resentment appears: that of the unjustifiable sacredly-supreme reality, scandal. But if I grasp—somehow, somewhere—what the question is; if I have that passion of the finite act—at once demand and generosity—, in which this act, in order to reach its highest fulfillment, desires its own annihilation; if I reach, before Christ, the limit of my being and of all finite being; if I accept this limit and let myself go; if I become aware—one cannot say in which way—that yonder the wholly Other summons . . . then that passion of my mind reaches an understanding with the demand of the absolute paradox itself. If I take precisely that which would bring about my ruin if my thought did not have the passion of annihilation, namely, the incommensurability—apparently absurd from the natural point of view—which is in fact the index of the highest value (impotent in the finite) of the incarnation—through an inconceivable and frightful movement of my mind I take precisely this absurdity itself as footing for the leap into the unknown and so come into a positive relationship to the wholly Other, to God.

This movement is called faith. It awakens before the revealing figure and its word. Its force is the absurd itself: *"Credo quia absurdum."*

What this movement reaches seems once more to be less than that of the Pascalian "Argument du pari": one simply lets go of the finite. The finite is simply no longer held fast as the essential; rather, one realizes that the essential, vis-à-vis the finite, must be "other."

158

Once more, not a proof in the real sense of the word.

On the contrary, the demands of a proper procedure of proof are counteracted wherever possible. But precisely in the manner of this counteraction there appears to lie a profound consistency. As soon as one opens oneself to it, one believes to recognize in it a particular "logic," which we will have to investigate.

III.

Profound differences separate the three endeavors. The first stems from the eleventh century, the second from the seventeenth, the third from the nineteenth. They contain the intellectual situation of their time: Augustinian scholasticism, philosophy of the concrete, anti-romantic-romantic decisionism. The first thought process lies embedded in a confession before God; the second, in reflections on how to found faith logically in the face of mundane skeptics; the third, in an apology of despairing Christianity against an existence which has become worldly. The decisive act is first the *élan* into the essential and real; then the risk into the unknown; finally letting go into annihilation.

Profound differences, then; but the affinity is still greater.

The first affinity among the three attempts is that of the intensive vitality of the thought. They are all thought not "objectively," from theoretical distance, but rather in "passion." They are a confession, an expression as much of existential decision as of objective exposition. The purely theoretical proof leaves the participant unmoved; it merely makes one pay attention to whether or not what is stated is correct. These "proofs," on the other hand, move one from the very beginning: by the way they begin; by the level of existence to which they appeal; by the form of their procedure. It belongs to the intellectual atmosphere as well as to the noetic quality of these thought processes, when Anselm, in the *Proemium* of the *Proslogion,*

159

reports under what almost unbearable demands on his entire being the idea of the proof of God had fought its way out of him. Likewise, when Pascal emphasizes at the conclusion of the "argument," that if the idea has made an impression, one might not forget that he who expounds it "has knelt down beforehand and afterwards in order to submit his all to this infinite Being." And finally, as far as Kierkegaard's *Fragments* are concerned, they absolutely vibrate with inner agitation.

Common too, measured by the norms of genuine proof, are the flaws in the logical progression.

And indeed, they become ever more numerous and decisive. In the ontological proof of God, the break lies between the intrinsic certainty of the idea conceived and the assertion of the objective reality of that which is conceived. In Pascal's argument it lies first of all in the assumption that in regard to the alternative "God exists—God does not exist," "God" could only be that God which faith indicates. Further, in the assumption that the possibilities of choice are but two: infinite fulfillment or definitive disaster. Finally and above all in the assumption that the stakes of the wager are really eternal "gain" or "perdition." Not to mention at all the problem which is broached by Nietzsche's thesis that real human existence is entirely bound to earthly finitude and must therefore, under pain of losing its essence, not want any "eternity." In Kierkegaard, finally, every logical certitude is abandoned. His "logic" stands in a negative relation to that which one would expect. It consists precisely in the consistency with which every positively logical capacity is abolished, and culminates in that concept which indeed represents the negation of all logic, that of the absurd. To be sure, it is precisely in this non-concept that one perceives most forcefully another "logic."

A further common trait is the "ontic" character of the thought experience. What is thought is not experienced simply as an idea, but has rather a weight which puts it in a position, for the consciousness of the thinker, to compete with concrete reality. The idea of God in Anselm, the system of probability in Pascal, the moment of the paradox or of the absurd in Kierkegaard are not "something merely thought," radically differentiated from the real; they have, on the contrary, as something thought, a density which allows the act of thinking, as a truly intellectual execution, to base itself on them as on reality; which makes it conscious of attaining reality through them.

Another thing in common is the great importance of the value factor. It is not a matter of establishing a mere existence or correctness, but rather of finding that value on which everything depends, the absolute value, and bringing it to bear.[52] The longing for this value stands as the decisive factor in the process of proof; it is indeed its first, experiential premise. The second is the conviction that it is impossible for this longing not to be realized, since otherwise the world would remain without meaning—an hypothesis which is itself experienced as simply impossible.

But the absolute value has as such a special position. It is not the highest in the scale of values, but rather, between the "highest" value and the absolute value—more rightly, the plenitude of value of the holy God—lies an abyss which is itself absolute.[53] This special position must also be expressed logically. The question of the absolute value must found a unique cognitive situation. It is precisely to this state of affairs that these procedures of proof attempt to do justice. Their individuality lies precisely in the way they approach it. They are borne by a special feeling for the absolute; for the special nature of the absolute vis-à-vis the finite; for the difference as well as for the affinity between these two designations; but above all for the character which they take on as soon as they are considered in relationship to one's own existence. The three proofs are borne by an existential dialectic of the absolute.

161

But finally: the thought processes which concern us have an intensively dynamic character. In them something is taking place. Not only do they presuppose in their thought material the concept of movement—as soon as one grasps them purely, they are themselves revealed as systems of movement. In a genuine "proof," the execution of the proof could be dispensed with mentally. One could well imagine the actual succession abolished in a comprehensive view directed towards the logically structured situation. With it, the didactic moment of the proof, the gradually convincing development, would drop out; but its meaning, the transparency of the various moments in their mutual logical relationship, would be preserved. Not in our thought processes. If one took away the execution of the movement, the actual thought progression from beginning to end, they would lose what is essential to them. In them the movement itself is just as essential as the result. The decision to take one's stand on the idea of God, with the conviction that one thereby gains a footing in the real God himself; the risk of staking one's life, beyond the impenetrability of the chances of the game, on the affirmation that God is "over there"; the leap into the nothingness of creation in the hope that God will be grasped—that this is accomplished is the essential of these proofs. They are kinetic systems.

And indeed, it is a special motive force to which they appeal. Its nature becomes clear if we bring to mind what has been spoken of in the preceding: the feeling for the existential density of ideality; for the absolute and what is specific to it; above all for its special character as a value. In addition, that special technique which—one could almost say—can break open the earthly clamps of logical relationships, take away the supports of the logical *terre à terre* and create a situation which can no longer be resolved but by a leap, a suspension, an ascension. All this points towards a special motive force: *eros*.

Eros does not belong to metaphysical lyricism. It is a real force of philosophical existence. To think, to think seriously philosophically and still more to think religiously, is to exist in thought. It means not only that I, the subject, stand here and look at what stands over there—nor, to be sure, that my subjectivity is at work, and, by means of its categorical structure, creates a world out of a chaos of feelings. Rather, something confronts me. In thought, I struggle with it for its truth. But it is thereby that I also struggle with myself, for my truth. When, in the cognitive struggle with the object, I make my way to its truth, my truth also appears: that truth by virtue of which I am true. Noetic eros is the longing to attain to the truth of one's own being through thinking carried out "in passion" with the truth of the object. Eros is the will to existential thought—and to the extent to which thinking becomes existential, the true eros becomes free.

Its meaning is realized in the movement from the finite to the absolute.[54] It presupposes the real similarity of the finite mind to God. Genuine similarity; to this extent, real relationship by nature, real ordination towards God at the moment of creation. But at the same time, mere similarity; hence the necessity of loosing oneself from one's egoistic entanglement and—at least in intention and endeavor[55]—of raising oneself above and beyond the "world" as the sum total of what is initially given, of what is one's "own."

That this tension of genuine similarity and mere similarity between personal man and—analogically stated—the personal God exists; that this God is the absolute value and—stated not *superlative* but *singulariter*—the *summum bonum,* and that man needs him, absolutely, as a matter of life and death, as his "salvation": this is what determines the essence of eros.

Its movement implies first and decisively that the finite be "let go of." Between the letting go of the finite and the grasping of the absolute—"between" is a purely logical term; in itself, that letting go is itself possible only in this grasping, and the latter only in that letting go, both a single act—between them lies the incommensurability of the "two quantities ordained one to the other" and the risk of the crossing.

163

The genuine proof of God—whether it starts out from causality, or from ideality, or from moral conscience, or whatever—looks predominantly at the positive side of the relationship, the similarity between the finite and the absolute; it is thus inclined to conceal the negative side, the incommensurability between them and the risk which every connection takes upon itself. The other, on the contrary—let us call it the kinetic proof, or better, the pointing upwards, the logical *eisagoge*—throws all its energy precisely in this second direction. For it, everything depends on pointing out the abyss, making one aware of the "brink" of the finite, making the otherness of what borders on it clear. But also on moving one to confidence that the absolute exits; on awaking eros; on making it realize that it here stands before its proper task and on spurring it on towards the accomplishment of it. The structure of these thought processes, not least of all the probably unconscious technique of their logical flaws, has the significance of bringing the situation of the "brink" to ultimate distinctness; but at the same time, of stimulating—by alternate checking and spurring on—the force of ascension of eros, that it might really let go, ascend, pass over to the other side and get a footing. But these thought processes have still something further in common: they are borne by the strongest religious concern.

Anselm was a monk. A sacred beauty lies over his figure. The *Vita* written by his pupil and companion Eadmer bears witness to his religious intensity.[56] It appears most convincingly, perhaps—as with Augustine—in his theological writings, in which the theoretical knowledge arises from the religious sphere itself, to then overflow once again into prayer. The *Proslogion,* which contains the ontological proof of God, is but one long prayer.

The preceding chapters of this book have shown of what passionate intensity was the religious life at work in Pascal; the next chapter will bring it once more to mind in the context of his interior itinerary. As far as the "Argument du pari" is concerned in particular, it concludes with the words: "If this discourse pleases you and seems forceful to you, know that it is written by a man who has gotten down on his knees beforehand and afterwards to beg this infinite and undivided Being, to whom he submits his all, that he also subjugate yours for your own good and for his glory . . ."

Kierkegaard, finally, offers the image of a man with all the worldly possibilities of the richly gifted romantic at his disposal. But then the religious sphere grows up, draws everything into itself, burns everything, until at the end only a glowing point is left: the will to stand up for the ever more sharply exaggerated essence of Christianity, in the struggle against a world which combines all the powers of the understanding, of art and of the senses in order to demolish it. But this combative attitude has its roots in that attentiveness for the voice of God, in that deep inner stillness which reveals itself in the most intimate of all Kierkegaard's words: the understanding with God.

But this is not yet the decisive point. It is rather in the fact that these three arguments themselves have a religious character. They are not only attempts to obtain an intellectual guarantee of the existence of God; rather, the thought process expressed by them is itself a religious act in the true sense of the word.

"Religion" is the living relationship of the concrete man to the living God. It presupposes that in some form or other, God is "given." The organ, to which God "gives" himself, is not easy to grasp. The analysis seems to be directed to advance through certain borderline phenomena—the *acies mentis* and the "fundus of the soul," past the moment of the "eye of the mind," of the "heart," of the "soul," to the "conscience," originally meant religiously.

God can be given to this organ in the form of emptiness. Then one's gaze goes into the dark, one's call into silence. "Nothing" is there; and yet this "nothing" has a quality, an orientation, a point of reference. "There" is God . . . But he can also be given in the form of fullness. Then God is positively

165

there; one's gaze goes into his countenance; one's voice feels that it is heard.

The religious relationship to the God who is so "given"— and indeed in all degrees of distinctness, intensity, and qualitative fullness—takes place in the religious act. On the basis of the difference in structure described above, this act can be differently structured: on distance, as a loving and an adoration from an intrinsic remoteness; or on contact, as a movement striving towards union.

This movement can take place in respect to the most manifold contents of the exterior or interior world, be borne by the most varied psychological acts, proceed in the most changing forms. But it always contains certain phases: first the letting go of the finite position, the swinging away from its "brink"—perhaps prepared by an ascension through the finite realm, in the various modes of the *ascensus mentis,* with its step-like orders and its inner dialectic. Then the gaining of contact with the sacred reality of the "beyond." Finally, the penetration into it.

This psychologically describable process leads to a theoretical question: How does man stand in relation to God, if God is to remain unquestionably God, and man, without lies and presumption, man? That is, the absolute abyss between God and man? As the task of thought, this question becomes the problem of the proof of God.

If it is thereby a matter of the relationship at a distance, then the question remains essentially oriented towards the thought content, towards the theoretical working out of the problem of whether, and how, God is also given in the experience of the finite. Then arises the real proof of God—and one can observe, moreover, in the manner in which it is conducted, whether it is a mere *exercitium intellectus,* or whether genuine religious experience underlies it. The crucial point will then lie in the experience of the finite and its fullness of meaning; the moment of analogy between God and the finite will form the means; and with great care not to leave any lacunae, the chain of logical links will be forged.

166

But if it is a matter of the relationship characterized by the religious movement, then it is above all the special character of the absolute in face of the finite which is envisaged in the question, it is otherness and distance, with the inclination to accentuate them to the point of incommensurability—not to a skeptical, but to a positive end. But it is not merely a matter here of the theoretical problem of the possibility of a movement from the finite to God; rather, the questioning itself is already movement, it is already the realization of that possibility which forms the object of the theoretical question. This questioning itself is thus already an "action." Strictly considered, it is an action undertaken with the greatest exactitude: an "experiment."

In the design of this experiment, it will be precisely those moments of incommensurability which prepare the force of eros for the decisive movement. The continuity of the logical process will be called into question—but in a positive sense, with the success of the movement in view. In order to unloose, psychologically speaking, the religious affect—astonishment, wonder, shock, fear, longing—, and thus, precisely by means of the logical flaws, to spur the religious movement to the decisive ascent. (The dialectical character of this incommensurability.)

There then arise systems like our three endeavors.[57] Anselm's ontological proof of God, Pascal's argument of the wager, and Kierkegaard's absolute paradox are expressions of the most powerful religious, perhaps even mystical, experience, which throws itself upon the question of the path from the finite to the absolute. There arises thereby a structure similar to a proof: the apparent demonstration that God exists, that he is This Person and This Thing. In reality, it is not a proof in the usual sense of the word. The real significance of the thought structure has to do with the realization of the movement. It creates for it, in part precisely by means of those logical flaws, a pathway, a direction, a system of stimuli.

This leads to an intermediary question.

167

The purpose of cognition is truth. But how is truth realized?

First and fundamentally in the specific, cognitive coming face to face with and "having" the object. Truth here means that I have the object really and properly in my inner gaze.

But this alone is not yet "truth" in the full sense of the word. It also means that I let the object approach me; I appropriate it to myself; that I make a decision in regard to it, and, in the knowledge of this object, actuate my own living being. That I, knowing this, become what I can become only in this very knowledge.

"Truth" is thus not only the objectivity, complete in itself, which comes into play in the cognitive act of the subject. The full cognitive content arises only in the cognitive movement. This does not in the least mean an establishment of the object through the thought categories of the subject. The "thing in itself" stands "outside" and is as such "complete." Knowledge is really encounter with the thing subsisting in itself. But the purpose of knowledge does not at all consist in the reflection of the "thing in itself"; its aim is rather that "world" come into being in the cognitive act. Something, then, which is this object of knowledge—but also I, the cognizing subject. Both together, and more than the sum total of them. The really "known" in its fullness is "the thing in me" and "I in the thing." It is the thing which, when known, becomes part of my life and in it becomes something new. I am he who, knowing, define myself by the thing, risk myself onto the thing, enter into the thing, linger in the sphere of its objective determination, and in it become something, which I can only become here. Here lies the importance of that which Kierkegaard announced in the face of objective cognitive theory: that the act is more important than the result, and indeed, more important cognitively; that the passion of the struggle for truth is more significant than the correctness of the cognitive content. What is false in this view is the exaggeration, especially if the objectivity of the thing and the objective justness of the act of comprehension are disputed. Correct is the emerging awareness that truth cannot be reduced to the correctness of the comprehension of the object, but means at the same time the constituting of the cognizing subject by means of this object, such as it is possible here and through this object. That truth lies not only in that which I comprehend, but also in that which I thereby do and become: existential truth. "World," on the other hand, is the unity which arises in the successful cognitive encounter of "the thing in itself" and "me."[58]

We must thus distinguish in the cognitive act between object and realization.

"Object"—more exactly, the form in which the object is given in the consciousness, its noetic equivalent—is the content of the ideas, concepts, judgments, thought contexts. "Realization" is the living act of imagining, conceiving, judging, itself. From the point of view of the object, the knowledge is all the more true as this act is more objectively and better ordered in the consciousness. From the point of view of the realization, the knowledge is all the more true as the living subject participates in the cognitive act in a more profound and specifically appropriate way; the more fully the zones of being in the subject corresponding to the object awaken; the more purely and powerfully the person engages himself in the appropriation of the object and the decision for the truth. When I know, then this does not only mean that I "grasp" an object, but that I myself become something through it and in it; that I define myself, in that I enter with my living being under the intellectual power of this essence, of this value, adopt an attitude towards it, stand up for it, etc. These acts are thus not only psychological prerequisites, in order that the noetic presence of the object come into being; they are rather an integral part of the phenomenon of the total truth itself, they help to constitute it. And indeed, they are all the more significant in it, the higher the order of the truth at hand, the closer it lies to the domain of the personal and of the values of salvation.

The fact of the object's being given, of its contents being unfolded, etc., has a form: logic. It is the logic of the object.

169

It has—if we want to use the precarious term—a "static" character, and signifies the relationships of order of the moments of being coexisting in the object. But does not the realization of the appropriation, of the self-engagement and self-actuation, that is, the act in cognition, also have its form? Certainly, a psychological form; psychology tells us how such an act is performed, what its types are, where its possibilities of differentiation lie, etc. But does it not also have its logical form? That is, a law for how the act must proceed for it to be, as such, not only strong or characteristic, but valid, containing value, realizing truth—that is, existential truth?

The problem leads further from here into the practical pedagogical question of what I must do to become capable of knowing correctly.

And it is significant that this question is posed by all three of the thinkers who occupy us here: by Anselm in his theory of the religious *experiri;* by Pascal in his theory of "custom" and its cognitive significance; by Kierkegaard in his theory of "training" in the Christian situation of contemporaneousness with Christ.

What was said above about "movement," starting with the analysis of the form of the experience of knowledge, here finds its fundamental justification:

Knowing is, as knowing, real process, real action, realization of existence. This process, this doing, this realizing of existence means not only, for example, the psychology of noesis, but is an integral part of the noesis itself. The degree of the yield of truth depends in part on the genuineness and intensity of this process as an act.

Now just as the problem of the object is different before the absolute as before the relative—in the case of the absolute, "idea" and "being" stand in a different relationship to one another than anywhere else: "idea" is here the equivalent of "being"—, so, too, the problem of the realization is here different. The higher the object, the less is it to be known by mere grasping of an object, and the greater the importance of the existential moment. Before the absolute object, not only a supreme engagement is necessary, but a specific, unique engagement, that is, the utter engagement: the religious decision.

If this is so, then what must be expressed in the "logic of realization" before the absolute "object" is that here not only a supreme measure, but the specific kind of self-engagement, the absolute, personal self-risk, is demanded from the cognitive act. In it, precisely, lies the real significance of our "proofs."

This leads to the idea of a logic of the religious realization.

Not as a theory of the attitude and education one must have in order to realize the religious act of cognition; that would be pedagogy and the theory of spiritual exercises. Nor as the indication of how practically that act can best be realized. That would be the description of its technique. But rather as the theory of its valid realization, which realizes existential truth.

This theory would be based on the insight into which "kinetic" value the individual concepts have; into the extent to which they signify movement, in the case of "realizing" thought. Into the direction of this movement; how strong it is; whether positive or negative, etc. On the insight, furthermore, that propositions are paths of movement. Thus on the insight into the kinetic value of the conceptual structure and the positional value of the individual concepts in it. On the insight, that there is no act without its place; that, in order to be able to realize an act, another must first be realized, and if it is to be completed, a third must follow; that an act, in order to be realized meaningfully, presupposes a "position," an existential level, a level which itself is only possible as the fruit of preceding acts —victories over oneself, exercises, developments—, and so on.

We have here the problem of a logic of meditation, of contemplation. It must force itself upon one, as soon as the nature of meditative thinking becomes clear and one regards its living and literary tradition as it is worthy of being regarded.

171

The old theories of meditation are more than pedagogies and techniques. They contain insights of kinetic, existential logic. The theories of gradation of antiquity and the Middle Ages are theories of the valid religious realization of truth. It seems to us that there is a whole descent of concepts and theories, which reveal their real meaning only if one grasps and fulfills them as the normative expression of movements. Begun by Neoplatonism, the lineage descends through Augustinian scholasticism into the nineteenth century.

The concept of eros, too, seems here to gain for the first time its full meaning. Perhaps a full insight into the nature of that logic only becomes possible when the nature of the eros movement is recognized as a movement of love. When one recognizes the interrelationship in it of being and value, of the absolute and the finite, the qualitative and the gradual; on which directional system it is based; the significance for it of curbing and spurring on, etc.

The three endeavors are systems of the religious logic of realization, of meditative logic.

Systems of thoughts, then, which have the function of indicating a certain direction to thought prepared for movement which entrusts itself to them, and of preparing it for the realization of the decisive movement. The very defects, from the viewpoint of objective logic, of the structure of proof, the inner flaws, seem to be a system of stimuli for the realization of the decisive movement in which one risks one's self.

CHAPTER VI

Pascal's Struggle

I.

Blaise Pascal grew up in an environment of self-evident faith, that of the well-to-do French bourgeoisie of the seventeenth century.[59]

The religious life of the times was richly developed. The sixteenth century had brought with it the effects of the Renaissance: the robust worldliness of a Rabelais, the unconvincingly mastered skepticism of a Montaigne, the philosophical deism of a Charron, the Stoicism of a Justus Lipsius, the incredulity of the *"beaux esprits"* and *"libertins,"* the atheism of a Vanini. Endless civil wars, proceeding from the religious tensions of the Reformation as well as from the shifting of the province into the modern unified state, had laid waste to the land and made life barbarous. Then a profound religious movement began. Henri IV opted for the Catholic Church; Protestantism was thus limited to small circles, and the unity of religious consciousness was maintained. Creative religious impulses found free scope in the life of the general public. At this time there also arose, in fact, great personalities, religious geniuses filled with pure Christian spirit, a Vincent de Paul, a Bérulle, a Francis de Sales—succeeded later by the generation of Bossuet, Fénelon and Bourdaloue—, who determined the feeling, the thinking and the whole way of living. Strong influences came from Spain, from the mystical movement of Saint Theresa of

Avila and Saint John of the Cross. And since Protestantism could not become a public influence, the reformatory impulsions traversing all of Europe had their effect as movements of a theological and practical nature within the Church.

The average religious life thus had unity, breadth, and strength. Powerful tensions were at work in it. Figures full of stimulating and forward-driving energy were in view. Possibilities of more intense religious life were open everywhere.

The attitude in Pascal's home was intent on clearly distinguishing between conscientious religious practice and deliberate striving for esteem, affluence, and scientific education. The young Pascal thus found around him an atmosphere of well-regulated bourgeois order.

This changed when the elder Pascal came into contact with two disciples of Jean du Vergier de Hauranne, Abbé de Saint-Cyran, in the year 1646. The latter was a peculiar personality with an ardent religious craving for renewal and strong charismatic endowment; but he was also obscure in thought, at once absolutistic in will and impressionable in feeling, fastidious and in many ways inhibited. He was connected through long years of common study with the Dutchman, Jansenius, later bishop of Ypres. The movement released by the two men, and known under the name of Jansenism, strove to establish the absolute primacy of faith over reason in Christian consciousness, and of a very strict ethical attitude based on the Bible over all worldly fullness of life in Christian conduct. The movement aroused the mistrust of the government; Saint-Cyran was imprisoned for five years at Vincennes, and died shortly after his release. The elder Pascal now felt himself laid hold of by this spiritual tendency; from him, the impulse passed over to the son, who in turn won over his sisters, Jacqueline and Gilberte, as well as the husband of Gilberte.

This religious contact has been called the first conversion of Pascal. It occurred during his stay in Rouen, during his work on the problems of the calculating machine and the vacuum, thus during a period of the most intensive creation. It is easily understandable that it does not penetrate profoundly; and while Jacqueline is greatly affected by the words of her brother, the latter remains himself thoroughly an "*homme du monde.*"

In the same period belongs an event which we would like to note: in Rouen lived the Sieur Saint-Ange, a former religious who pursued a very peculiar, semi-rationalistic theology, but was otherwise a harmless man. Pascal, at that time twenty years old, attacked him in consort with two still younger friends. With a tenacity to which documents still preserved bear witness,[60] Pascal established the weaknesses of his doctrine, brought the matter before the ecclesiastical authorities, and forced the much older man to recant.

There here appears in the still quite young man a feeling of such heightened responsibility for theological exactitude, and at the same time such an outspoken spirit of polemics and such a will to being right, that one takes notice.

II.

In 1647, his twenty-fourth year, Pascal becomes sick. From this time on, he is only occasionally able to carry on consistent or exacting work. Jacqueline becomes very close to him, and becomes his special helper. At the same time, his religious life begins to become more profound.

With the desire of finding more attentive medical care and direct contact with the intellectual creation of his time, he moves to Paris, accompanied by his sister.

At this time, relations are knotted with Port-Royal des Champs which were to become fateful for both parties.

The name designates a Cistercian abbey founded in 1204, situated southwest of Versailles, which from 1609 on had

175

been brought from complete decadence to a high spiritual standing through the determined labor of the young, high-minded abbess, Angélique Arnauld. From 1619 until 1622, Mère Angélique stood under the at once strong and wise guidance of Saint Francis de Sales. In a letter from the year 1655, thus from the period of the most acute struggle over the Jansenistic position, she still speaks of the *"extrême douceur, retenue et sagesse du bienheureux Evêque de Genève."* Thirteen years after his death, in 1635, the religious leadership was taken over by the man of whom we have already spoken, the mystically gifted, ardent, strict, but also obscure, stubborn, perhaps pathological Abbé de Saint-Cyran. The theological direction fell to Antoine Arnauld, the youngest brother of the abbess, who was a strong mind, strict doctrinaire, and sharp polemicist.

Around the monastery community, which included important personalities, there gathered a circle of like-minded followers —the entire epoch, indeed, tended towards the formation of intellectual social groups: salons of *"beaux esprits,"* private academies, research societies, etc. To this circle belonged above all the so-called *"solitaires"*: men who had withdrawn often from brilliant positions in life in order to live completely dedicated to religion—doctors, lawyers, educators, theologians. Their inner tendency has already been described: in opposition to the socio-cultural attitude towards the world, a strongly emphasized Biblical and supernatural faith and a similar ethic with rigoristic tendencies—both based on a conception of redemption and grace which approached that of Calvin, yet without wanting to depart from the orthodox line.

Pascal, as already mentioned, entered into close relation to this at once humanly and religiously vigorous center—but also at the same time to the mundane life of Paris. While he, instructed by Montaigne and Méré, lives *"en homme du monde"* —we may perceive an upshot of it in his "Discours sur les passions de l'amour"—, and at the same time, inasmuch as his weakened powers allow it, continues his scientific works, Jacqueline decides to enter Port-Royal as a nun. She must indeed postpone the plan, since her father declares himself opposed to it; and even though he then consents, he nevertheless demands that she wait until after his death.

In the year 1649 the family moves to Clermont-Ferrand; in 1650 it returns to Paris; in 1651 the elder Pascal dies. The daughter now seems free to follow her choice. A situation then develops which in itself could seem immaterial, if it did not throw a special light on Pascal's character. He who had been angry with his father because of his negative attitude to Jacqueline's wishes now raises objections himself. First of all, certainly, because he would not like to lose the sympathetic company and understanding help of his sister; but also, and this is what is surprising, for financial reasons. If she enters the convent, she takes her fortune as a dowry to Port-Royal; but Pascal wants to keep it joined with his, because both would thus be assured of being well provided for. He is also thinking of the industrial exploitation of his calculating machine, for which he would naturally need ready means. Perhaps, indeed, his ideas go still further, if a recent interpretation is correct, according to which he was thinking at that time of a union with Mlle. Charlotte Gouffier de Roannez, and hoping to obtain, through the help of her family, a high office, and with it a brilliant career. If this is true, then these plans would have to be considered as the high point of his aspirations as a man of the world. They would have brought with them an extraordinary strain of his financial means, and the return of his sister's property would have been difficult for him. Be that as it may, Jacqueline, just as energetic and even more resolute than her brother, goes to Port-Royal in spite of his resistance. The abbess declares herself prepared to receive her without dowry, which must once more get at the family's self-esteem. The relationship becomes more critical, until Pascal comes into contact with his sister again on a visit to Port-Royal and gives her back her property.

177

III.

The time during which Pascal sees before him all the possibilities of an intellectual and social existence, lasts, calculated very liberally, from the removal of the brother and sister to Paris in the year 1647 until 1654, the year of the *Mémorial.* Within this whole period, a shorter one stands out, during which "the world" became so strong in him and the religious life lost so much in interest for him, that Port-Royal could later speak of a period of "disorder." It lasts about a year and a half, from mid-1652 to the end of 1653. Into this period falls his encounter with the young Duc de Roannez, intendant of Poitou, who united great wealth and influence with lively intellectual interests and religious inclinations. He was entirely taken by Pascal, and they became such close friends that, in fact, the great world with all its splendor opened before the young scholar.

His scientific research continues. He turns from physics more towards pure mathematics; he investigates problems of numbers theory, of infinitesimal calculus and the theory of probabilities. In a *mémoire,* which develops his plans and dedicates his work to the *"Celeberrima Matheseos Academia Parisiensis,"* he says of the problem of the game of chance: ". . . *res hactenus erravit incerta; nunc autem quae experimento rebellis fuit rationis dominium effugere non potuit. Eam quippe tanta securitate in artem per Geometriam reduximus, ut certitudinis ejus particeps facta, jam audacter prodeat; et sic matheseos demonstrationes cum aleae incertitudine jungendo, et quae contraria videntur conciliando, ab utraque nominationem suam accipiens, stupendum hunc titulum jure sibi arrogat: aleae Geometria."*[61] These words reveal the self-assurance of this scientific mind, so powerful *experimento et ratione.*

At the same time, guided by Montaigne and his friend the Chevalier de Méré—who first formulated the concept of the *"honnête homme,"* and of whom Mme. de Maintenon passes

178

for the accomplished pupil—, Pascal studies man. Observation and inner talent, Stoic philosophy and Jansenistic pessimism operate together. Enlightened at once by appreciation and disappointment, by longing and renunciation, his gaze penetrates ever more profoundly into human existence, and he forms those views about the nature of man of which we have already spoken.

During the same period, Pascal plunges into the world of Stoic thought and feeling. In the times of civil war and the shaking of all order, the spirit of *ataraxia,* of apathy which surmounts fate, the strict, virilely proud ethic of Epictetus and Seneca, had been for many a support. Pascal's master, Montaigne, had educated himself in contact with it. Jansenius, through his teacher, Justus Lipsius, had stood under the influence of the Stoic mentality. Thus Pascal, too, received a great deal from it. His "Entretien avec M. de Saci sur Epictète et Montaigne" (P. O., p. 146) as well as many fragments of the *Pensées* give evidence of it. To be sure, he here unmasks it as inhuman and arrogant; but he is thereby struggling against something which is alive deep in his own inner being.

In December of the year 1653, very suddenly it seems, a crisis sets in. The life of society and the possibility of a great career become worthless to him. In a letter of December 8, 1654 (*Oeuvres,* IV, p. 15), Jacqueline writes retrospectively that he has "since more than a year ago a disdain of the world and an almost unbearable disgust with all people who belong to it." Even if one accepts the declarations of the very zealous nun of Port-Royal with a certain prudence, one must still consider them as evidence of profound inner events. At the same time, one senses the violence of this inner life, the pressure under which it stands. Still more clearly in the immediately following words: ". . . which, in accordance with his stormy temperament, should lead him to great excesses, yet he practices in all this a moderation which gives me the highest hopes."

To what extent exterior moments played a role can hardly be decided. If Pascal had plans concerning Mlle. de Roannez, the ducal family must have rejected them. We here grope in the dark; the official Pascal tradition seems to have repressed or obliterated everything which was apt to shake the orthodox image of a pure spiritual man, ascetic, and confessor of Jansenism. The path through life of Mlle. de Roannez took a strange course. At the age of twenty-three she went through a powerful religious experience and, advised by Pascal, wanted to enter Port-Royal. Her mother was opposed, so her brother, the Duc, took her with him to his estate in Poitou. Pascal's correspondence with her, of which only fragments remain, probably belongs in this period. She then succeeded nevertheless and entered Port-Royal in 1657. After several years she gave in to the pressure of the family, left the abbey, and married the Duc de La Feuillade. After a profoundly unhappy married life, she died in the year 1683 . . . Now, however everything may have taken place: whether Pascal's crisis began purely from within, and only an inner necessity expressed itself in the outer failures, if such occurred; or whether Pascal really wanted to follow another path through life, found it blocked, accepted the failure, and, directed by it, set out in a new direction—in any case, there begins a detachment from the "world," which in a personality of such force of desire, planning, and domination, could take place only with the most arduous struggles.

A second letter of Jacqueline's, dated January 25, 1655,[62] informs us of how the inner crisis becomes more profound. Pascal is in a state of helpless shock. It certainly means a great deal, when the writer says of the proud man: "*Il me vint voir et à cette visite il s'ouvrit à moi d'une manière qui me fit pitié!*" He confessed that "in the midst of his occupations, which were great, and amid all the things which could contribute to making him love the world, and to which one was right in believing him very attached, he was so provoked to leave all that, both by an extreme aversion he had of the follies and amusements of the world, and by the continual reproach which his conscience made to him, that he found himself so detached from all things that he had never been so in the same way, nor anything approaching it; but that on the other hand, he was in such a great abandonment on the part of God that he felt no attraction to this side; that he nevertheless strove towards it with all his power, but that he felt quite well that it was more his reason and his own mind, which drove him to what he knew was best, than that of God, and that in the detachment from all things in which he found himself, if he had the same sentiments of God as before, he believed himself capable of undertaking everything [in order to follow God], and that he must have had horrible attachments [to worldly things] at that time in order to resist the graces which God gave him and the movements which he awakened in him."

It is at once the depression and the stagnation of the inner life, the feeling at once of straying and of a new standing which is demanded, the depreciation of what was hitherto valued and the presentiment of higher—but from the former position, in-accessible—values, as they make their appearance especially in creatively living men, whenever one level of existence is laid aside, but the new level has not yet come forward clearly and reliably; or, to choose another image, when the preceding figure of the personality has been lived through to the end, but the next has not yet arisen from within. So much from the psychological point of view. Spiritually, from the point of view of faith, it is certainly the Living God who is there, but in the manner of privation; the fullness of his proximity is not felt, but rather emptiness and "*aucun attrait de ce côté-là*"; the movement of the inner being which seeks him finds no abode —and yet, in spite of everything, an awareness exists that something is there, a point of meaning, a force, not tangible enough that the existential consciousness could feel itself supported by it, and yet so powerful that from its point of view all things are depreciated.

If we may believe Jacqueline, what appears there demands a letting go, an annihilation, a giving up of one's own self. What makes one capable of it, however, is not one's own insight and effort, but the experience of the "other": the Archimedean

181

point which appears "*de ce côté-là*" in oneself, and thence the liberating elucidation, the insight into one's own being, the quiet decision, of which we have often spoken already.

Pascal comes back; the visits to his sister become "so frequent and so long," that she esteems "to have no longer any other work to do." In her opinion—and she is certainly right—, it is a matter of growth "in humility, in submission, in defiance and disdain of oneself, and in the desire to be annihilated in the esteem and memory of men."

The crisis in the inner happening reported by the letter lies at this spot. When Jacqueline immediately thereafter says: "This is his situation at this moment," then she means the end of January, 1655. Beforehand stands the experience, unknown to her, of November 23, 1654, in which the enormous inner stagnation dissolves—or more correctly expressed: in which Pascal receives the force to accomplish the *metanoia,* the breakthrough. But the preceding sentence: "I saw him grow little by little, so that I no longer knew him," speaks unknowing of the effects of the experience.

Our first chapter investigated this event and saw in it the decision which determines everything which follows in Pascal's life. It is an event which marks an end and a beginning. An experience of light and fire; a certitude-bringing collision with reality; an overpowering, ever newly expressed joy. In it, Pascal encounters God as he who comes and acts, who has revealed himself in the history of the Old and New Testaments. Not the God of the philosophers, be it the absolute being of theory or the infinite mystery of presentiment, but the "God of Abraham, of Isaac, and of Jacob," "the God of Jesus Christ."

Pascal encounters Christ, the Redeemer and Lord. He experiences him as turned towards him. What happens to Christ happens to him for his, Pascal's sake. What is done to him by men, he, Pascal, has done it to him. The relation of the redemption is experienced in its most exact reality: it is for my sake

182

that this happened to Christ. What was mine, guilt, he adopted; what is his, justice, is given to me for my own.

Indeed, this consciousness contains a certainty which rivets the attention of him who reads not only in a literary way, but with an attentiveness sharpened by Christian experience. Pascal is blissfully certain—but is this certainty not too great? . . . And what does it mean, when, after the phrase *"grandeur de l'âme humaine,"* we find the sentence from John: "Just Father, the world has not known you, but I have known you"? In the Gospel, it is Christ who speaks these words—but it is difficult to avoid the feeling that in the present context, they are spoken by Pascal.

In this experience, the particularity of the "order" of revelation and grace vis-à-vis that of nature and culture becomes clear. It is the fruitful experience which gives him the capability of differentiating definitively and of determining, from the point of view of this supreme distinction, everything which precedes it. The total arc of human existence stands out; in it, every separate moment receives its place.

At the same time, he makes the resolution to follow "the paths taught in the Gospel"; to practice "total and sweet renunciation," that is, the renunciation of the fundamental values of existence: marriage, property, the smugly sovereign disposal of one's own will: "Total submission to Jesus Christ and to my director."

This resolution, in this soul, in this character! . . . And what spirit will predominate? To what disposition, to what economy of inner life, to what kind of religious pedagogy will this *"humeur bouillante"* entrust itself, since it would need a direction endowed with superior intellectual force, sovereign knowledge of man and perfect wisdom? Pascal's fate is here preparing itself. It will certainly be great—the only question is what it will cost, and whether it will finally lead to fulfillment or destruction.

183

IV.

For Pascal, it was now only a matter of drawing the conclusions from the event—which was seminal, as God's touch always is: it unfolds its contents only in the trusting obedience to the directions found in it, in the living through of the happenings of exterior existence interpreted in terms of them.

That "growth" at the decisive spot for Pascal's character, which Jacqueline reports; that pressing on from self-love and self-assertion to detachment from himself, to Christian self-condemnation and humility, was already the realization of such a conclusion. And indeed, Pascal wanted to place himself under a concrete authority with "*soumission douce et totale*," as the experience of the *Mémorial* had directed him. For this he turned to Port-Royal. He wished this community, which he regarded as the standard of Christian life, to take him under its direction—and recognize him, precisely thereby, as a religious personality.

But this was not easy. First of all, the community and its friends could not forget that he had once been passionately attached to the world, and had gone so far as to withhold his sister's inheritance from her. But there was another, more profound reason for distrust. The spirit of Port-Royal was oriented more towards prayer and Christian action than towards the intellectual penetration of Christian truth. Its faith had something of blind abandonment, of "*Credo quia absurdum*," about it. When it urged the renunciation of science, then it meant thereby not only the sacrifice of what might be "world" in the striving for knowledge; rather, the critical penetration and systematic elaboration of the believing consciousness were suspicious in themselves. Now, in Pascal it encountered the very incarnation of the scientific will to knowledge. To be sure, he had sacrificed the "world," in the sense of enjoyment, success, self-affirmation; to be sure, he had begun to detach his heart from all desire, he wanted to seek only God and the service of God in his neighbor. But he held fast to what he had recognized as

184

truth, as genuine value, and bore it into the new sphere of life. He held fast to the values of the *"esprit géométrique"*—so much so that until the end of his life, to the extent that his ravaged forces permitted it, he produced mathematical works of a high order. So, too, the values of the *"esprit de finesse"* and of *"honnêteté"*—so much so that significant tasks of philosophical knowledge and pedagogical work ensued for him. It is with the same spirit of critical and systematic penetration that he turned to the *"ordre de la sainteté,"* in order to understand its essence, in contrast to the other domains, but applying the results obtained in them. Port-Royal never acknowledged this attitude. It accepted him as a religious personality, though after marked hesitation; as an intellectual figure it always regarded him with reticence and without real understanding. Even in the religious sphere, indeed, the relationship was not unequivocal; for the fact that in the last year of Pascal's life it was shaken— not to say, perhaps more accurately, shattered—, is not only due to the particular dissensions of the moment, but reveals tensions existing from the beginning on. Pascal never became one of the "Messieurs de Port-Royal." He would have liked to be one. Perhaps he never entirely saw what an abyss separated him intellectually and religiously from the community which he so passionately revered. He wanted to have a share in it, with a longing whose roots lie not only in the sense for human and religious value, but also in a very profound spiritual eros. In order to understand it, one must appreciate the pure beauty which lies over new religious foundations, and at the same time remember that Pascal, grown up without a mother, was despite all his intellectual power and combative force a man without a home. In this community he felt the warmth of a sacred hearth, and wanted to share in it, but in vain. To be sure, he fought for Port-Royal; he took up the Jansenist ideas, and thought out his own problems in terms of them; he has been made the hero of Jansenism. Yet he remained lonely. In the decisive hour, Port-Royal rejected him with terror. As for his personal convictions, we are of the opinion that he stood

185

in a complicated relationship to the concepts and ways of thinking of Jansenius and Arnauld: he used them, but meant something else fundamentally.

Jacqueline's letter cited above lets us witness the difficulties
on the part of Port-Royal—especially if one has become attentive and reads between the lines. For Pascal, it is at first a
matter of finding a spiritual director. The successor of Saint-
Cyran at Port-Royal, Singlin, seems the natural choice; but he
resists, as he says, out of shyness, taking "persons of learned
condition" under his authority.[63] After an interval, during
which—characteristic of the relationship of the brother and
sister—Jacqueline is entrusted by him with the direction of her
brother, Singlin takes over the responsibility.

In agreement with him, Pascal decides to go for a time to
Port-Royal, in solitude; not least in order to withdraw from
the commerce with friends, about the closest of whom, Roannez,
Jacqueline says that he "occupied him completely." He occupies
"a room or cell among the solitaries of Port-Royal, from which
he has written to me with an extreme joy at seeing himself
treated and lodged like a prince, but like a prince in the judgment of Saint Bernard, in a solitary place where one vows to
practice poverty in everything in which discretion allows"
(*Oeuvres*, IV, p. 66). She then reports how very austerely he
lives, entirely concentrated on prayer, self-examination, and
the study of Sacred Scripture.

The import of this retirement was above all the fact that
Pascal lived under binding direction. His mind, filled with
violent self-assurance, experienced the liberating influence of
obedience. The truth about his own existence no longer came
only from his own judgment, subject to all the possibilities of
self-delusion which he has himself so forcefully described, but
also and decisively from the regard and the judgment of
another, who had assumed the co-responsibility for the development of his Christian life.

186

But the authority which thus entered into his life was none other than the Church. It is important to see this in its entire import. What Pascal sought in the *"directeur"* was not only the religious endowment of the physician and educator of the soul —as one goes today, for example, to an important psychoanalyst, who is at the same time a religious man and experienced master of life. He was the priest of the Church; the man whose judgment and wisdom in direction are upheld not only by his personal endowment, but by the force and authority of the Church. When the spiritual director speaks, he speaks out of the consciousness and the mission of the Church—otherwise he is at best a good pedagogue, at worst a bearer of disaster. The spiritual director is the Church in the concrete.

Under Singlin's direction, Pascal transforms the structure of his life. Gilberte Périer reports in her account of his life (P. O., p. 16) how he puts the *"voies enseignées dans l'Evangile"* into practice. He attempts to detach himself from whatever is not absolutely necessary for life. He renounces pleasure, limits his needs, takes upon himself the most disagreeable and painful medical treatments in the spirit of penance. He sells part of his household goods and gives the proceeds to the poor. Prayer and meditation receive an ever greater place in his life.

The text "Sur la conversion du pécheur" develops the experience of that fundamental revaluation of values which determines this transformation of existence (P. O., pp. 196ff.).

But he immediately begins to observe again, and indeed, in the newly attained domain. In his own inner being he has experienced the reality of Christ and of grace; he experiences ever anew the reality of Christian existence, of its essence, its laws of development, its forces and values. In the commerce with Port-Royal he sees the phenomenon of the Christian life taking place in the form of original and important personalities. The *Pensées* show many traces of his experiences and observations.

187

He also applies himself to pedagogical problems. The text "De l'art de persuader," appended to "De l'esprit géométrique (P. O., pp. 184f.), poses the question of how a conviction comes into being—of how, in particular, rational knowledge is related to sentiments of value and feelings of sympathy—, and attempts to construct an art of persuasion out of these insights. A theory, then, of how the realms of the "*raison*" and the "*coeur*" can be combined in order to bring forth genuine "*coutumes.*"

We see at the same time—and it is a thoroughly charming spectacle—the great theoretician of the most spiritual things taking pains to find a better method for teaching children to read. He establishes that the poor creatures do not learn the letters correctly, since the latter carry signs which do not coincide with their phonetic value. He thus finds that it is more accurate to designate the letters with their mere phonetic value, so that the letter to be learned is given immediately by the sign.[64]

It is perhaps from this period that stems that beautiful fragment of a religious meditation, which has come down to us under the title "Mystère de Jésus" and which is inserted among the *Pensées* (fr. 553, pp. 574–578).

It is a meditation on Christ in Gethsemani, one completely filled with the consciousness of the solitude in which the Redeemer stands. "Jesus is the one person on earth, not only to feel and share his suffering, but to know it. Heaven and he are alone in this knowledge." But he who meditates knows about it, for the essence of meditation consists not in standing before the event considered in historical recollection, but rather in standing in it in living participation. One is nonetheless a little startled when sentences like these occur: "Jesus will be in agony until the end of the world: one must not sleep during that time." Gethsemani always exists; everyone is always asleep. One must keep watch with him—who must? He, Pascal. This is Christian, as soon as it says: "You, Blaise Pascal, must keep watch." But when one is dealing with a mind accustomed to

188

being among the elect, one who knows among the innumerable who do not know, in possession of the *"pensée de derrière la tête,"* which enables him to speak to others as they speak, although aware that everything is otherwise—how far is one then from the formula: "I, Pascal, am he who keeps watch among the multitude which sleeps?"[65]

Jesus then turns to him who prays, and there follow sentences of wondrous, intimate warmth: "Console yourself, you would not seek me if you had not found me." One can not really seek God, Christ, if not by his grace, which draws one to itself. "You seek, and that is why you have already found," Jesus thus says to Pascal! . . . "I thought of you during my agony, I have sweated such drops of blood for you." Once again, profound words; but can one have such a certainty in genuine Christianity: "such drops of blood for you?"

A wondrous closeness becomes perceptible: "I am more a friend to you than such or such, for I have done for you more than they, and they would not suffer what I have suffered from you, and would not die for you at the time of your infidelities and cruelties, as I have done."

The image of sin wells up: "If you knew your sins, you would lose heart." We have seen what a powerful experience of the evil in man Pascal had, and we can imagine what anxiety about eternal salvation must have ensued from it: "Then I will lose it, Lord, for on your assurance I believe their malice. — No, for I, through whom you learn it, can heal you of them, and what I say to you is a sign that I want to heal you. To the extent that you expiate them, you will know them, and it will be said to you: Behold, your sins are forgiven you."

An ultimate mystery of love and unity holds sway: "I love you more ardently than you have loved your abominations." It is the community of love with the Redeemer: "I see my abyss of pride, of curiosity, of concupiscence. There is no relation from me to God, nor to Jesus Christ, the just. But he has been made sin through me; all your scourges have fallen upon him. He is more abominable than I, and far from abhor-

189

ring me, he considers himself honored that I go to him and help him. But he has healed himself and will heal me *a fortiori*. I must add my wounds to his, and join myself to him, and he will save me in saving himself." The basic fact of Christian consciousness, then. The great experience of the *Mémorial,* source of astonishment and rapture, was indeed the recognition of who God is: not the mere absolute being, but he, of whom man can experience nothing unless he comes and reveals himself. God is He. And he is engaged in action oriented towards man, towards me. He reveals himself in the historical figure of his messengers, in the person of the Redeemer. Christian existence is not the content of a system, but of an event, of the action of God. But this action is meant for me. Here, in the "*mystère,*" this divine intention unfolds. God has not only acted, he has engaged in human history. He has not only stood above history as a sovereign, but has entered into it. God in himself has no destiny; the incarnation means that he has taken destiny upon himself. What man has done and does, he has taken as his destiny and never shakes it off. But the man meant here is the sinner: I myself. He has let my existence become his destiny. But it has been thereby drawn into the glowing, creative recommencement, and out of it has come for me a new beginning, that of redeemed existence. It is love, on which Christianity knows itself to be founded: that the redemptive God accepts the existence of man as his own, and that out of it a new beginning dawns for man. Infinite communion: what is mine becomes his, and therefore what is his becomes mine.

It becomes the consciousness of a continuous community of existence: "To do the little things as if they were great"; not from an ever so respectable wisdom, according to which the great would be small and the small great, but rather "because of the majesty of Jesus Christ, who does them in us, and who lives our life; and the great things as if they were little and easy, because of his omnipotence." Thence a confidence which overcomes all weakness: "It is to tempt me, more than to test you, to think whether you would indeed do such and such a thing in the future: I myself will accomplish it in you when the time is at hand." Still more profoundly: "Your conversion is my affair; do not fear, and pray with confidence as if for me."[66]

Thence a reversal of valuations:[67] "Do not compare yourself to others, but to me. If you do not find me in those to whom you compare yourself, you compare yourself to someone abominable. If you find me in them, compare yourself to me. But whom will you compare? Will it be you, or me in you? If it is you, it is someone abominable. If it is I, you compare me to myself. Now I am God in everything." This is that life which unfolds in the remains of Pascal's letters to his friend, Roannez. The faith aspires to mystical experience, in order to thereby become a force in daily life.

And yet a final point must be stressed in this rich text. In the *Mémorial* it is said: "Total submission to Jesus Christ and to my director"; here: "Ask your director, when my own words are for you the occasion of evil, and of vanity or curiosity." What is here expressed is the fundamental Catholic and Christian consciousness, that there is no immediate relationship to the Father, but that the Father is only accessible to us through the Son; but also that there is no relationship at each one's pleasure to the Redeemer, who rather stands in the scope of the Church and is accessible only through her to the individual. Detached and taken for itself, the word of Scripture can be "the occasion of evil, and of vanity or curiosity." Pascal's Christian experience has a forcible directness; but what it discloses is the fact that God in himself is hidden and is only revealed in the Mediator. The God—supposedly—attained directly is an illusion. He is only genuinely attained in Christ. But even the relationship to the Mediator itself is not autonomous; in it stands the bearer of authority, who lifts it out of the danger of subjectivity. This bearer of authority is the Church. Just as God is not freely accessible—he is rather revealed only in Christ for what he is, the Father—, so, too, Christ is not freely accessible, but is related to an order, a sphere, an historical fact, the Church, and is thence defined ever anew.[68] For so it also

191

states: "I am present to you through my word in Scripture, through my spirit in the Church and through inspirations, through my power in the priests; through my prayer in the faithful." Ever anew, Pascal links the Christian realities to one another. He who has such an enormous force of personal experience, of standing on his own, sees that there is here an order, whose overthrow would not be a sign of independence and force, but of disorder and presumption; and out of the most profound knowledge of a necessity and a danger, he takes pains to secure this order ever anew.

V.

And now the complicated and so very human story, charged with sadness and evil, the magnificent and at the same time distressing story of Pascal's struggle must be told. In November, 1654, the event of the *Mémorial* occurs; in August, 1662, Pascal dies at the age of thirty-nine. This entire period is filled with a single, wearying struggle, setting in ever anew after pauses and rising finally to the paroxysm in a tragic moment. Everything contributed to this struggle: general tensions of the time, and specific personalities; theological ideas and political forces; the movement set in motion by Saint-Cyran and Jansenius; the community of Port-Royal and the circle assembled around it; Pascal's family and the Molinist theologians of the Jesuit order; other theological groups and their mutual oppositions; the clerical and political public of the country; cultural and social events; the motives and movements which had been awakened by the Reformation; the tensions between France and Rome. All this cannot be narrated here, or else the chapter would become a book. The reader who would like to know more must therefore rely on the sources and the extensive secondary literature; but he must not forget in the process, that in this matter even more than in others, the picture which each writer gives depends on his attitude towards Christianity.

192

Here we can only say as much as is necessary in order to understand Pascal's inner itinerary.

Many antitheses work against one another in this struggle.

There is above all one, which already appears at the beginning of Christian thought: whether the initiation of the religious relationship is placed entirely in God or whether man's own activity is called upon; and indeed, not only in the sense that the believer struggles and labors—the seriously minded man does so in any case—, but rather, that the human factor has positive meaning in the Christian domain as such. In the first case, there emerges the tendency to depreciate man; grace governs the entire believing consciousness; a very powerful feeling of sin appears; the relationship to the world becomes pessimistic; the economy of Christian consciousness tends towards a separation of the life of faith and worldly existence; at the same time appears a tendency towards the radical, the extreme. In the other case, the attitude takes on an optimistic character; man seems trustworthy; his activity is encouraged; religious and worldly existence enter into close and manifold relations; Christian existence takes on an aspect of appeasement, it tends towards conciliations, it seeks mediations and transitions; "Christian culture" is envisaged and desired; at the same time, the effort is directed towards finding spheres in which the immediate human and cultural impulse can validly operate, without at once being brought under the norms of revelation, etc.

This touches upon a second antithesis: between that disposition which everywhere emphasizes the Christian note, subordinates all human activity and creation to it, so that the whole of existence is directly determined by religion—and the other, which precisely out of Christian conviction asserts a relative autonomy of the various worldly domains of reality and value. This difference, too, comes into play already in the first Christian times, and has an effect in all domains, especially the ethical. While the second disposition demands direct ethical experience and ethical culture in the real sense, the first tends

193

towards an absolute primacy of religion. What is specifically moral is then easily absorbed into religion; there occurs, if one may so put it, a short circuit on the part of the religious conscience—a danger to which corresponds, on the other side, that of a detachment of morality from the religious context, of the secularization of ethical culture as well as of all culture *per se*.

There would be yet more to say on this point.

The reformatory surge which goes through Europe carries high the religious absolutistic structure. It emphasizes the primacy of faith over knowledge; not only the sovereignty, but the incommensurability of grace vis-à-vis human existence and capacity. The world abandoned by religion is all the more decisively taken possession of by the likewise abandoned worldly creative effort. For the fact that, out of an exaggerated faith, world and man are separated, as "sin," from the domain of the sacred, that every possible relation between the Holy God and fallen man, between grace and world, faith and reason, is denied, is the first step; the second is the declaration of this man in this world as autonomous. But while this religious structure reaches supremacy in the Reformation and definitively breaks up a series of living relations, on which the totality of Christian existence rests, it operates within the Catholic domain in an attenuated form and maintains, except for a few borderline phenomena, the vital cohesion.

The movement which proceeds from Saint-Cyran and Jansenius is at first a striving for a more vigorous Biblical and supernatural Christianity, the decisive primacy of grace, and a very strict manner of living determined at once by faith and by a fundamental bourgeois puritanism. Then the struggles begin. What was at first an experiential and living religious attitude hardens into a doctrine; the resentment over the mutually inflicted injustice of polemics poisons feeling and judgment. Thus arises little by little Jansenism as it has become known historically, which despite all efforts to delimit itself from Calvin, is but a mitigated Calvinism, and bears a full measure of guilt for the failure of Christianity in the face of the Enlighten-

194

ment of the eighteenth century. In the face of this movement stands the still young but already powerfully developed Jesuit order, which energetically champions the concern of human freedom and independent action. It attempts to make room in the domain of faith for the newly awakened consciousness of individual responsibility and the will to labor in the world. In establishing a relative, though very formal autonomy of human judgment and action, it wants to parry the demand for an absolute autonomy, and unite the freedom so powerfully experienced by the period with the obedience towards the authority of God or the Church. Above all in ethics. Absolute autonomy would here mean that man acts purely according to his own judgment—if he does not altogether reject every ethical obligation, as did the widespread skeptical and libertinistic tendency. On the other hand, the moral doctrine of the order strives to maintain the objective validity of the positive commandments of God and the authority of the Church, but at the same time to create a sphere of individual freedom. This freedom is placed in the interpretation of the commandment; that is, the individual must come to an understanding of the measure of obligation which proceeds from the commandment, and is entitled to bring his freedom of movement into play in face of the law. But by dint of that unilateral force which new ideas *in statu nascendi* have, a technique for this develops, which despite the purest intention of the theory, can in practice lead the conscience to withdraw from the word and spirit of Christian duty.

The two positions were sharply opposed to one another; hence each was very sensitive to the weakness of the other. The movement of Port-Royal could but react passionately against the possibilities which could result from the—incorrectly employed—Molinist principles. Thus above all against the danger of so emphasizing the inherent significance of human reason and freedom, that the primacy of grace would be thereby diminished, the weight of sin lessened, and the pure initiality of justification restrained. Further, against the danger of rationalizing Christianity; of introducing juridical categories into ethical

195

and religious thought; of relaxing the strictness and simplicity of Christian duty by a technique of mitigations, of intermediary concepts, of shifts in intention; of doing away with the conflict, rationally unsolvable in the last analysis, between Christian challenge and worldly existence. Against the danger, then, of sliding from what is essentially Christian into a universal rationality and of secularizing Christian moral life . . . The Jesuits, for their part, could but look with apprehension upon the way in which, on the part of the disciples of Jansenius and Saint-Cyran, the tension between revelation and reason, between grace and human self-reliance, between the Christian ethos and the world was so intensified that the unity of believing existence threatened to split apart. They could but foresee that man would no longer be able to maintain the consciousness at once of a sinfulness formulated in this way and of the impulse to living creative effort; that the opposition would break asunder into a desperate faith on the one hand and an equally radical ensnarement in the world on the other; that a religious overburdening would arise, which would of necessity produce grave disturbances, and then bring about its opposite, skepticism and wordliness. The Jansenist doctrine of predestination was to prove especially fateful. It was originally intended, to be sure, to protect the genuine sovereignty of grace; but it then very quickly went so far as to claim that man is completely corrupted by original sin, his disposition simply evil, his will necessarily abandoned to the strongest motives of the moment; that God indeed redeemed "men" *in abstracto,* but in fact only certain of them; that out of the impenetrable mystery of his will he chose some for eternal salvation and bestowed on them his grace to such an extent that it brings them irresistibly to the love of God and to Christian life; and determined the others just as sovereignly to perdition, or more precisely, abandoned them to the annihilation to which, in reality, they had fallen prey through original sin, and does not bestow on them that efficient grace, so that they irresistibly fall prey to blindness and evil. An absolute mystery is thereby rationalized in the direction of a defi-

196

nite structural motif, so that it comes into contradiction with natural human as well as Christian consciousness. To the reproach of excessive shrewdness, of overly subtle distinctions, of too extensive indulgence vis-à-vis the world, they opposed that of pride in the faith, of self-righteousness, of pharisaism, of spiritual violence. And they could point to the fact that the danger of insincerity in the technique of mental reservation was outweighed by a far more profound insincerity: that which must ensue from the very pretension to "pure" Christianity and from its consequences for the relationship to existence.

The loss of the struggle, as stated above, cannot be described. It concentrated around the book by Jansenius, which, excessively simplifying and systematizing Augustinian thoughts, had constructed the theology sketched above: the *Augustinus,* published in 1640. The altercation began immediately. The theologian of Port-Royal, Antoine Arnauld, stepped in with an apology for the book in 1643, followed by still two more—three texts in which the doctrine of French Jansenism developed. The theological faculty of the Sorbonne in Paris rejected the book, and formulated their point of view in the five *Propositions.* The government adhered to the Sorbonne, the clergy took sides both pro and con.

In the course of the struggle something tragic takes place for those who highly esteem the disposition of nascent Jansenism and the old Port-Royal. What had originally been alive in it was not a doctrine, but a powerful experience, a high-minded self-abandonment, and an ardent life of prayer. Saint-Cyran himself was above all a man of the spiritual life. Arnauld, on the other hand, was a doctrinaire and a polemicist. A living Christian approach thus became a polemically fixed doctrine. The positions became overly simplified and extreme, the concepts became rigid, the attitudes obstinate, the possibilities of heresy came more and more to the fore. A movement of progressive but orthodoxly intended faith became a sect.

197

VI.

Where does Pascal stand in all this?

It is clear that many things must have drawn him to the Jansenist form of thought. For in fact, he had already occupied himself with its problems at an early date; his attitude towards the Sieur Saint-Ange was already determined from this point of view. At a critical moment in the struggle he intervened with a *Lettre écrite à un provincial par un de ses amis, sur le sujet des disputes présentes de la Sorbonne* (*Oeuvres,* IV, pp. 119ff.). It was published on January 23, 1656; seventeen others followed it, the last of which was published in March, 1657. Fragments of further letters were found among Pascal's papers after his death (*Oeuvres,* VII, pp. 169ff.).

The first ten letters were written by someone living in Paris to a friend in the provinces, and report about the events; above all about the discussions he has had with typified representatives of the parties concerned. From the eleventh on, the letters are addressed to the "*Révérends Pères*" of the Jesuit order, or to certain of them who were particularly prominent in the struggle. At the beginning the letters are short; they then become longer and longer; the eighteenth is a veritable treatise. The first four deal with the initial question of whether the five disputed propositions had been championed by Jansenius at all, or in what sense the individual concepts had been used by him. Then the attack commences: the "modern" moral theology of the Jesuits has abandoned the foundations of Christianity; it means the sacrifice of revelation to philosophy, of Christianity to worldliness. The meaning of Christian life as a life of grace is depleted; human autonomy has taken its place. The attack becomes more and more caustic, and each new letter takes up the answers published in the interim. The last two letters return to the initial question, the problem of grace, and attempt to grasp it from a more profound starting point. Then they suddenly stop short.

Pascal did not work alone. He relied on the writings of Arnauld, and his friends helped him as well. Among them the

198

Chevalier de Méré, who without being interested himself in the subject of the dispute, advised him to give up the general theological formulation of the first letters and to proceed to the attack against the concrete opinions of his adversaries, for this would appeal directly to the general public.

The impression made by the *Lettres provinciales* was enormous, as might be expected. After the publication of the first letter, the bookseller of Port-Royal was arrested. The author himself remained anonymous and thus eluded the civil authorities.

Pascal wrote under a pseudonym: Louis de Montalte. One senses a special significance in this fact. Not only the awareness of danger, but something more profound: that the concrete personality, living through the various sides of its existence, releases out of itself, as it were, the combatant; that it frees him from the restrictive, but also protective context of society for an absolute operation, for the combat *per se*. This does not mean that Pascal wanted this, or abandoned himself to an impulse in this direction. His later writings were also published under pseudonyms: Salomon de Tultie and Amos de Dettonville, anagrams of Louis de Montalte. The conscious motives are thus prudence and, for the later writings, the renunciation of one who no longer wishes to be prominent personally. The matter would have to rest there for the interpretation of the incident with these motives—if the circumstance under discussion did not take on through the manner of the combat a special emphasis in the context of Pascal's personality and life, an emphasis which is yet to be elucidated.

Pascal's intention was to lead the discussion away from concepts to the phenomenon itself; to speak not from the point of view of traditional theology, but from immediate Christian experience and the new canon of the "*honnête homme*"; and not as a specialist to his colleagues, but as a layman to the "*gens du monde*" with their healthy judgment and "*sens naturel.*" This

199

provided a great advantage; the matter could be grasped straight-forwardly and discussed in human terms, without technical expressions and academic debates. But it also brought with it a serious disadvantage, for the matter at hand was in fact not only questions of Christian consciousness, which could be comprehended by common sense, but at the same time complicated theological problems laden with the heritage of century-long controversies, the treatment of which presupposed thorough training and great knowledge. To transpose them really and without loss of substance into the sphere of the *"gens du monde"* would thus have presupposed not only an acute understanding and great pedagogical as well as literary ability, but also a superior philosophical and theological education, which Pascal just did not have. In this respect, he was a layman in the derogatory sense of the word. The danger of the layman, the resentment against the specialist, was thus very urgent; all the more so, since here a passionately concerned religious man, who had the highest opinion of his intellectual qualities, stood opposed to the tradition-bound experts' science which allegedly destroyed the essential.

To this danger was added another: The specialist begins with the object and its complications; what guides him is the objective judgment about what exists; he is thus careful and prudent. The layman begins with his disposition; the value judgment guides him; he wants "purity," decisiveness. As a result, he pushes the value situation to the extremes and simplifies the state of affairs. Thus with all the pathos of his sincerity and moral seriousness, he easily becomes insincere and unjust. "Sincerity is the most spiritual of virtues," a profound proverb goes. The layman has a tendency to make a simplistic attitude out of it, and a peculiar kind of demagogy easily takes the place of sincerity.[69] With this, we come to a final danger which particularly menaced Pascal. He was a polemicist of the highest rank. But as soon as it is a matter of religious truth, of things of decisive significance for the salvation of the soul, it is risky if the combatant is too good a combatant. There is a danger lest he take pleasure in the combat as such and let himself be carried away. And if he is a man of unbalanced temperament, with inhibitions at work within him, then this danger receives a new and more serious character: a certain complex of act and function, with its particular instincts and value judgments, may detach itself from the total personality, gain something like autonomous existence, and force the rest into its service. From this there can develop what psychology calls the demonic. But faith knows that the most profound dangers of the person and his salvation can hide behind such psychological processes, and the demon receives a very real meaning.

The *Lettres provinciales* are polemical masterpieces. Borne by a profound seriousness and a passion which springs up ever anew; incisive in the exposition of the problem; marvelous in their power to make things transparent; concrete, close to life, of superior logical and artistic ability. In them a moving drama takes place. The intellectual positions become figures and powers which struggle with one another. The reader feels himself drawn into the struggle, called upon to take a position, as helper, as defender, as judge. They are masterpieces in the line of "De l'art de persuader" and "De la logique du coeur." And since the ordering of ideas and the language, the motivation and the emotional state stem entirely from the world of the "*honnête homme,*" the problems discussed are suddenly transformed from objects of inaccessible theological expertise into questions which concern everyone and in which everyone can put in a word from immediate experience and healthy human understanding. Nonetheless, measured by an ultimate norm, they are bad. Not only because they are insufficient theologically, because they do not do justice to the position of the adversary, because they quote incorrectly, and whatever can be impartially objected to them—worse than all this is their fundamental polemical presupposition and the attitude which ensues from it.

An absolutistic way of thinking will also push the other to an extreme, even if he is not radically disposed at all. A combative mentality will make a point of seeking the adversary, and will find, awaken, or else fabricate him everywhere. If it is a case, moreover, of an interiority which measures itself by an absolute norm and thereby experiences itself continually as unworthy; whose character indeed consists precisely in being able to accept a norm as ultimately valid only when this norm hopelessly transcends it, and its own being comes into the situation of being desperately lost; if this norm is absolute power, and man thus stands before it in the attitude of helpless abandonment and fear, which can only be redeemed in the equally extreme attitude of personal election—then all this must also have its effect in the relationship to others. Such a consciousness will be incapable of accepting the other man straightforwardly. It will immediately presume certain intentions in him, suspect associations and plots, and will adopt an attitude composed of uncertainty and apodictic affirmation, of fear and violence, of distrust and aggressivity.

This attitude is highly developed in Jansenism; one has even spoken of its "*monomanie du complot*." The mentality of the Jesuit order was foreign to it, its historical mission incomprehensible; one thus did not stop with the conviction that the theology of the order was in error, but came to have the goading feeling that it was conspiring against the predestined bearer of sacred truth and therefore against this truth itself.

The same attitude is found in Pascal; but like everything which he has in common with his environment, it too receives in him not only a far greater dynamism, but an entirely different existential character. A tendency to the mania of conspiracy becomes in him a very somber, evil potentiality. Here lies the evil of the *Lettres provinciales*. They are based on the assertion that the Jesuits are not only mistaken, but knowingly stand opposed to the truth. That they are not only in the wrong, but deplete and falsify Christian morality in order to come into power, in order to rule over the learned, the rich, the nobles, the courts, high politics—in short, the world. The combat is guided from this point of view. There awakens that demonism of combat of which we have already spoken: the adversary was not only accused of having fallen away from Christianity, but of having knowingly betrayed the sacred truth for the sake of power. This interpretation of the adversary then justifies that absoluteness of combat which this will craves. A combat begins which wills the destruction of the adversary. And which stylizes the adversary in such a way that against him, the combat of extermination becomes possible and legitimate.

After the first movement of wonder one becomes disenchanted, and apprehensive about the one who combats in this way. If Christianity were really to be endangered by the adversary—will it be saved by this spirit of combat? And what becomes of the man who combats in this way?

The combat did not come to an end with the *Lettres provinciales*. There followed complications upon complications. To the literary discussions were added outward measures, in favor first of one party, then of the other. Pascal intervened more than once in the course of events, above all through drafts for several of the so-called "*factum*" in which the Parisian clergy adopted a position against the new moral theology and practice. Here the course of ideas receives a new character; the polemic and theological treatise are replaced by the politically oriented writing.

The fragments remaining from letters to the Duc de Roannez and his sister also stem from this period. They show how profoundly Pascal is involved and what solitude he feels around himself.

He speaks there of the "strange secrecy into which God has withdrawn" (no. 4, P. O., p. 214). We sense the special tone of sentences like this: "Let us pray God to make us know him and serve him in all things; and let us give him infinite thanks that, after hiding himself in all things for the others, he has revealed himself in all things and in so many ways for us." And again: "Ordinarily God hides, and reveals himself rarely to

203

those whom he wants to engage in his service" (no. 4, P. O., pp. 214 and 215).

The notion of an abandonment of God emerges: "*Sans mentir, Dieu est bien abandoné.*" But the elect stands by him: "*Il me semble, que c'est un temps, où le service qu'on lui rend est bien agréable*" (no. 3, P. O., p. 213).

But at the same time, almost as a warning to himself, the sentence: "Let us pray to him to have pity on us and on the entire Church, outside of which there is but malediction." The predestined individual confronts the sacred totality, the Church, and anchors himself in her. He senses the growing tension of the connecting bond and seeks to secure it.

It is not immediately evident why the *Lettres provinciales* were broken off. The seventeenth had just taken up the question of grace—the central religious and theological question of the entire dispute—from a more profound starting point and with more complete inclusion of its problems. A full discussion was in store. The public was waiting in suspense, and nothing had yet happened from the side of public authority which would have made the continuation impossible. The reasons must therefore lie deeper than in tactical considerations.

Perhaps Port-Royal itself changed its attitude towards the letters in the course of publication. At first it rejoices; perhaps it then began to feel that there is too little love in Pascal's combat. Perhaps also too many literary and intellectual qualities, too much culture. This objection exists. It is ambiguous; the Philistine can hide behind it, but it can also be the expression of a very Christian instinct. It is indeed suspicious when the problems of Christianity are handled with an overly detached, overly objective, overly sovereign intellectuality. The danger then arises that things slip into "philosophy" or aesthetics. And behind it a still more profound danger, that the proximity of the scandal of the cross is abandoned. As stated, the objection is ambiguous; but Christian things, if they are to remain pure, must not abandon the range of 1 Cor. 1, 18–31. Aesthetic splendor, intellectual power, spiritual triumph—if the norms are taken as strictly as Pascal himself wants to see them taken, all this is questionable to the subtle Christian sensibility. In any case, the great intellectual and artistic style of this manner of discussion did not lie in the intention of Port-Royal.

But then Pascal's own attitude towards the problem shifted. At the beginning of the discussion, he simply upheld the Jansenist position, and just as simply rejected the Molinist position. Like Port-Royal, he saw in Scholasticism only abuse, in Thomas Aquinas a feeble compromise, and recognized as foundations of theological judgment only the Fathers—understood Jansenistically. But then he became aware of the complexities of the problem. The sensitive Nicole, who like Pascal never belonged to the circle of the "Messieurs de Port-Royal"—he was called Arnauld's Melanchthon—, had sought on the latter's incentive an understanding with the Thomists, who had indeed for their part a feud with Molinism. The result was a broadening and deepening of the position which brought about the indignation of the strict Jansenists. But Pascal was on friendly terms with Nicole, and through him learned to consider the theology and philosophy of the Thomists in a new light. He evidently sensed the force of synthesis of this magnificent thought and became aware that his own initial position was extremely primitive. Above all, he probably saw a new possibility of differentiating the problem of efficacity, of distinguishing between the causality in the physical order and that in the intellectual, and again that in the order of freedom and love. He must have thus begun, to the dismay of Port-Royal, to consider the Jansenist and Molinist positions as partial positions of an antithetically structured total system. The problem would have thereby come for the first time into the real range of Pascal; it would have become a problem of concretion, and as such, object of the dialectical method which he handles with such mastery. If Pascal had been able to develop it in a suitable form in accordance with its full antithetical nature, there would

205

have arisen a theory of grace which would perhaps have further developed, in respect to anthropology and psychology, that of Saint Thomas Aquinas.[70] As the seventeenth and eighteenth letters show in comparison to the first, the development tended to free the problem of grace from the purely Jansenist simplification and narrowness and place it in the total context of Christian reality. In the measure in which this broadening of perspective took place, the *"petites lettres,"* even if they had meanwhile grown in length, must have no longer appeared to him as the appropriate form of treatment.

Finally, however—and here our interpretation is based on the line of his Christian development, as it is determined by the *Mémorial*—, there seems to be something inner and religious behind this breaking off: Pascal frees himself from the constriction of polemics. What we have called the demonic slackens. Pascal becomes free again. Not definitively; the working out of natural inner dispositions, in whose crises and resolutions the personal struggle for freedom and salvation proceeds, takes place in thrusts, until the definitive breakthrough or until the catastrophe. The breaking off of the *Lettres provinciales* seems to signify the conclusion of such a phase, the realization of the Christian theme of the Pascalian existence posed by the *Mémorial,* which as a liberating "delivering up of the soul" demands that which was directly opposed to his intrinsic danger: humility.

VII.

The place of the *Lettres provinciales* is taken by another project, which was to realize this inclusion of the problem of grace into that of the whole of Christian existence: the plan of an apology of Christianity.

This plan shows once again how little Pascal may be considered together with his circle. Jansenism tended ultimately to the incommensurability of God and world, of grace and nature. It preached, admonished, warned, sought to shake and to

206

awaken; but an "apology" in the strict sense of the word, a rational foundation and elucidation of the act of faith on the basis of strict method and with the claim to scientific validity— all of which is a partial concern of Christian culture—could but be foreign to it and awaken its distrust. The plan presupposes the possibility of a methodical and theoretical comprehension of Christianity; but precisely this, Pascal's most essential intention, could but go against the instinct of Jansenism.

The man to whom the apology addresses itself is neither an abstract humanity, nor a detached rationality, but rather a type precisely determined by his historical standpoint, by his sociological and cultural conditions. He is a man who feels a certain respect for religion, but is otherwise entirely devoted to the world. A man with alert senses, refined sensibility, clear judgment; Méré's nobly minded and highly educated *"honnête homme."* The planned demonstration of Christian truth was to be addressed to this man. Natural science and mathematics, knowledge of man, esteem of worldly values, *"esprit de finesse"* and *"coeur,"* religious experience and methodical work of the understanding were to be combined to this end. The work was to arise from superior intellectuality, intensive experience, and exact method. A Francis de Sales would have been able to value the undertaking; Port-Royal could hardly begin to understand its most profound intention and the will to action operating in it.

Pascal's "Jansenism" is in the last analysis something different than the world of thoughts and motives of his friends. It is the problem of his own existence, expressed, indeed, with the words and formulas which the historical and individual situation placed at his disposal. But the same words mean something different in the mouth of different personalities. Pascal was bound to the movement by a thousand ties, but he was too great to be absorbed into it. Despite the best intention to belong to it, he was always alone and solitary.

207

We must yet refer to a religious experience which was of importance for Pascal's knowledge of Christian reality in general, as well as for the plan of the apology in particular. At the time of the work on the *Lettres provinciales,* the experience of the *Mémorial* was deepened by another, namely the miracle of the holy thorn.[71] The young Marguérite Périer, Pascal's niece, suffered from a malignant fistula of the tear gland, which had already attacked the bone of the nose. On March 24, 1656, she was abruptly cured by the contact with a relic considered to be part of Christ's crown of thorns—and in regard to the cure itself, it must be noted that Marguérite reached an age of over eighty years. The incident provoked great sensation; it was followed by others of a similar kind. They were greeted by Port-Royal as signs which divinely confirmed its position, and were called in question by the opposition for the same reason.

Pascal was profoundly laid hold of. Above all, he saw divine reality declaring itself in the event, thus "experience" in the strict sense of the imparting process, as in the experience of the *Mémorial.* But at the same time he believed he saw here the phenomenon of the "sign," of divine intervention becoming clear in history and even forming religious history. In the *Pensées* one can trace how from this point on the notion of miracle—in itself and in the context of Biblical history—concerned him.[72]

We cannot go further into the plan of the apology itself here. It is one of the greatest losses of intellectual history that it was not carried out. A synthesis of Christian consciousness would have arisen, such as we do not today possess. An expression of Christian consciousness, which would have been borne at once by the most intensive religious experience and the most acute rationality, by existential seriousness and the broadest spiritual vision; which would have been answered for by scientific method as well as by the self-engagement and destiny of a singular personality.

The work would have brought a solution of the task, which

Kierkegaard—with certain limitations—set for himself, and which is seen again today: to present Christian truth on the basis of the problem of man. More exactly, to develop the coherence of Christian truth on the guideline of human existence structured in stages, of its different levels, of its specific crises, etc. The state of consciousness of a typical man of the seventeenth century, the century in which the modern era had definitively broken through—see Chapter II above—, would have become clear; a man who in this intellectual situation had opted for Christianity and adhered to it with the most personal effort. The culture of the *ancien régime* would have presented itself, and in such a superior mind that something definitive would have become clear about culture in general.

Pascal would have here developed for the first time his image of man, of the world and of the reality of faith. Here, too, his views on the problem of grace and of Christian conduct would have found their full development on the basis of a sufficiently broad system of levels. Pascal presented his plan to his friends. It was appreciated and approved; it is open to question, whether his real intention was seen.

Shortly thereafter his illness worsened. The tragic history of the plan has already been reported: how the extensive preliminary studies which the book would have demanded became impossible; how Pascal's power of recollection declined, and he, after having been used to making no notes, but rather to working out everything in his ever-present memory, now wrote down his thoughts; at times in detail, mostly in short indications, on the first sheets or bits of paper at hand; how he at times could not even write himself, but had to dictate, so that the inadequacy of the writer betrays itself in the mistakes.

What thus came into being has come down to us as the mass of the *Pensées*. They were assembled after his death. Some things were probably lost or left aside, some others added which belonged elsewhere. The originally intended structure cannot be reconstituted; the arrangement of the various editions is already in fact an interpretation.

VIII.

The new illness, of which we were speaking, led Pascal to return again to Paris. The site of Port-Royal was very unhealthy; he seems not to have stood it any longer. The change brought at first an improvement. New creative force awakened.

Into this period falls above all the theory of cycloids—those curves which are described by a nail in the rim of a wheel when the wheel turns. The discovery attracted the greatest attention, and formed for Leibnitz, who received a copy of the manuscript, a foundation for his formulations of infinitesimal calculus.

But this scientific masterpiece—just like the research on the problem of the vacuum in its time—was also involved in a combat, which leaves a disagreeable impression, but which is of importance for the evaluation of Pascal's interior life. Pascal, pressed by his friends, had announced a prize for the solution of the problem, and had committed himself, in case no satisfactory solution were forthcoming, to give it himself. The discussion with two of the claimants, but especially with the Jesuit Père Lalouère, awakes a similar impression of violence and injustice as that conducted previously with Père Noël.[73] Pascal's conduct betrays a state of the most extreme irritability—all too comprehensible in a man sick unto death, who has years of the most painful corporal suffering, difficult inner struggle, and irritating outer combats behind him. Here it is not a matter so much of the claims to priority of a great researcher as of the cause of the Jansenist movement, in whose service the work of this researcher has been placed. Père Lalouère is thus not only the rival in the scientific contest, but also the Molinist and opponent of Port-Royal.

And yet another impression sets in in the observer who views Pascal not only with respect before his towering mind, but also with concern for the man: this human soul was not in the right hands in its surroundings. Pascal could have applied Tertullian's phrase to himself: *"Miserrimus ego semper uror caloribus impatientiae.*" He was extravagantly gifted. What wonderful power of mind, when this man, worn out by struggles and close to death, as soon as he has somewhat recovered, constructs the theory of cycloids with incredible rapidity; creates soon thereafter—as will soon be said—a new chapter of the Christian doctrine of values; then solves the technical and organizational problem of an omnibus enterprise—and all this while he is busy with deeply probing research for the apology! But he is not only incredibly gifted; his gifts have something about them which excites terror. It is not only the expression of family pride when Gilberte Périer tells how Pascal's father, when he found the twelve-year-old at his work of mathematical discovery, "was so appalled by the greatness and power of this genius that he left him without saying a word" (P. O., p. 6). The mind can have many qualities; it can also be frightening. In Pascal's mind there is something frightening. A somber depth rumbles beneath it. An all-consuming ardor burns in it. This mind has a wild grasping force. When one occupies oneself with it for a long time, it suddenly becomes clear to one what it lacks. It has no relationship to living nature. Not a word which would reveal a sensibility for what is moving, flowing, growing in nature; or for landscape; or for tree and flower. But he has no spontaneous relationship to art either. Architecture, painting, sculpture mean nothing to him; music is apparently the most foreign to him. His sphere of existence and element are neither living nature nor art. What he sees is nature as object of intellectual conquest, and man with his work. Thus "mind" in a particularly strict sense of the word. And Pascal lacks one more thing: humor. We know no passage which would reveal even a tinge of it. Irony, sharp, biting satire, to be sure; in the *Lettres provinciales,* its trenchancy sparkles, its slash whistles. But no humor. No one in his entire family seems to possess this fundamental human, metaphysical, religious force, which makes one capable of experiencing evil existence with a sensitive heart, without being damaged inwardly. All of Jansenism seems to lack it. It is serious, unflinchingly serious—but is it not a very serious judgment of this kind of Christian "seriousness," if it must be said that it lacks humor? The goodness, the freedom, the understanding acceptance of that which exists? Nature, music, humor—Pascal really lacked everything which in a special sense makes the mind "human": that which frees, that which gently transforms, that which helps. Hence the frightful pressure, the overheating of the mind, the threat of destruction. In addition, this sick body with its overexcited nerves and the barbarous curative methods of the time! Only when one takes all this into consideration does one realize how endangered Pascal was. How much he would have needed a kind, liberating human friendship; a calm and liberated depth of soul, which would have taken him into its care; a love, which would have soothed him. But there was nothing of the kind around him. The people around him make a strange impression. They are serious, strong in character, morally strict, ascetic—everything; they seem to lack only one thing: the warm, luminous force of the heart which understands and helps. They seek the "glory of God," the confirmation of the Jansenist cause—one would like to ask them whether they cannot see and feel. But so it remained, until the end, when in this pitiless atmosphere the demonic element and this "mind without music" rose to its paroxysm, and no other way was left open to it but that into the solitude of complete silence!

After the magnificent and at the same time distressing case of the cycloids, Pascal's forces collapsed again; he suffered a kind of "*anéantissement*," and sought rest in the country. In the middle of August, 1659, a slight improvement appeared, but only early in 1660 did it become more permanent. Pascal traveled to his native city, Clermont, and gained strength enough to be able to return to Paris in the fall.

"Trois discours sur la condition des Grands" (P.O., pp. 231ff.) remain from this period. They are addressed to a boy from a great family, perhaps the son of the Duc de Luynes, who belonged to the Jansenist movement, and in whose palace Pascal often stayed. The talks develop the canon of the *"honnête homme"*—a proof of how much these values meant to him right to the end—and relate it to Christian existence. They thus carry on the notion of the "orders" of existence, and thereby make a contribution to the Christian doctrine of values.

There is an interesting contrast to this problem, when Pascal asks himself whether one could save those who have no means of having a carriage of their own from having to walk in the mud of the Paris streets. He thus conceives the plan of an omnibus organization, and does not rest until a society with the necessary civil privileges is constituted and a time-table worked out. He himself wants a financial gain in the process —now, to be sure, in order to be able to help others. The affair succeeds, and an amusing letter from Gilberte Périer tells how the first voyage took place on March 18, 1662, amid enormous excitement (P. O., pp. 247ff.).

In this period of final invigoration, yet another brief personal happiness is allotted to him with the children of his sister, whom he loved a great deal.

IX.

Soon new and very grave complications gathered together. The general ecclesiastical attitude developed more and more against Jansenism. A bull of Pope Alexander VII had renewed in its time the condemnation of the *Propositions* by Innocent X, and emphasized that they were upheld in Jansenius's *Augustinus*. The assembly of the French clergy of March, 1657, had thus decided that all members of the clergy had to furnish a declaration—the famous *Formulaire*—according to which they condemned the five propositions mentioned above, and rejected Jansenius' book as containing these propositions. This decision had remained on paper and the whole matter had been left in silence. The Jansenists, as at the time of the first papal bull, had employed the method of distinction between the *quaestio juris et facti.* They had acknowledged the condemnation of the five propositions, but contested, on the other hand, that those propositions were contained in the *Augustinus.* That is, while an error of the pope in fundamentally dogmatic decisions is excluded, here, where it is a matter of the establishment of facts, a mistake could be admitted. But a new assembly of the French clergy took the matter up again, and in April, 1661, passed severe executory resolutions.

Port-Royal now saw itself faced with grave decisions. Supported by the vicars general of the absent Archbishop of Paris, who was favorably disposed towards Jansenism, Port-Royal at first attempted a compromise, which was based on the distinction mentioned above, and, it seems, stemmed from Pascal himself (*Oeuvres,* X, pp. 75ff.). But then misgivings arose on the part of the ecclesiastical authorities, as well as of the nuns themselves.

The events became more and more complicated and cannot even be outlined here. In any case, it came to a rupture within Port-Royal itself.

In a sphere in which the consciousness of election played so great a role, in which absolute certainties and the feeling of ethical superiority were so strongly developed, where everything was taken so infallibly seriously and all humor was lacking, oppositions and dissensions were bound to arise. For distrust, underhanded goings-on, and intrigues were in fact not as rare as would have been expected with the constant emphasis on the highest Christian fundamentals. It has already been pointed out several times that Pascal's position in the community of Port-Royal was ambiguous. One trusted him, and yet did not quite know where one stood with this superior mind, difficult to judge, and made irritable by his constant illnesses. His collaboration on the formula of compromise made many into his enemies, among those who were unpretentious, merely religious, strict, as well as among the politicians of the community. When the formula appeared, only Arnauld, the theoretician, and Nicole,

214

himself suspected of Thomism and thus of defection, still stood beside him.

And now suddenly an abrupt change: Pascal believes to see that the misgivings of the nuns are justified, and dissuades them from signing. In an extremely incisive exposition, he declares the distinction between the *quaestio juris et facta* impossible, and every such attempt an abandonment of the faith (*Oeuvres,* X, pp. 171ff.).

This means a break with Arnauld and Nicole—without the other group being thereby won. Pascal begins to stand alone. Between him and the allied Arnauld and Nicole a conflict develops, which is at bottom a conflict between Pascal and the concrete Port-Royal, its way of thinking, and its relationship to the Church. Pascal brings the problematical nature of this relationship to the fore, pushes it to an extreme, and forces it to its ultimate consequences. And whereas his adversaries, who are at bottom much more disposed than Pascal to forming a sect, become advocates of the official attitude of the Church and exhort to assimilation, Pascal, who loves the Church with painful fervor, pushes, in the continuation of a vehemently mounting polemic, towards such an opposition to the sovereign of the Church, that he comes close to rupture.

The frightfulness of the struggle only becomes clear when one reads in Pascal's correspondence with his most beloved friends how passionately he placed himself in the unity of the Church; and not only of an invisible, spiritual Church, but of the visible Church which has its sovereign in the pope. There it says: "For it is the Church which merits, with Jesus Christ who is inseparable from it, the conversion of those who are not in the truth; and it is then these converted persons who come to the aid of the mother who delivered them. I praise with all my heart the zeal which I have recognized in your letter for unity with the pope. The body is no more living without the head, than the head without the body. Whoever separates himself from the one or the other is no longer of the body, and no longer belongs to Jesus Christ. I do not know if there are people in the Church more attached to this unity of the body than those whom you call ours. We know that all virtues, martyrdom, austerities and all good works are useless outside of the Church and the communion with the head of the Church, who is the pope. I will never separate myself from his communion, at least I pray God to grant me this grace; without which I would be lost forever."[74]

Pascal's state of health deteriorates again, and this time definitively. Jacqueline, who had always stood so close to him and helped so much, has been dead since the end of 1661. Pascal is completely alone. Only Domat stands exteriorly beside him— a man of stern and violent character.

The conflict intensifies rapidly to unprecedented severity.[75] The first to reply to Pascal is Nicole. In the form of detailed "answers," he examines the individual statement of the "Ecrit sur la Signature." By means of the distinction already mentioned between the *question de droit* and the *question de fait,* he again attempts to establish that the authentic doctrine of Jansenism had not been condemned by the pope, because the contents of the *Augustinus* had not been correctly understood (*Oeuvres, X,* pp. 198ff.). If one rejected the distinction mentioned, one would be in danger of charging the pope and the bishops with condemning the truth. Arnauld, too, replies with a series of "maxims" for the proper interpretation of a decision of the Church (pp. 212ff.).

The rejoinder is composed by Domat and approved by Pascal. It shows that in the present cast, the distinction under discussion is impossible, that the sense and intention of the pope's doctrinal declaration are clearly directed against the doctrine of grace of Jansenism. It thus seems impossible to avoid the consequence that the pope is mistaken, and must be resisted.

Arnauld replies (pp. 253ff.). The first part deepens his methodological viewpoints. The second formulates a sharp reproach: may *"ces Messieurs"* bear well in mind what they are doing! They are attacking the defenders of the Jansenist doctrine of grace from behind. While the latter are taking pains to show

216

that the Church, despite all condemnation *in quaestione facti,* recognizes it *in quaestione juris* and thus abides in the truth, the former want to have it believed that the entire Church condemns it as heresy: *non tali auxilio nec defensionibus istis tempus eget.* They, the few, "three or four," take their stand against the well-advised many, and threaten to lead them on a way which "is dangerous not only for the people, but for the truth itself" (p. 261).

A reply by Domat-Pascal seems to have been lost; it must have reproached Arnauld with contradicting his own earlier views.

The latter answers (pp. 262ff.) that it is unavoidable, in the course of an intellectual effort stretching over many years, that certain views would be abandoned or reformed. He then formulates the various possibilities of a positive attitude to the Jansenist doctrine. For *"ces Messieurs,"* according to their declarations, there is only the "frightful consequence," that the pope and the bishops, thus the entire Church, had laid down a false doctrine.

Pascal and Domat answer this challenge with a *"grand écrit,"* which has not been preserved. It must have been of the most extreme severity of language and content.[76] Owing to Arnauld,[77] the authors reproach their earlier friends and comrades in arms with treason to the sacred cause; with disavowal of their earlier convictions; with sophistry, cowardice, and anxiety over earthly interests. They firmly maintain their thesis regarding the dispute over grace and the position taken by the pope. They assert that never "has there been a sentence and a condemnation more clear, more unequivocal, more precise, more explicit, more decisive, more contradictory, more definite, more expressed and more understandable than the condemnation of Jansenius and of the doctrine in the bulls and the *Formulaire.*" The pope "wanted to condemn" the doctrine of grace—which they presuppose to be the truth; he had "the diabolical intention to condemn the sense of Jansenius, whatever it might be."

217

We must come back once more to the *Lettres provinciales*. They wage a war against certain theoretical views and practical religious attitudes. Their theses themselves are not to be dealt with here. It is the business of theological examination to decide what was correct and what was false in them—and the task of historical inquiry to determine what Pascal as well as his adversaries really meant at that time, during the breakthrough and mutual struggle of new impulses, forms of sentiment, notions, and problems. Something else concerns us here. Throughout Pascal's polemic runs the assertion that the adversary stands opposed to the truth. Not only that he is mistaken, nor only that he persists in error, but rather that he does not want the evident truth; indeed, that he falsifies sacred doctrine in order to gain power over people.

It has already been stated that Jansenism tended to see plots everywhere; it had a sort of mania of persecution, which must indeed be understood as the reverse side of the belief in personal election. The same tendency was present in Pascal, who united an intense consciousness of personal election with a sensitivity, which was by itself already the sign of an ultimate uncertainty. This tendency is connected to that which has several times already been called his danger: the demon of combat; the will to combat *per se*. The latter, the combat of annihilation, becomes possible, or even receives a religious consecration, the moment that the adversary becomes the absolute adversary: he who stands opposed to the truth as such, betrays it and misuses it. It is the satanic adversary; Dostoevski's Grand Inquisitor; the Antichrist. Here lies the most profound injustice which Pascal committed against those whom he attacked: out of adversaries in the struggle for truth, out of adversaries who were mistaken—as he had to be convinced—, indeed set on error, he made adversaries of the truth, who resist the better insight because they have some aim in view. But herein lies also the most extreme danger for Pascal himself; for the demon of destruction, into which the evil in him concentrated, signifies at the same time self-destruction. When Pascal seeks a broader

218

level of discussion in the last two *Lettres provinciales;* when the polemical opposition relaxes and strives towards something constructive, when the "letters" finally break off, this is evidently a sign that Pascal is coming to himself. But the final decision has not yet fallen, it is only postponed. The demon has not yet appeared in all its force.

The crisis now brews again. Its structure is the same as in the combat of the *Lettres provinciales*—of those which precede the last two: combat *per se,* without the readiness to transcend one's own standpoint in a larger and freer comprehension; without the readiness to admit the adversary into the community of the will to truth. But by the fact that it is no longer a group within the Church or a theological tendency against which the affect turns, but rather the head of the Church himself, of whom he had after all said to his most intimate friends that he would never separate himself from him, because this separation would mean eternal perdition—the demonic danger thereby reaches its acme.

When Arnauld reproaches him with the change of his attitude as concerns the *Lettres provinciales* and the enormity of his assertion, Pascal's excitation grows without bounds. He replies with the *"grand écrit"* mentioned earlier, which must have been of a violence never before attained. And, mysterious recompense: the same reproach which those who were attacked formerly made against the triumphant *Lettres provinciales,* that they dealt imprecisely with their sources, were arbitrary and violent in assertion and judgment, is now leveled against Pascal by his former friends and comrades in arms.[78]

In January, 1662, a new crisis in Pascal's illness sets in; we are told that he fainted during a discussion on the pending questions. The exaltation of the combat, which surpassed all his strength, is followed by a profound exhaustion. As soon as one takes the roots of his existence as they really are, the spirit of his piety and his most profound religious intention, as the *Mémorial* determines them, —then one can say nothing else

219

than: Pascal comes to himself, definitively. He renounces any further word of combat. He keeps silent.

Pascal now accomplishes his third and definitive conversion. The first brought him into contact with religion *per se*. The second brought about the decision in favor of revelation, of the "God of Jesus Christ"; it gave him the awareness of being called, and awakened the readiness to follow. In the third he must have become aware of his most profound danger: of the possibility of destruction which came out of his own nature; out of the compulsion of rational consistency, the compulsion to be right, the will to power through knowledge, the spirit of combat. In this hour, Pascal must have caught sight of his demon and freed himself from it.

What he thought further about the problems under discussion can no longer be decided, but it is of secondary importance for what is essential. Whatever views he had, they were in any case borne by a different spirit and had a different Christian and existential meaning than hitherto. It is also impossible to decide the much discussed question—beginning with the report of the priest who counseled him during the last six months of his life and administered the last sacraments to him, Père Beurrier[79]—, which has to do with whether Pascal revised his attitude to the judgment of the pope, but it likewise does not reach into that innermost domain which occupies us here. A genuine declaration was not demanded of him, so he cannot have refused it. However he may have taken his stand in other respects, in any case it took place in a different spirit than before. But if it is unjust to interpret a man into a refusal, which he himself would have characterized as perdition—so is it likewise unjust to doubt, without a compelling reason, the sincerity of his will to belong to that Church, which for him was that, which has already been stated several times. Pascal renounced theory and polemics. He concentrated himself completely into prayer, and took pains to liberate himself from everything earthly and to serve his neighbor.

The accounts of the final period of Pascal's life go to the

heart. It is six months of terrible suffering, but filled with profound peace—and what does that mean, when a Pascal feels peace! The accounts tell of spiritual exercises which last several weeks, "in penitence, mortification, silence, and the examination or review of his entire life, and then he made a general confession." They tell that he "sold his carriage, his horses, his tapestries, his beautiful furniture, his silver, and even his library, with the exception of the Bible, Saint Augustine, and very few other books, and gave all the money from the sale to the poor; he dismissed all his servants and put himself in pension at his sister's, Mlle. Périer's, in order no longer to have the care of a household."[80] They tell that he lives deep in Sacred Scripture; that he had "a marked love for the Divine Office,[81] but above all for the small hours, because they are composed of Psalm 118,[82] in which he found so many admirable things, that he felt delight at reciting it. When he spoke with his friends of the beauty of this Psalm, he was transported in such a way that he appeared outside himself." It is the long Psalm of contemplative intimacy, which through 176 verses circles around the luminous reality of the word and the will and the truth of God.

The *Mémorial* had closed with a phrase which speaks of obedience; of that obedience, which for a mind like Pascal must have been the most difficult: "total submission to Jesus Christ and to my director." In this period Pascal must have experienced anew the Christian meaning of obedience, and perhaps, indeed, for the first time drawn the real consequence from it.

In his life, the expressions of an obstinate will to be right, to fight inexorably to the end, and to conquer, come back repeatedly. A single line runs from the discussions with Père Noël regarding the theory of the vacuum to those about the announcing of prize for the solution to the problem of the cycloid; from the action of the twenty-year-old against the Sieur Saint-Ange, through the struggle of the *Lettres provinciales* against the Molinist theology, to the paroxysm of his accusation

221

that the pope wanted to destroy the evident truth. But this line is interwoven with another: an ever new self-integration into the Church. The *Mémorial* speaks of Christ coming to meet man, and of the obedience to him and his representative, the spiritual director, who is a priest of the Church . . . In order to practice this obedience, Pascal places himself under the direction of M. Singlin . . . The "Mystère de Jésus" speaks of the inside, one could almost say, of the mysticism of obedience. It shows with imperturbable clarity the sacred economy of divine things; down to the clairvoyancy of that statement, that without the Church even the word of God can bring about ruin . . . The *Lettres provinciales* emphasize his unconditional will to unity with the Church . . . The letters to Mlle. de Roannez, written in the most profound intimacy that Pascal knew, contain that confession, of the most intense pathos, which has been cited . . . The *Pensées* never speak of a direct relationship to God or Christ without the Church; on the contrary, they contain many statements which link Christ, and through him, God, to the Church in an entirely self-evident way. For Pascal's relationship to God and Christ, the Church is something similar to space with its coördinates for the relationship of the eye to the object. Only in the Church can Christ be properly seen, because he stands essentially in her . . . This is the contrary line.

From the first arises Pascal's temptation—which is, however, something thoroughly different from an anti-Church affect. It is not the revolt of an individualistically oriented piety against authority; nor the protest of a religious doctrine of incommensurability, which places everything visible in a paradoxical relationship to what is invisible and essential, in opposition to the pretension of normative Christian definition—but rather at bottom the revolt of a mind confined in itself, filled with enormous self-assurance, against everything which opposes it *per se*. Thence ensues a struggle whose ultimate consequence would not be the break-through to a direct personal relationship to

222

God, nor the separating out of a sphere of desperate Christian freedom through the renunciation of all continuity between grace and the world—but rather the triumph of the victory. But of absolute victory; that is, of the destruction also of the combatant himself if he does not find the solution in the peace of the "abandonment of the soul."

In the silence of the final months Pascal must have experienced the solution of this compulsion. This silence is the execution of the *Mémorial* and the "Mystère de Jésus."

The problem of this life can only be understood from the Catholic point of view. It dissolves as soon as one approaches it in a Kierkegaardian Protestant way. Then Pascal's intention becomes a pitiful attempt at that, which Luther or Calvin accomplished in great fashion. In reality, such a struggle is only to be understood, if behind the attack against the pope there stands not some half-Protestant affect, but the revolt of confined finiteness *per se*—and the solution of this conflict of existence lies in the solution of the cramp of rebellion.[83]

The silence of the last six months before his death, interrupted by no further remarks on the pending questions, reveals this solution. It is not easy to find something greater than this silence after this life. Only from this standpoint does all the struggling receive its ultimate meaning. The understanding of the Pascalian existence depends on the understanding of this silence.

The account of the end is moving. One might reread it in Gilberte Périer's biography.

On July 2, violent colics set in, which will last almost without interruption until August 19, robbing him of all sleep.

The longing for the sacraments immediately awakens in Pascal; for confession, which he makes four days after the change for the worse; for extreme unction; but above all for the Eucharist. For him, the Eucharist, along with the word of Scripture, stood in continuity to the incarnation of Christ; it was for him the last word of Christianity and the most profound

223

expression of the community of the Church. He asks for it with impetuous longing, and there is a terrifying force of revelation in the way in which the Jansenist environment denies the sacrament to one who was suffering so terribly, under the pretext that only those close to death may receive the viaticum. One consoles him by telling him that the pains are only temporary, but he "asked with such incredible entreaties that one give him communion, and that in the name of God one find means of remedying all the inconveniences which one had hitherto alleged to him; and he pressed so much for this, that a person who was present reproached him, that he had anxiety, and that he should give himself over to the sentiment of his friends; that he was feeling better, and that he had almost no more colic; and that, since all he had left was a '*vapeur d'eau*,' it was not just for him to have the holy sacrament brought to him; that it was better to wait until this action could be done in Church." Does Pascal still have anything in common with this mentality? Is he not isolated?

He then expresses this request, of a truly sublime simplicity of faith: "Since one does not want to accord me this grace [the Eucharist] . . . not being able to communicate in the head [of the Mystical Body of the Church, that is, Christ], I would very much like to communicate in his members [the faithful], and for that I have thought of having here a poor sick man, to whom one would render the same service as to me, and hire a nurse especially for him, and finally, let there be no difference between him and me." The request cannot be fulfilled; so he presses his sister "to do him the favor of having him carried to the hospital for the incurables, because he had a great desire to die in the company of the poor" (P. O., pp. 38f.). This request, too, finds no fulfillment. We may doubt to what extent one took it seriously and asked oneself whether, coming out of this extraordinary existence, it might not have a real and necessary meaning.

Then the condition deteriorates suddenly; a new and violent colic seems to bring the end. Finally the priest is called. The moment he enters, the sick man comes to himself and can receive the Eucharist. Immediately after the religious observance, the convulsions set in again, and after twenty-four hours of terrible suffering, on the nineteenth of August of the year 1662, at one o'clock at night, Blaise Pascal breathes his last.

Notes

[1] *Der Mensch und der Glaube. Versuche über die religiöse Existenz in Dostojewskijs grossen Romanen* (Leipzig, 1933), Nachwort.

[2] Editions: *Oeuvres de Blaise Pascal, publiées suivant l'ordre chronologique, par Léon Brunschvicg, Pierre Boutroux, Félix Gazier,* vols. I–XIV (Paris, 1914–1925). Based on the critical edition, a pocket edition by Léon Brunschvicg: *Pensées et Opuscules,* in several editions. As far as possible, the quotations in the present work are taken from the pocket edition (6th ed.; Paris, 1912), with the abbreviation "P. O." Otherwise, they are from the complete edition (*Oeuvres*), whereby the Roman numerals indicate the volume.

The *Mémorial,* p. 142; registers to it, *Oeuvres* IV, pp. 7ff. The copy on paper has been preserved; of the copy on parchment, there remains but the exact copy made by Abbé Périer (see p. 23).

[3] He thus belongs among those who have grown up without the enveloping maternal sphere and thence retain forever a homelessness of the heart. The greatest of them is Dante. By the example of an Augustine one may see what they lack and what a difficult compensatory task is imposed upon them.

[4] Published in 1640. *Oeuvres* I, pp. 243ff.

[5] It is fascinating to see what happens to an idea when it comes out of Montaigne's sphere into that of Pascal: how it receives a different weight, a different depth, a new dynamics and pathos.

[6] On all this, see Chapter IV of this book. See, too, Guardini, *Der Mensch und der Glaube,* Nachwort.

[7] P. O., pp. 695ff. [The translation, as of all quotations from Pascal in this book, is by the present translator. The material in square brackets is retained from the many such explicative interpolations in the author's own translation. —Tr.]

[8] See the interesting letter of the young Pascal to Queen Christine of Sweden, in which he recommends the calculating machine and develops the analogy in detail (P. O., pp. 111ff.).

[9] "Whence it seems, since the one is truth where the other is error, that one would form, by uniting them, a perfect morality. But, instead of this peace, there would result from their combination but a war and a general destruction: for one establishing certitude, the other doubt, one the grandeur of man, the other his weakness, they destroy the truth as well as the falsity of one another. So that they cannot exist alone because

226

of their defects, nor unite because of their oppositions, and thus they shatter and annihilate one another in order to make room for the truth of the Gospel" (P. O., p. 160).

[10] A phenomenon which Pascal caught sight of in an experience complementary to that of the *Mémorial,* the healing of his niece, Marguérite Périer.

[11] One must perhaps even translate: "as often as he changed clothes" (P. O., p. 141).

[12] The passages cited are: Ex. 3, 6 (Mt. 22, 32)—"My God and your God"; Jn. 20, 17—Ruth 1, 16—Jn. 17, 25—"They have forsaken me the fountain of living waters," Jer. 2, 13—Mt. 27, 46—Jn. 17, 6—"I will not forget your words," Ps. 28, 16.

[13] This does not mean that there is no Christian truth and science of this truth expressible in genuine concepts, that is, theology; but the nature of this science, and the nature of its object, must be pointed out. Nor do we mean that for the Christian there is only the direct relationship to Christ, thus neither Church nor dogma. The Church is indeed "the prolongation of the incarnation in history"; her content is Christ, and she herself nothing more than the way in which Christ becomes the form and contents of the life of redeemed humanity, σῶμα χριστοῦ.

[14] Even when it is received from the preaching and liturgy of the Church, from dogma and theology.

[15] Jn. 14, 6. It remains to be asked whether Pascal knew the concept of the "God of the philosophers" at all. He did not work with it. The religious problem posed itself to him only after his decisive Christian experience. But that he knew that concept proceeds, for example, from the blunt declaration of war against the Cartesian conception of God, *Pensées* frs. 76–79 (P. O., pp. 360ff.). Descartes above all represents the "philosophical attitude," against which Pascal turns.

[16] The experience and the phenomenon of Providence are expressed in very living terms in a letter written during Pascal's last years: "When by our own impulsion we want something to succeed, we become irritated against obstacles, because we sense in these hindrances that which the motive which makes us act did not put there . . . But when God truly makes us act, we never sense anything without which does not come from the same principle which makes us act; there is no opposition to the motive which urges us on; the same mover which brings us to act brings others to resist us, at least it permits it; . . . this uniformity does not trouble the peace of a soul" (P. O., p. 245).

[17] Pascal himself gave a great example of such a procedure in his research on the vacuum.

[18] Here, too, an extreme situation, in which a highly refined art of intellectual government stands hard on the border of a spiritual Machiavellism.

[19] The whole forms a continuation of the Greek doctrine of μεσότης and the medieval doctrine of the *mediatas.*

[20] The concepts "nothingness" and "the infinite" have, as follows from the context, a dialectical meaning; the former means the "infinitely

227

small," the latter, the "infinitely great." In addition, this antithesis scintillates over into another: the "infinite" is the whole, the universe; "nothingness" is the last indivisible part, the absolute atom. But the universe, as will become clear further on, is not the graspable cosmos, but rather endless, illimitable, and unmasterable reality. Finally, the antithesis receives yet another meaning: "nothingness" is the "beginning," the "infinite" is the "end." Here nothingness is taken as pure but operative potentiality—see, for example, the way in which the tree is contained in the seed: it is not there, and yet it is there—, infinity as the illimitable multitude of the effects of the initial cause in the immeasurable multiplicity of things and events.

[21] Fragment 386 shows a man in suspension between the waking and sleeping states of consciousness (p. 504). Indeed, according to fr. 434 it is not at all possible to affirm that the waking state is the essential. "Who knows whether this other half of life in which we think we are awake is not another sleep a little different from the first, and from which we awake when we think we sleep?" (p. 529).

[22] *Oeuvres*, II, p. 138. See the introduction to the treatise on the vacuum.

[23] Man's position becomes so uncertain that one must ask what the cause of his existence is: "Is he created by a good God, or by an evil demon, or by chance?" Here, too, the center and the system of coordinates of order become lost: not of spatial, but of axiological order. The focus of value disintegrates; the feeling of axiological indeterminability, of singularity, sets in. This is expressed in fr. 72, in which man is called "*le plus prodigieux objet de la nature*" (p. 357). And stronger yet in fr. 434: "What a chimera is then man? What a novelty, what a monster, what a chaos, what a subject of contradiction, what a prodigy!" In the word "*prodige*" lies hidden the passion of the Renaissance for the encounter with the unknown, the adventurous, the grandiose, and even the monstrous. "Judge of all things, imbecile worm of the earth; depositary of the truth, sink of incertitude and error; glory and refuse of the universe"—so that his reason becomes "a paradox to itself" (p. 531).

This radicalization of suspension to the pure facticity of place and time has a parallel in Pascal's sociology. Since it is not possible to find a sociological locus recognizable as true to nature and a corresponding order for human existence, the pure facticity of the positively established law sets in. Order can no longer be founded on an essence, on a "conformity to nature," but rather rests on the groundless authority of positive law.

[24] The conclusion is thus brought nearer, that grace and sharing in divine life belong to the nature of man—a conclusion which would destroy the purity of the concept of grace and draw God into the context of worldly necessity. Pascal did not draw this conclusion; on the contrary, he would have rejected it most sharply. This leads to the complicated question of how the relationship of nature and grace is to be conceived at all. The following is intended as a hint.

In the history of the concept of grace, various structures are operative, determined by the moments of existence which are especially emphasized and made the guiding motifs of its interpretation. Among them, two are important for our question. Developed in the most extreme logical consequence, they present themselves somewhat as follows.

The first sees in man a real man only when he stands in the union of grace with God. Without this union, the "mind-endowed living being" is not yet a real man. Consequently, indeed, from this point of view even his original intellectual character becomes questionable, and true "intellectuality" awakens only in the contact with the Holy Spirit, in being called by the personal God. The living being is but raw material, the preliminary stage or miscarried reject of man. Exactly opposed is the other conception, according to which man, in his body-mind unity, is a thoroughly complete being. Being called by revelation, faith, and communion with God are then but a relation of meaning between man—in essence complete in himself—and a God standing "face-to-face" with or "above" him. If in the first type, grace became an essential and necessary element of human nature, then in the second it becomes a mere intention posited by a decision, a pure relation of meaning. The two structures form a sharp opposition, but stand at the same time in dialectical relationship to one another. And indeed, we have presented them here in their extreme case, that is, in the way in which each conceives man grasped by grace as soon as it goes to its extreme and thereby destroys the living totality of its object. Thus, as it were, the pathological form of the structures concerned—in which, however, their specific direction of meaning becomes especially clear. It becomes clear at the same time that they grasp the object really intended from two opposed sides. It lies between them. Each of them destroys it, though in an opposite direction, in that it takes into consideration a particular motif of thought and being, while excluding the opposite, and pushes it to the extreme. These extreme cases form, as it were, the patterns of possible heresy. The thought motif operative in them, however, does not have to take the step into heretical exaggeration and dissolution. "Normally," that is, guarded by the obedience of faith, it will remain in the living relationship to the center of the whole—just as a constructive or functional principle of bodily life, which produces sickness when it grows too rapidly, normally stands in the proper relationship to the other moments, that is, forms an organism. There then arises a theory which, in accordance with the predisposition of the thinker, is structured by the predominance of certain motifs congenial to him, but is at the same time integrated into the limits and relationships of the whole; that is, it is orthodox.

The extreme case makes clear the peculiarity of the corresponding structure, but also the danger inherent in it of destroying the content of faith in its living totality. It characterizes the way in which the legitimate interpretation, working with a given thought motif, frees itself from the obedience to revelation, departs from the respect of the sacred mystery, and becomes mere religious speculation.

Now in the sphere of the extreme case—to come back to our question—, the concept of "nature" means something other than in the central realm of the living concretion. In the latter it is a genuine theological concept, in the former, openly or covertly, a philosophical or psychological concept. The transition is, of course, often difficult to ascertain.

Pascal's conception is based on the first of these two structures, but remains, if we are not mistaken, thoroughly in the central realm. This may be questionable in a given remark; on the whole it seems clear. The importance which freedom and the person have in his view—with regard to God as well as to man—seems to indicate this. See also pp. 111ff.

He does not start out from an abstract concept of human nature and declare that grace belongs to its consummation, but rather from the image of man of revelation, from man as God intended him. This man is "created for God," and his existence is that of relation with God. It is of this man that Pascal speaks when he says that man only becomes "real" when he stands in communion with God. He does not simply assert that without grace, man is incomplete in his nature; that would be naturalistic, monistic, conceived from the point of view of the world. Rather, he says: the man, of whom revelation speaks, is he who has been received into communion with God. He speaks of this man alone; and again, not abstractly, in the form of a doctrinal system, but in living conversation with a given listener: the skeptically rationalistic educated man of the seventeenth century, in whose feeling and consciousness the image of the emancipated man was being prepared. To him he says that man cannot be conceived in the way in which modern times conceive him with ever more acute logical consistency: as autonomous "nature"; as unity of essence and being, meaningful and complete in itself. One can conceive a plant, an animal in this way, but not man. His divinely established determination consists precisely in surpassing the sphere of inner-worldly reality, the organic, psychological, sociological, and cultural domains; in receiving from the God of revelation the points of reference of his existence, and in determining anew all psycho-physical, social, cultural life according to it. But this is not something which could be added to the humanly essential, something which could also be foregone; rather, the decision about faith and grace is the decision about salvation or perdition, about the meaning of existence *per se,* in the strictest sense of this word. If "man" is that which God wills him to be, then the man who rejects this will is not "man." He is not autonomous man, complete in essence and meaning, who merely places himself in another relationship to God, but rather enters into contradiction with the meaning of his existence established by God, and therefore absolutely established; precisely in his autonomous self-assertion, he is a semi-being, having lost his true self; something for which there is no real category— least of all that of modern-day "nature."

[25] Certainly, a great deal can be brought to bear against this conception from the anthropological point of view; but the decisive question remains that of what chances it has of mastering the totality as well as the tensions of real human existence. The recognition seems to be on the way, that it is not the "empirical" images of man which are truly in conformity with reality, but that it is precisely they which are unreal. A peculiar inverted idealism guides them—a somber resolution not to see

the real man. In fact, the most deficient metaphysical and religious theory of man still does more justice to reality than all merely empirical theories. To be sure, within the metaphysical, religious approach begins a new and now much more profound division.

26 See, too, the beautiful thoughts, worked out in such a lively manner, of fr. 430, especially pp. 522f.

27 See a very profound particular trait in fr. 800: "Who taught the evangelists the qualities of a perfectly heroic soul, in order to portray it so perfectly in Jesus Christ? Why do they make him so weak in his agony? Do they not know how to portray a steadfast death? Certainly, for the same Saint Luke portrays that of Saint Stephen stronger than that of Jesus Christ" (p. 700).

28 The word "*intelligence*" is perhaps also to be translated by "wisdom" of structure and function.

29 Pascal undertook, in fact—in the *Lettres provinciales*—to treat the most difficult theological questions not as an expert of academic theology, but simply "*en honnête homme*"; whereby, to be sure, he met with the misfortune of the non-expert, that of disastrously underestimating the range of the questions discussed.

30 Cited by Fortunat Strowski, *Pascal et son temps* (5th ed.; Paris, 1921), vol. II, pp. 264 and 261.

31 We recall that Pascal carried out a literal mechanization of the intellectual process, a conversion of cognitive elements into a machine, when he constructed the calculating machine—an automaton in the full sense of the word.

32 Pascal's teacher, Montaigne, already knew this. But it is a great difference, whether an idea stands in the clear, realistic, courageous, but at the same time cool, thin intellectuality of Montaigne—without obligation in the final analysis—, or in the burning, arduous, excited sphere of Pascal. It receives a different specific weight, a different dynamics, and at bottom a different quality. When the two men say the same thing, it means in reality something different.

33 The difference between this and the skepticism of Augustine is significant. In the latter it arises from the incongruity between the forcefully experienced absolute character of the truth and the act experienced as finite; in Pascal, from the insight into the significance of motive for the genesis of concrete knowledge, and into the way in which human motivation is ultimately endangered by sin.

34 Yet we must not confuse this attitude with the purely formal aestheticism of the end of the nineteenth century, in which "form for form's sake" means bankruptcy. Where there is no longer any reason, any value to give meaning to things. Form hangs suspended in nothingness. Under it gapes despair. In Pascal, the whole is thoroughly positive. It stands in the service of a conscious and decided faith.

35 And in conclusion: "Justice and truth are two points so fine that our instruments are too blunt to touch them exactly. If they approach them, they blunt the point and press down all around, more on the false than on the true. Man is thus so fortunately fabricated that he has no proper

principle of the true, and several excellent principles of the false . . ."

[36] Parentheses of the original.

[37] Thus something completely other than the incognito of the *Philosophical Fragments*. See, too, the sixteenth of the *Lettres provinciales* (*Oeuvres*, VI, p. 276).

[38] "*Amor che nella mente mi ragiona*" (*Convivio*, III, Canzone); "*Donne ch'avete intelletto d'amore*" (*Vita nuova*, XIX).

[39] Here, by the way, it also becomes clear what the oft-quoted formula means, that the heart has its reasons, which the reason does not know. Anything but emotional subjectivity and uncontrollability of feeling! Rather, two realms of intellectual, objectively valid evidence, which sustain one another without being able to be dissolved into one another.

[40] *Opera omnia*, ed. Gabr. Gerberon Mon. Congr. S. Mauri I. Venet. MDCCXLIV, pp. 41ff. The two works about to be mentioned: *ibid.*, pp. 50ff. and 53ff. The present English translation is that of S. W. Deane, *Saint Anselm: Basic Writings*, Open Court Publishing Co. (2nd ed., LaSalle, Illinois, 1962). The three texts mentioned here are from pp. 7ff., 145ff., and 135ff., respectively.

[41] [The German term "*ontisch*" refers to being itself, as opposed to "*ontologisch*," which refers to the study of or thought about being. —Tr.]

[42] Here lies the relationship of the ontological argument with the final proof of immortality in Plato's *Phaedo*. It, too, has a logical lacuna, as soon as one understands it "logically," —or more exactly, from the thought experience of distance-thinking. The defect consists in concluding, from the affinity of the soul to the Idea, the indestructibility of its real being. In reality, the argument is based on something particular: the Platonic cognitive experience, in which the Idea—which is the veritable reality—is touched upon and a living, real participation in it attained.

[43] Just as it is a unique case to pronounce the name of God. This has always been felt by believing consciousness, as long as it was living.

[44] What is meant is the mathematical infinite as the possibility of going ever further.

[45] Everything: the infinite fulfillment through the divine value which surpasses all measure. Nothing: what is it to be lost, "everything which is mine," is finite and loses all significance, according to the formulas placed at the beginning, in face of the infinite.

[46] It may be noted that the "Argument du pari" in no way represents the substructure of Pascal's own faith. It is the attempt to concede to the skeptic the most extreme difficulty of proof, and thus to take up the problem of proof at its most advanced position. To be sure, in the fact that he dares this undertaking at all, and in the way in which he carries it out, the whole Pascal lies once more hidden.

[47] Søren Kierkegaard's *Samlede Vaerker*, udgivne af A. B. Drachmann, J. L. Heiberg, og H. O. Lange (Kjobenhavn, 1923), vol. IV, pp. 197ff.

[48] "Collision" [in German "*Anstoss*"] has from the outset the double meaning of that against which one collides ("*anstossen*"), and of that which is shocking ["*das Anstössige*"], that is, approximating the Biblical concept of "scandal."

49 The English translation is from the Princeton University Press edition of the *Philosophical Fragments* (2nd ed.; Princeton, 1962), pp. 46–59.

50 The romantic definition of the highest fulfillment through annihilation, of the consummation of life through death.

51 We cannot go into closer analysis of Kierkegaard's Christology here.

52 *Per se,* it is not indeed a question of the absolute value in the philosophical sense, or of the redemptive value of natural religious experience, but rather of that which the New Testament means by the pearl, the treasure in the field, the visions of preciousness of the Apocalypse, the reward in heaven, eternal life, etc. That is: of the character and fullness of value of the Living God revealed in Christ, and of his kingdom. The reflections of this chapter, however, are directed to the content of the three "proofs" considered from the point of view of the philosophy or psychology of religion, and we ask the reader to keep this in mind.

53 The consciousness of this relationship and of the problems which arise from it stirs for the first time in Plato's uncertainty in face of the idea of the good and its relationship to other ideas—precisely the spot where the philosophical idea of God will later begin.

54 But also—what the Greek eros did not yet see, and which could only become clear in the light of Christian agape—in the movement, in the loving return of the absolute to the finite, whereby alone true comprehension of things, of human existence, of history, etc., becomes possible.

55 To what extent this is possibly naturally, to what extent it presupposes grace, indeed the real coming of God into the world, cannot be discussed further here.

56 *Opera,* annex to the second volume, pp. 5ff.

57 What has been said already gives an answer to the question which has perhaps occupied the reader. Perhaps he has become accustomed, for example in the context of the way of thinking of dialectical theology, to see in the emphasis of the impossibility of going from the world to God the characteristic note of Christian thought. In this case, applying the category of the absolute to God, seeing the finite in a positive relationship to God, speaking of "analogy," accepting any possibility whatever of positive statements from the finite towards God, appears *a priori* as unchristian. Only that way of thinking is recognized as Christian, which breaks off every continuity; sets the finite in absolute dissimilarity, indeed in a specific contradiction, conditioned by sin, to God; sets up as the unique situation that of being sentenced; admits statements only in the form of the paradox. The role of theoretical thinking about God is, then, that of being on guard lest this very thinking establish itself, and the religious decision in "fear and trembling" remains as the unique legitimate act. A long study of these problems, especially of Kierkegaard, has shown us their weight. We are also aware of the inner power of this way of thinking. Only we think we see that it is not itself the "Christian" way of thinking, but merely a certain psychological structure: that which rests on a particular affinity to the discontinuity of being. In its view, indeed in the first way in which it experiences being, including its own, it is the

moment of dissimilarity, of discontinuity, of tension, of contradiction, which comes to the fore. One can specify its categories, its methods, its crucial points, its technique of accentuation and attenuation, etc. . . . One can trace its psychology to the roots of its attitude, to its fundamental affects of anxiety, of defiance, of shock at the body and the world, its particular forms of bad conscience about existence, etc. One can show that it stands in exact antithesis to an opposite structure—precisely that which it perceives as unchristian. In reality, this feeling is not in the least the protest of the Christian consciousness against what is pagan, but rather a structural hate against the opposite structure; one could almost say, a hate of blood and feeling against the other race of thought. But for that very reason, it is also clear that this difference has nothing to do with Christianity and paganism. For this very structure can also become pagan, and everything seems to indicate that the possibility of this already lies ready. This way of thought is thoroughly positive when it recognizes itself for what it is: structure, no more, no less. And when it lets itself be taken in charge by the faith, it is a possibility in Christianity. A real possibility, but nothing more than that. The same is true of the other structure, which begins with continuity, with the direct possibility of declarations.

58 The existential moment of cognition is naturally only roughly sketched here, to the extent that the context demands.

59 It is inevitable that this chapter repeat some of what has been said in the preaching, especially the first. For the historical context, see, among others. Fortunat Strowski, *Pascal et son temps,* vols. I–III (3rd, 5th, 6th eds.; Paris, 1921–1922).

60 *Oeuvres* I. pp. 349ff.; there, too, the official report, countersigned by Pascal, on two "Conférences ou Entretiens Particuliers" in the affair.

61 *Oeuvres* III, p. 307. ". . . It [the problem of the game of chance, that is, of probability] had hitherto wandered in uncertainty; but this time, after having proved itself refractory to experiment, it was not able to escape the ascendency of reason. For by the means of Geometry [mathematics] we have transformed it into a [calculable] art with such certainty that, sharing in mathematical certitude, it is henceforth in a position to progress with audacity; and consequently, uniting in it the demonstrative force of mathematics to the uncertainty of chance and conciliating these two terms which seemed contrary, it receives its name from both, and rightfully lays claim to this stupefying title: the Geometry of chance."

62 *Oeuvres,* IV, p. 61. The letter seems to us—apart from its contents —particularly revealing, because it shows that Pascal had not yet told his sister, who was so close to him, anything about the experience of the *Mémorial* which had meanwhile taken place. To judge by the surprise caused by the parchment sewn into the coat of the deceased, he did not speak of it later either, one more proof of the decisive importance of the event.

63 Letter of November 16, 1654, from M. Singlin to Mère Marie des Anges; *Oeuvres,* IV, p. 64n.

64 See Jacqueline's letter to her brother, *Oeuvres,* IV, pp. 77f. "Our Mothers [nuns] have ordered me to write to you, so that you may tell me all the circumstances of your method for teaching reading by *be, ce, de,* etc. . . . in which the children do not have to know the name of the letters . . ." Port-Royal, which greatly occupied itself with pedagogical matters, had published in 1660 a *Grammaire générale et raisonnée,* in which Pascal's method was utilized; *Oeuvres* IV, p. 78n.

65 Perhaps this is somewhat exaggerated; perhaps words or turns of expression are given a sense, stemming from a certain total conception, which is not contained in them. It is difficult to avoid this danger, and yet to push the analysis as deeply as possible.

66 [The author's translation attempts to clarify Pascal's phrase: ". . . *prie avec confiance comme pour moi*" (p. 576) as follows: ". . . as if you were praying for something which I am to accomplish." —Tr.]

67 In fr. 555, p. 578, which is closely related in meaning.

68 See in this regard the explanation of Dostoevski's Legend of the Grand Inquisitor, in Guardini, *Der Mensch und der Glaube,* pp. 578ff.

69 Dostoevski's Grand Inquisitor is an especially powerful example of this—but also Kierkegaard's "Instant." The *Lettres provinciales* belong in this succession.

70 Thus Strowski, III, pp. 137ff., 153ff. His view seems to lie thoroughly in the line of Pascalian possibilities.

71 See Jacqueline's letter of March 29 and 31, 1656, to her sister; *Oeuvres,* IV, p. 327.

72 *Pensées,* sections XII and XIII.

73 The documents and exchange of letters, *Oeuvres,* VII, p. 337; VIII, *passim;* IX, pp. 167ff.

74 Letters to Mlle. de Roannez, no. 6; P. O., pp. 218f.

75 For its history, see the documents, *Oeuvres,* X, pp. 176–267: "Discussions sur la Signature."

76 It is not for nothing that a letter addressed to Domat in 1676 warns him that, if he wishes the reconciliation with Port-Royal, he should burn the manuscripts on the question of the "Signature" given him by Pascal, since it is to be feared lest one "misuse them in a manner prejudicial to the truth and to the memory of M. Pascal" (*Oeuvres,* X, pp. 194ff.).

77 Strowski, III, pp. 371f., 374ff.

78 In a letter of Nicole on the whole dispute, *Oeuvres,* X, p. 344.

79 *Oeuvres,* X, pp. 384ff.; beforehand and afterwards, letters from various sides.

80 Declarations of Père Beurrier, *Oeuvres* X, p. 391.

81 For the breviary. The passage, from Gilberte Périer, *Vie de Blaise Pascal,* P. O., p. 34.

82 According to the numbering of the Vulgate.

83 There is a similar dwarfing of a great existential problem: in the interpretation of Saint Francis of Assisi. He, too, is understood—especially by Sabatier—according to the scheme of the tension between the consciousness of a direct relationship to Christ and the objective au-

thority of the Church. His life thus becomes an unsuccessful attempt to break through into the supposedly desired evangelical freedom; his strength is not sufficient; under a thousand torments, the Christian consciousness capitulates before the still triumphant power of the Church. As if a figure thus split in his innermost being could have had the effect that Saint Francis had! In reality, the problem of Saint Francis moves on a much deeper level, which the outsider does not perceive at all. With him, it is never a question of whether the objective authority must be broken—and not only because the time for it had not come, but essentially so. Francis rather holds fast to his mission, and at the same time accepts the objective impossibility of its immediate realization; he goes the way of sacrifice, which is the form of the realization of divine love.